Revolution, radicalism and reform

England, 1780–1846

D1392445

Richard Brown

CAMBRIDGE
UNIVERSITY PRESS

To my mother, who died in the early stages of writing this book

PUBLISHED BY THE PRESS SYNDICATE OF THE UNIVERSITY OF CAMBRIDGE
The Pitt Building, Trumpington Street, Cambridge, United Kingdom

CAMBRIDGE UNIVERSITY PRESS
The Edinburgh Building, Cambridge CB2 2RU, UK
40 West 20th Street, New York, NY 10011-4211, USA
10 Stamford Road, Oakleigh, VIC 3166, Australia
Ruiz de Alarcón 13, 28014 Madrid, Spain
Dock House, The Waterfront, Cape Town 8001, South Africa

http://www.cambridge.org

First published 2000

Printed in the United Kingdom at Redwood Books, Trowbridge, Wiltshire

Text design by Newton Harris Design Partnership
Map artwork by Kathy Baxendale

Typeface 10.5pt Minion   *System* QuarkXPress®

A catalogue record for this book is available from the British Library

ISBN 0 521 56788 2   paperback

ACKNOWLEDGEMENTS
Haymakers (enamel on Wedgwood), by George Stubbs (1724–1806), Lady Lever Art Gallery, Port Sunlight, Merseyside, UK/Bridgeman Art Library, Board of Trustees: National Museum and Galleries on Merseyside: p.3; The Fotomas Index: pp.5, 7, 22, 31, 38, 39, 41, 50, 76, 84, 118, 126, 153, 158; *Portrait of William Pitt the Younger* (1759–1806), *c.*1782 (oil on canvas) by Gainsborough Dupont (1754–97), Private Collection/Philip Mould, Historical Portraits Ltd/BAL: p.12; *Portrait of George III (1738–1820) in his coronation robes, c.* 1760 (oil on canvas) by Allan Ramsay (1713–84), Private Collection/BAL: p.14*t*; Mary Evans Picture Library: pp.14*b*, 49, 64, 79, 93, 103, 108, 143; *Portrait of Mary Wollstonecraft Godwin* (1759–97), engraved by W.T. Annis, pub. 1802, (engraving)(b/w photo), Private Collection/BAL: p.23; *Portrait of Sir Robert Peel* (1788–1850), (engraving, b/w photo) by English School (19th century), The Illustrated London News Picture Library, London, UK/BAL: p.60; reproduction of *The monster meeting*, 20/9/1843, at Clifden in the Irish Highlands, showing Daniel O'Connell MP, addressing his supporters, by Joseph Patrick

Haverty, courtesy of the National Gallery of Ireland: p.73; *Horatio, Viscount Nelson* (1758–1805), 1793, by Sir William Beechey (1753–1839), Guildhall Art Gallery, Corporation of London, UK/BAL: p.90; Hulton Getty Picture Collection: pp.94, 106, 142, 156, 164, 176; *Portrait of Arthur Wellesley, 1st duke of Wellington*, 1814, by Sir Thomas Lawrence (1769–1830), Apsley House, The Wellington Museum, London, UK/Topham Picturepoint/BAL: p.96; *Portrait of Thomas Malthus* (1756–1834), political economist, 1883 (oil on canvas, b/w photo) by John Linnell (1792–1882), Private Collection/Roger-Viollet/BAL: p.163; The Royal Archives © Her Majesty Queen Elizabeth II / W. E. Kilburn: p. 197.

We have been unable to trace the copy of the engraving on page 169, and would be grateful for any information that would enable us to do so.

Picture research by Sandie Huskinson-Rolfe of PHOTOSEEKERS.

Contents

Britain in the 1780s

Focus questions

◆ In what ways was Britain a country of economic diversity?

◆ How was British society structured?

◆ How did Britain's political system work?

◆ How important was religion?

Overview

In the 1780s **England** was, in some respects, very modern. It was a country experiencing rapid industrial change, where the growing population was being drawn to the expanding towns and cities of the north and the Midlands. It was a land criss-crossed by the canals and newly surfaced roads that were fuelling economic growth. But in many important respects it was still an old country, where communications were slow and many people still worked on the land. In the 1780s, the tensions between change and continuity were unresolved and, in some ways, they remained unresolved six decades later, in 1846.

In what ways was Britain a country of economic diversity?

Population

Britain's population had been growing since the first half of the eighteenth century. By the first national census in 1801, it had reached 15.7 million and by 1831, 24.1 million. The superficial cause of this increase was straightforward: after the 1750s, the **birth rate** increased and the **death rate** fell. But historians disagree about the reasons for these changes. A decline in killer diseases like smallpox, improving living conditions and economic prosperity (which encouraged early **marriage**) resulted in higher life expectancy – it is likely that it was a combination of these factors that caused growth in the population.

Broadly, **England** was divided into London (the metropolis) and those areas outside London (the provinces).

The **birth rate** is measured as births per year per 1,000 of the population.

The **death rate** is measured as the number of people who die each year per 1,000 of the population.

The age of **marriage** fell in the eighteenth century from around 28 years to 26 years for women. This increased their child-bearing period.

What were the main reasons behind the growth of the population in the early nineteenth century?

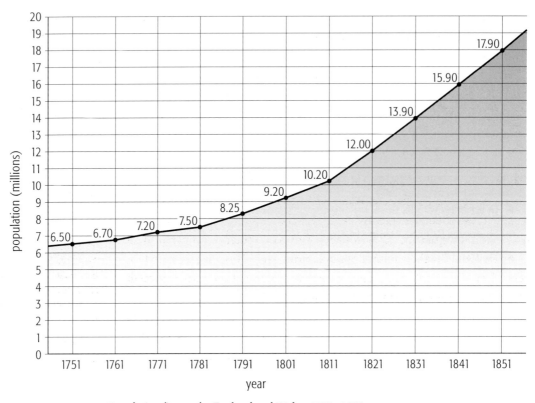

Population figures for England and Wales, 1751–1851.

Population growth stimulated demand for raw materials, manufactured goods, food and services that could be provided by the growing reservoir of available labour. Manufacturing industries, whether in the areas of dynamic growth like cotton textiles or in traditional **artisan**-based trades, expanded. The service sector saw particular growth, with increased demand for domestic, medical and legal services and the creation of new professions to support expanding industries, towns and agriculture.

Artisans were skilled workers.

Population growth stimulated urban growth as people moved from the rural areas to the newer urban centres of production and to London. Urban growth had its costs as well as its benefits. It heightened squalor, with many migrants finding they had exchanged rural for urban slums. Poor living and working conditions resulted in death rates remaining high in towns, especially among the labouring population, and in increasing exploitation in the workplace. This led to a growing gulf between the rich and the poor.

What were the main results of population growth?

An agricultural revolution

Between 1750 and 1850 sweeping changes took place in British agriculture in response to the increased demand for food from a rapidly expanding population.

Farming dominated the British economy in the 1780s. The previous century had seen major changes in farming:

- Turnips and crops like clover ended the need for fallow land.
- Cheaper iron-making led to major developments in ploughs, though it was not until after 1850 that agricultural machines were widely used.
- Selective breeding increased the quality and quantity of meat and dairy produce.
- **Enclosure** of arable land led to the better use of land.

The growing needs of the population as well as the increased profitability of farming during the **French Wars**, when imports of grain from Europe were often restricted, made it profitable to make better use of arable land. By 1820, 25 million **quarters** of corn were produced annually, compared to 15 million in 1760. Yet this was not enough. From the 1760s, Britain relied on foreign imports of wheat to feed its growing population. Urban growth could not have been sustained without this.

The French Wars marked a high point in British farming. Farmers invested heavily in improving their land, funded by high grain prices. After 1815, however, falling prices and cheaper continental imports brought

Enclosure turned the large open or strip fields in Britain into smaller fields demarcated by hedges or fences. In England and Wales, land was enclosed for arable farming. In Scotland, land was cleared of people to make way for sheep.

In what ways had farming in Britain been transformed by the 1780s?

The **French Wars** lasted, on and off, from 1793 to 1815. First Britain fought against revolutionary France and then against Napoleon Bonaparte.

A **quarter** was 28 pounds or 12.7 kg.

Haymakers by George Stubbs, 1785. An idealised view of rural life.

problems for arable farmers that led to successful demands for **protection**. This resulted in the passage of the **Corn Law** in 1815. Urban and industrial Britain saw the Corn Law as a means of keeping food prices artificially high and of supporting farming at the expense of the manufacturing industry.

High costs certainly made wheat farming difficult when prices were low. Many arable farmers complained of economic depression between 1815 and the mid-1830s. Those who survived did so by significantly reducing their labour costs. Many agricultural labourers, especially in southern England where little alternative employment was available, found themselves in **distress**.

The role of agriculture in the English economy was showing signs of declining national importance by the 1820s. This was less so in Wales, Scotland and Ireland, where farming remained important.

The Industrial Revolution

Between 1750 and 1850 the British economy experienced very rapid and pronounced growth in manufacturing and a sudden acceleration of technical and economic development. The proportion of the **labour force** employed in industry, whether in the manufacturing or service sectors, increased and the proportion employed in farming fell. The textile, iron and coal industries underwent dramatic change as new technologies and new markets stimulated growth on an unprecedented scale.

But this traditional view of the Industrial Revolution is only part of the picture. The success of cotton textiles was not typical of manufacturing industry. In other sectors, growth was modest. There was no great leap forward for the economy as a whole. There was growth of a far less dynamic nature in a whole range of traditional industries like furniture-making and hat-making. Most employment in manufacturing industries, such as ship-building and gun-making, remained small-scale and these trades were hardly affected by new technology.

It was the wider use of **division of labour** that allowed output to grow. Economic change was the result of the combination of old and new processes. Steam power did not replace water power at a stroke. Work organisation was varied and factories coexisted with **domestic production**, artisan workshops, large-scale mining and metal-producing industries. As late as 1851, the majority of people employed in Britain worked in the unmechanised sectors of the economy.

The market – local, regional, national or international – was at the heart of the economy in the 1780s. The transport of bulky goods was made easier by the development of the canal network in the second half of the eighteenth century and by railways after 1830. These changes helped reduce the cost of transport. Coastal and river transport became increasingly important,

An engraving of the upper ironworks at Coalbrookdale showing horses pulling a steam engine cylinder made at the works.

although Britain remained a predominantly horse-drawn society until the late nineteenth century.

The last half of the eighteenth century saw a growing demand for consumer goods. The experience of London was paralleled in the growing cities of the Midlands and the north. Population growth stimulated demand for cloth, leather for shoes, bricks, pottery, iron pots and pans. Growing consumption influenced, and was in turn influenced by, trade and economic growth.

What were the major features of the British economy in the 1780s?

How was British society structured?

The working population

The labouring population, who made up the bulk of society, consisted of those who earned their wages largely through manual work. There were, however, important differences within the working population. Agricultural labourers formed a major part of the workforce in rural Britain. Even within this group, there was a distinction between labourers in the low-waged southern English counties, where there was little alternative employment, and those in the higher-waged northern counties, where farmers had to compete for labour with expanding urban manufacturing industries. Within rural communities, the social hierarchy was based upon levels of skills that paralleled levels of income. Bird-scarers, usually children, were at the base of the hierarchy, while ploughmen were at the top. Only the better-educated shepherds had greater status.

The same hierarchy of skills existed in industrial Britain and the distinction between skilled and unskilled or general labourers was important. Artisans were highly paid and relatively secure in traditional trades largely unchanged by the Industrial Revolution. They guarded their skills, developed through the process of apprenticeship, against semi-skilled workers who were paid less. Skilled factory workers, like the fine-cotton spinners and weavers of Lancashire, benefited from new technology. Others, like handloom weavers and framework knitters, became redundant. The creation of new skills during the Industrial Revolution led to the gradual creation of new skilled elites: foremen, overseers and technicians as well as managers.

Semi-skilled and unskilled manual labour was more vulnerable to economic fluctuations and to unemployment or under-employment. Men were generally able to push women to the lower-paid margins of manufacturing. Women found work in the sweated trades, like dress-making, where they worked long hours for little pay in small unregulated workshops, or as domestic servants, for which there was a growing demand.

The Industrial Revolution resulted in great diversity in the experience of the working population. Some workers, like navvies, experienced rising wages while others, like handloom weavers, saw incomes decline or jobs disappear.

The middle classes

The middle classes were increasingly defined as a class in the late eighteenth century. They were distinguished from the aristocratic elite by their need to earn a living and from the labouring population by their property, however small, represented by houses, manufactured goods, tools or by educational investment in skills or expertise. If they were successful in their trade or business, they might be able to buy land and so enter the landed classes. As a class, the middle classes benefited from the changes in the economy and, although they were not exclusively urban, they were increasingly found in the growing towns of the provinces.

Their sense of class identity came from their growing acceptance of a common social and political ideology. This had three strands:

- First, **evangelicalism**, whether Anglican or **Nonconformist**, provided a firm religious foundation grounded in a 'call to seriousness'. It emphasised the virtues of hard work, plain and moral living, respectable family life and, above all, conscience. This contrasted with the aristocracy, who were widely accused of immoral behaviour.
- Secondly, the ideas of **Jeremy Bentham** attacked the inefficiency of aristocratic society. Tradition, restriction and influence, the values particular to aristocratic landed society, were compared, unfavourably, with the middle-class virtues of order, discipline, merit and application.

How was the working population divided up?

Evangelicalism brought a sense of religious commitment to existing religious groupings. It was based on moral earnestness and belief in salvation through conversion and faith.

Nonconformists were people who did not conform to the Church of England or dissented from its beliefs. In the eighteenth and early nineteenth centuries, they were called Dissenters. After 1828, when they were given the same rights as Anglicans, they tend to be called Nonconformists.

Jeremy Bentham (1748–1832) was a philosopher who believed in 'the greatest happiness of the greatest number'. He used this to make judgements about how society and its institutions worked.

- Finally, **political economy**, with its focus on the freedom of the market and the virtue of enterprise, provided an economic justification for the growing power of the middle classes. The middle classes promoted their ideology with missionary zeal.

In the 1780s the middle classes encompassed, at one end, city bankers and large industrialists with incomes from investment and profits of over £500 per year and, at the other extreme, small shopkeepers and clerks with annual earnings of only £50. The provincial elites were a small group of men and their families who controlled growing industrial complexes. In London, the elite were the merchant bankers. On familiar and sometimes marrying terms with the aristocracy, they were not representative of the middle class as a whole.

The lower middle class was composed of smaller manufacturers, shopkeepers, milliners, tailors and local brewers as well as a rapidly growing number of clerks in both business and government, schoolteachers, an emerging managerial class, accountants, pharmacists and engineers. Aware of their status, they maintained an important distinction between themselves, as employees who were paid either fees for their services or a monthly salary, and wage-earning manual workers.

The landed classes

In the 1780s power – economic and political – still lay in the possession and exploitation of land. Landowners did not simply farm their own land or rent

What formed the basis of middle-class ideology?

Political economy or classical economy was developed initially by Adam Smith in *The wealth of nations,* published in 1776, and taken further by other writers like Thomas Malthus and David Ricardo. Smith and his successors argued that economic growth was best achieved when there was a free market in goods and services, with countries trading with each other freely without customs duties or tariffs restricting trade. They believed that the state should keep its intervention in the economy to a minimum; this was known as the idea of *laissez-faire.*

Capital and Labour, a *Punch* cartoon showing the relationship between rich and poor.

it out to tenant farmers. They exploited mineral deposits on their estates, providing stone, slate, sand, brick-clay, timber and coal for growing industries. They rented out their urban properties in response to a growing housing shortage. They invested in government stocks, the Bank of England, in industry and transport.

Since they monopolised the offices of state, landowners benefited from being in power. They controlled patronage, rewarding the loyalty of friends, family and clients openly and without moral scruple, to maintain their political power. They were adaptable, if conservative, in outlook. A **peerage** of 300 wealthy families dominated the landed classes.

The **peerage** consisted of individuals who had a seat in the House of Lords.

The **squire** was the major landowner in a parish; he often controlled the appointment of the parson.

In what ways was landed society divided in the 1780s?

On one level, **paternalism** meant being supportive to those with less wealth. On another, it meant acting as a father disciplining people as if they were children.

Beneath great landowners were the gentry. They dominated the counties as **squires**, justices of the peace, Poor Law officials, churchwardens and backbench MPs. Below the gentry, landed society forked into a hierarchy of owner-occupiers or freeholders, with incomes ranging from £700 down to as little as £30 per year, and tenant farmers, who found their profits threatened by falling food prices. The latter group were the most vocal supporters of the Corn Laws.

The basis of landed society was mutual obligation within a hierarchical framework: those lower down on the social scale deferred to those above them and those higher up adopted **paternalistic** attitudes to those below. This was acceptable to most people in rural England and Scotland, where the landlord usually shared the same nationality and culture. This was less the case in Wales and Ireland, where landlords were often from both an alien culture *and* religion.

By the 1780s, however, the bond of dependency between landlord, tenant farmer and labourer was beginning to break down. There had always been popular disturbances like food riots when people reminded those with power of their responsibilities and of the need for just wages and just prices. Food riots in the 1790s, the rural slump after 1815, the riots in the Fens in 1816, in Norfolk and Suffolk in 1822 and, particularly, the Swing riots across southern England in 1830 (see Chapter 10) challenged established values. Each rising was largely unsuccessful and harshly repressed. The market, not appeals to custom and established practice, increasingly determined the social behaviour of the landed classes.

How did Britain's political system work?

Legislation is introduced by acts of parliament, sometimes called statute law. Before legislation passes all its stages in parliament, it is called a bill.

The United Kingdom, based on a single parliament at Westminster, was quite new in the 1780s. Wales was united with England by **legislation** in 1536 and 1542. The Act of Union with Scotland took place in 1707. However, Ireland did not lose its independence until 1800. The British constitution comprising monarchy, House of Commons and House of Lords had been held up, particularly by continental writers, as a model of how a country should be run. But the American War of Independence (1775–83) and the outbreak of revolution in France in 1789 led to increasing radical demands for reform of the system.

The electorate

In England and Wales in the 1780s, about 435,000 people out of a population of 7.5 million (just over 5 per cent) could vote. In Scotland and Ireland, less than 1 per cent of the total population of 6 million could vote.

The Septennial Act of 1715 established seven-year parliaments (although general elections were also held on the death of the monarch, a practice finally ended in 1867). The House of Commons was made up of MPs from the boroughs or towns and the counties. Both boroughs and counties sent two MPs each to parliament. In the counties, all **40-shilling freeholders** were entitled to vote, which meant that some of the counties had a considerable number of voters. Yorkshire, for example, had about 20,000 in the 1780s. Bedfordshire had nearly 4,000 just before the Reform Act of 1832, which was average for an English county. The situation was much more confused in the boroughs. In some, the vote was only given to the corporation or town council. In others, it was given to those who owned or occupied certain types of property or to local tax-payers or to all those who were not getting alms or charity.

Counties had larger electorates than boroughs and were more democratic because the size of the electorate was important in determining the level of corruption surrounding an election. The 'rotten boroughs', like Dunwich in Suffolk where 32 electors chose the two MPs, were an important issue of the day. Rotten boroughs had been important centres of population, trade or industry in the medieval period, but they had declined in importance over the centuries. Where there were a small number of voters in a borough, they were able to sell their votes during elections. The price varied: some electors accepted straightforward bribes, while others preferred to negotiate benefits for their town or corporation. Successful candidates were expected to show their gratitude. An elector had two votes, but could give both votes to one candidate. Since elections were expensive, great efforts were made to avoid a contest whenever possible.

More than 40 per cent of the English boroughs had electorates of less than 100 and two-thirds had electorates below 500. This made it easier for candidates to affect the results of an election through corruption. Some boroughs were under the control of a particular family or patron. Although control by patrons was accepted, the electorate could not be taken for granted and they had to be carefully cultivated.

40-shilling freeholders
were those people owning land rated at 40 shillings.

The electors voted in public on a stage known as a **husting**. Elections took place over several days.

Returning officers were responsible for conducting elections in constituencies. In the eighteenth century they were not impartial organisers but often supporters of one of the candidates.

How did the electoral system work?

Elections

Eighteenth-century and early-nineteenth-century elections were noisy, rough and held in public. Drunkenness and rioting were common events. Voting took place on an open **husting** and unpopular preferences were greeted with catcalls, whistles or overripe fruit. Opponents were lured into taverns where they were made drunk and locked up until voting was completed. Since there was no voting register, documents were often forged to give the vote to those who did not have it. Dead men were impersonated, votes were cast twice and the **returning officer** often embarrassed his opponents by transferring the hustings to some inaccessible and unadvertised spot. Known enemies were disqualified on trumped-up charges. Once all the votes had been cast, there were still disputes over whether individuals had the right to vote.

Parties

Before 1832, working out election results was complicated by the vagueness of party lines, the number of uncontested elections (where there was only one candidate) and the presence of independent candidates. National political parties, like those we have today that offer distinctive political programmes and have organised national and local party machines, did not begin to emerge until after the Reform Acts of 1832.

However, from the 1780s the number of MPs consistently supporting **Tory** or **Whig** positions in votes in the House of Commons did increase. But to talk about the Whig and Tory parties is deceptive. In neither case did the term mean a tightly knit political group, although both Whig and Tory supporters came from the aristocratic landed elite. It is important not to project our modern view of political parties back into the eighteenth century. The Whigs and Tories in the 1780s lacked significant organisation at central and local level and their ministers made little attempt to control their supporters through party discipline. Historians have argued that the term 'groupings' might be a better way of describing the parties of the late eighteenth century.

Prime ministers remained in office if they had the support of both the monarch and the House of Commons. They had at their disposal large amounts of political patronage, which they used to maintain their authority and to manage parliament. Pursuing planned policies was difficult and throughout this period prime ministers tended to react to situations rather than determine them. Changes in policy were only possible when they were widely supported across the political establishment or if the policy was uncontroversial.

The term **Tory** was applied to those who upheld the rights of the crown, resisted the removal of disabilities from Roman Catholics and Dissenters, and opposed parliamentary reform. Under Sir Robert Peel, the term Conservative replaced Tory.

The **Whigs** were defenders of parliamentary government and accountability of ministers to parliament. They were in favour of religious toleration and became supporters of moderate parliamentary reform in the 1820s.

How important was religion?

Organised religion in the 1780s played a dominant role in people's lives. Christian principles formed the bedrock of society and its system of morality. Baptism, marriage and burial were key events in people's lives. The pulpit was an important means of communication. The churches provided education, especially for the poor, in the form of day and **Sunday schools** and people often learned to read from the Bible. The language, images and messages of religious belief were present throughout society. Chapel or church were at the heart of many communities and provided a focus for spiritual and practical support.

The fundamental religious division was between Roman Catholicism and Protestantism, the religion of the state throughout Great Britain. The Anglican Church (or Church of England) was the established church, except in Scotland where the Presbyterian Church had the same role. The Anglican Church was created by parliament in the sixteenth and seventeenth centuries and its archbishops and bishops, a conservative body largely unwilling to allow reform, sat in the House of Lords.

The strength of the Anglican Church had always lain in rural England. By the 1780s, however, the close relationship between squire and parson, which had kept rural society under control, was threatened by weakening social ties and widespread criticisms of clerical abuses.

The Church was weak in the growing towns. It failed to accommodate growing congregations, which left a religious vacuum among the working population that was filled by Nonconformity or Dissent from the 1760s and 1770s.

Anti-Catholic feelings ran deep in British society and Roman Catholics were, until 1829, denied the same civil rights as Protestants. In Ireland, Catholicism was the religion of the majority. It was seen as a means of expressing nationalist aspirations and was consequently viewed by the authorities as subversive. In Wales, Calvinist Methodism increasingly took a similar stance.

Sunday schools began in the 1780s. They were designed to keep working-class children off the streets and provided a limited education.

What different types of organised religion were there in the 1780s?

What separated supporters of the established church and Nonconformists?

Summary questions

1 Identify and explain any *two* factors that marked out Britain as an 'old country' in the 1780s.

2 Compare the importance of at least *three* issues in ensuring change in Britain after 1780.

2

William Pitt, 1783–1801

Focus questions

◆ What was the basis of Pitt's authority between 1783 and 1801?

◆ Why did Pitt dominate politics between 1783 and 1793?

◆ How successfully did Pitt face the challenges of the French Revolution between 1789 and 1801?

Significant dates

1783	Pitt becomes prime minister
1788–89	Regency crisis
1789	Outbreak of French Revolution
1793	War with France begins
1798	Irish rebellion breaks out
1800	Act of Union with Ireland
1801	Pitt resigns; Henry Addington becomes prime minister; French war ends with Peace at Amiens
1804	War with France resumes
1805	Battle of Trafalgar takes place
1806	Pitt dies

William Pitt the Younger
(1759–1806).

Overview

William Pitt dominated British politics in the late eighteenth and early nineteenth centuries. When he became prime minister, America had just gained its independence, Britain was isolated in Europe and its finances were in a perilous state. Pitt restored national finances, revived trade and introduced important reforms in the first ten years of his government. All this led to a 'national revival' in Britain.

The second part of his ministry was dominated by the French Revolution. Britain led the coalitions of European countries that fought, not altogether successfully, against revolutionary France. At home, Pitt had to deal with demands for radical parliamentary reform, which he rejected with considerable firmness.

Ireland proved his undoing. The 1798 rebellion was followed by the Act of Union in 1800 that brought the government of Ireland directly under the control of Westminster and ended the Irish parliament in Dublin. Pitt had committed himself to delivering emancipation to the Irish Catholics in return for their agreement to the removal of the Irish parliament. He was unable to make good on this commitment because of King George's opposition and, as a result, he resigned in 1801.

What was the basis of Pitt's authority between 1783 and 1801?

After 1760 there were ten years of instability as George III sought a prime minister to run the government whom he found acceptable. Stability was eventually provided by the administration of **Lord North**, which lasted from 1770 until 1782. As a result of the crisis in the **American colonies**, his government also collapsed.

Successive governments did not have the king's support and were unable to forge reliable majorities in the Commons. Effective government proved difficult though 'economical reform', which aimed to reduce the parliamentary patronage at the disposal of the government, was pushed through and peace was agreed with America in 1783.

In early 1783 North formed a coalition government with the Whigs, now led by **Charles James Fox**. George III had little choice but to accept the coalition because it had the support of the House of Commons.

Pitt 'the Younger'

William Pitt (1759–1806) was the son of William Pitt the Elder (1708–78), who was prime minister between 1766 and 1768. He entered parliament in 1781 and was chancellor of the exchequer in the short-lived government of Lord Shelburne from July 1782 until early 1783. He refused to support the Fox–North coalition and he joined forces with the king to defeat the passage of the India bill, which attacked the rights of the **East India Company** and royal patronage. After the India bill was defeated, the king dismissed the Fox–North coalition government in December 1783, arguing that the coalition government had lost the support of the House of Commons and was therefore no longer fit to govern. He then asked Pitt to form the new, albeit minority, government.

Pitt became increasingly confident as he won the votes of many independent MPs and majorities against him began to fall. Between December 1783

Frederick, Lord North (1732–92), was an able domestic Tory politician, but his mishandling of the American crisis and conduct of the war led to his downfall.

The relationship between the 13 **American colonies** and Britain caused growing concern in the years after 1763. Neither the king nor successive governments understood the depth of feeling in the colonies about their relationship with Britain. The result was war in 1775 and the declaration of American independence in 1776.

Charles James Fox (1749–1806) entered parliament in 1768 but, apart from two short periods in office, he remained in opposition as leader of the Whigs. He opposed the government's American policy in the 1770s and welcomed the French Revolution. During the 1790s, he emerged as the champion of British liberties in the face of Pitt's repressive measures.

The **East India Company** was powerful in India, where it ruled large tracts of land. The Whigs, who wanted to see it brought under the supervision of parliament, tried and failed to do so in their India bill in 1783.

How did Pitt become prime minister in late 1783?

George III (reigned 1760–1820).

The **1784 general election** results were: Pittites 315, Foxites/Northites 213 and Independents 30.

What role did George III play in the politics of 1782–84?

and March 1784, Pitt was able to govern without a majority for two reasons. First, he had the complete support of the king and, secondly, he also had support outside parliament, where he had a reputation as a reformer and as an individual who was seen to put the country before the narrow political advantages of party. In March 1784, when the opposition's majority had dwindled to one, George III dissolved parliament and called a general election.

The king's intervention was both unconstitutional and controversial, but he argued his actions were justifiable. Although the king had infringed the independence of parliament, he had considerable popular support and many people thought that he had averted a threat to the constitution. They believed that the opposition, led by Fox and North, had threatened stable government when they challenged the right of the king to choose the ministers he wanted.

Pitt's support within parliament came from those who believed in strong, stable government. They preferred to have improved administrative structures, particularly if these produced more efficient and cheaper government rather than expensive programmes of reform. Pitt was content to work within the system and never attempted to fashion popularity in any way independent of the king.

The events of 1783 and 1784 showed that the support of the king was essential if a government was to survive, as he still had considerable influence.

The 1784 election

The **1784 general election** was highly successful for Pitt as it gave him the majority necessary for effective government. The election was important for two reasons:
- First, Pitt had restored the principle of a minister governing with the support of both the king and the House of Commons.
- Secondly, despite the loss of party members and sympathetic independent MPs, the Whigs had not been destroyed as a political force.

By the end of the 1780s, the term 'leader of the opposition' was coming into use. It applied to Charles James Fox, the Whig leader in the Commons, rather than to the duke of Portland, the Whig leader who sat in the Lords. The public's perception of 'government' versus 'opposition' was heightened by the personal rivalry between Pitt and Fox.

Pitt may have won in 1784, but this did not mean that the following decade was without political tensions. Throughout the 1780s the opposition Whigs more or less maintained their voting strength, and between 1784 and 1786 Pitt was defeated on four substantial issues: defence, parliamentary reform, and economic unions with the United States and Ireland.

Charles James Fox (1749–1806).

Why was the 1784 general election so important?

The regency crisis, 1788–89

When George III was stricken by an attack of apparent **madness** in late 1788, the Whigs were in a state of disarray. They had been associated with **George, prince of Wales**, for six years. The Whigs saw the succession of the prince as their route to office – once he became king, he would dismiss Pitt and appoint Fox and the Whigs. For his part, the prince was happy to use the Whigs to embarrass his father. This state of affairs proved to be a two-edged sword for the Whigs: they were obliged to apply to parliament for additional money to clear the prince's unpopular debts, while the discovery that he had secretly married the Catholic **Maria Fitzherbert** in 1785 alienated Portland and other aristocratic Whig leaders.

These tensions within the Whigs surfaced in 1788 shortly before the king's illness and made it clear how dependent the Whigs were on the prince if they were to achieve power. The fact that Fox relied on the future king for power highlighted the hypocrisy of his attacks on Pitt, who owed his position to the existing king.

Pitt knew that if the prince of Wales became **regent**, he would almost certainly dismiss him and his government. This prompted Pitt and his supporters to draw up a Regency bill in late 1788 that closely limited the power of the regent. The Whigs delayed the passage of the bill, arguing that the limitations placed on the regent's powers (especially his right to make new peers) was an unfair restriction on the power of the crown. They argued that the prince should have unlimited power and should not have to seek parliament's approval for his actions.

Pitt's majority held and he was able to push his bill through parliament. In mid February, when the bill was in its final stage in the Lords, the king made a rapid recovery, thus ending the process. The opposition had been defeated, Pitt had preserved his ministry and won the thanks of the king and large sections of the public.

In spite of this crisis, however, the Whigs recovered quickly and entered the 1790 general election well organised, thanks to the management of William Adams, the party's election manager.

The development of the Tories and Whigs as political parties

The French Revolution transformed British political life. One way in which this manifested itself was between 1790 and 1794, when tensions within the opposition Whigs led to divisions within the party. The publication in November 1790 of Edmund Burke's *Reflections on the revolution in France* (see page 22 for a discussion of Burke's beliefs), in which he laid down principles subsequently identified as central to the ideology of Conservatism, provoked division within the Whigs.

Recent research suggests that porphyria (a condition caused by blood deficiencies) was the cause as the symptoms of **madness** and porphyria are similar.

George, prince of Wales (1762–1830), eventually succeeded his father in 1820 as George IV. He was regarded by many contemporaries as feckless with money and his debts mounted in the 1780s and 1790s. In the 1780s he was an attractive figure who appealed to those denied power, but in middle and old age he was regarded as a conservative figure.

George, prince of Wales, married **Maria Fitzherbert** illegally: the Royal Marriages Act of 1772 made it illegal for a member of the royal family to marry without the permission of the monarch. The Act of Succession of 1701 forbade marriage to a Roman Catholic.

What happened during the regency crisis of 1788–89?

When a monarch is unable to carry out their duties, a **regent** becomes the effective head of state, appointing ministers and governments. George III recovered in 1789, but when his final breakdown occurred in 1811, the prince of Wales became prince regent, a position he held until he became king in 1820 on the death of his father.

In May 1791 Fox, who was an enthusiastic supporter of the Revolution, parted company with **Burke**. Fox and Burke had long been political and personal friends and their parting reflected a growing concern that the Whigs were becoming a radical, reforming group. Burke took only a few supporters with him, but the rift within the party widened during the following year.

In April 1792 a group of radical Whigs formed the Friends of the People in an attempt to commit the party to parliamentary reform. The Whigs had to make an uncomfortable choice: Burke had emphasised the dangers of well-meaning reforms leading to revolution and, increasingly, the debate within the Whig party polarised over whether it should emphasise reform and liberty or order and public security.

Fox did not join the Friends of the People although he sympathised with its aims – he had become increasingly convinced that Pitt intended to undermine English liberties. In December 1792 he was driven to defend both the French Revolution and parliamentary reform as he had come to believe that Britain had more to fear from the influence of George III than from the French Revolution. As a result, 30 conservative Whigs distanced themselves from Fox and Portland and declared their support for the government.

The execution of the French king, Louis XVI, in January 1793 and the outbreak of war with France the following month aggravated Whig problems. Fox opposed the war, while Portland regarded it as a regrettable necessity. Later that year (in May) Fox supported a motion for parliamentary reform in the Commons, but Portland opposed it.

The result of these tensions was that Fox found it impossible to keep the Whig party together. By late 1793, the conservative Whigs had separated from the party and had joined forces with Burke. Then, in July 1794, Portland formed a coalition with Pitt: he and four other conservative Whigs entered the cabinet. This marked a realignment of political forces.

The formation of this coalition is often described as marking the birth of the modern Tory party. The French Revolution and the outbreak of war with France in 1793 brought to a head the fundamental divisions in British politics, between those who wanted to resist change (the Tories) and those in favour of fundamental constitutional reform (the Whigs) that was to dominate political debate for the next century.

However, the division between the two parties was never absolute and, when they were under pressure from the public (especially the threat of public disorder), the Tories *were* prepared to introduce reform. In that respect, the events of 1794 can be seen as the beginnings of the modern Tory party. However, it must be remembered that between 1794 and 1801 the members of the coalition government were united primarily by a fear of France and by their support for the existing system rather than by any fundamental political principles.

Pitt did not really see himself as a Tory, rather, as he said on many occasions, as an 'independent Whig'. In spite of this, Portland and the conservative Whigs never lost their long-standing distrust of Pitt. Between 1794 and 1801, Pitt could count on the support of over 500 of the 600 MPs in the House of Commons. His personal support had increased in the 1780s and early 1790s to around 420 MPs and Portland's Whigs made up the remaining 80 supporters.

The coalition between Pitt and the Whigs was one of convenience, grounded in the need to win the war with France and to limit the threat of revolution in Britain.

Fox and his supporters, numbering about 60 MPs, stood apart. Between 1794 and 1797, they demonstrated a commitment to peace and reform, calling for an end to the war and for religious freedom and parliamentary reform. When in 1797 **Charles Grey's** reform motion was defeated in the Commons, the Foxite Whigs renounced regular parliamentary attendance, though they never completely seceded. Pitt's resignation in 1801 brought them flooding back to parliament.

Charles Grey, 2nd Earl Grey (1764–1845), adopted a radical approach to parliamentary reform in the 1790s, but he was far more conservative in nature when he was prime minister between 1830 and 1834.

The fall of Pitt

The fall of Pitt in 1801 was a matter of conflicting constitutional principles. Pitt had committed himself to Catholic emancipation in order to win the support of the Irish Catholics for union between the Irish and English parliaments. He was unable to fulfil his promise because of King George's opposition to Catholic emancipation. As a result, he felt honour-bound to resign in 1801.

He had been in power for nearly 18 years and had fought a hardly successful war for 8. He was physically and mentally exhausted. His management of the cabinet had, since the mid-1790s, become increasingly high-handed and he had begun to take the king's support for granted. The king's refusal to accept Catholic emancipation may have been his way of re-establishing royal influence. The crisis of 1801 clearly showed the continuing importance of the monarch in politics. It is also important to remember that the king's attitude reflected the anti-Catholicism of public opinion at the time.

Why did Pitt fall in 1801?

Why did Pitt dominate politics between 1783 and 1793?

Pitt was a cautious and unsuccessful reformer in the early 1780s. In 1785 he unsuccessfully attempted to abolish 36 rotten boroughs (see Chapter 1) and to transfer their seats to London and the counties. He failed to achieve economic union with Ireland and dropped the idea of economic union with America.

These failures confirmed that Pitt was unable to push through the reforms he had hoped to make because they were so widely opposed. Parliament was prepared to accept Pitt as an administrative reformer, but not as a radical one.

The framework of government within which Pitt operated was overwhelmingly administrative. This meant that the government reacted to problems as they arose instead of planning ahead and initiating programmes of a reforming nature. Pitt was primarily an administrative reformer responsible for a 'national revival' between 1783 and the early 1790s in which he restored national finances and improved Britain's trade, making the country more prosperous.

Restoring national finances

In 1783 the government's expenditure exceeded its income by £10.8 million, largely because of the cost of the American War and inefficiency in collecting excise duties. The government had difficulty in raising loans and confidence in the eventual recovery of national finances was low. Between 1783 and 1791, annual governmental revenue increased by almost £4 million, half of which came from new taxes, the reduction of smuggling and fraud, and the remainder from an increasingly efficient system of tax collection.

Pitt's initial priority was to increase revenue and his first target was smuggling. It is difficult to estimate the effect smuggling had on national finances, but perhaps a fifth of all imports was contraband. Pitt adopted a two-pronged strategy:

- He introduced restrictive legislation which made smuggling less attractive and extended the authorities' right to search suspect cargoes.
- Parallel to this was a massive reduction of import duties. The Commutation Act of 1784 reduced the duty on tea from 119 per cent to a uniform 25 per cent; this was followed by reductions of duties on wines, spirits and tobacco.

Pitt did not destroy smuggling, but he made it a far less profitable and a far more risky business.

Pitt was one of the most efficient tax-gatherers ever to govern England. His taxation policy was based on the prevailing view that all should pay a share, but that the poor should not be overburdened. Luxury goods – horses, hackney carriages, gloves, hats, ribbons, candles, servants and hair powder – became the major items on which taxes were levied.

Pitt's taxation policy was largely acceptable to tax-payers, but could be both unpopular and misguided. It is possible, for example, that the window tax (which was a tax on glass panes) may have held back the development of the glass industry. A projected tax on coal was withdrawn because of opposition, and taxes imposed on linen and cotton in 1784 had serious economic implications and were immediately withdrawn.

In 1783, the **national debt** stood at £238 million with interest charges amounting to about a quarter of government spending. In 1786 Pitt wanted to reduce this by extending the 'sinking fund', into which annual sums were paid to reduce the national debt. It had existed since 1716, but its value had been reduced by ministers raiding it for other purposes. It was placed under the control of a board of six commissioners. The scheme worked well, with a £10 million reduction in the national debt, until the outbreak of war with France in 1793. The reform of the sinking fund was perhaps more important in restoring national confidence than in reducing the national debt.

A country's **national debt** is the total outstanding borrowings of its central government.

Administrative efficiency

Offices, whether **sinecures** or not, were given as rewards for political services, not on merit. Pitt wanted to reduce waste in government and needed competent administrators. As radical reform would have encountered widespread opposition, Pitt operated cautiously.

Sinecures were well-paid jobs for which a person was paid for doing little or nothing.

Sinecures and **placemen** were allowed to lapse on the death of their occupants. Most of the posts the public accounts commissioners recommended in 1786 should be abolished, disappeared within the next 20 years. Efficient departmental management was gradually built up, but with a greater degree of Treasury control.

Placemen owed their jobs to the government or crown. In both cases, they were expected to support the government of the day.

In 1785 a Treasury Commission of Audit was created to oversee public expenditure. The Board of Taxes was reinforced by staff transfers from the Treasury and the Excise Board. The creation of a central Stationery Office in 1787 ensured economies in the supply of stationery to departments. Pitt tightened naval spending, relying heavily on its comptroller of the Navy Office, **Sir Charles Middleton**, to implement his policies. People with talent were promoted and were encouraged to develop administrative policies on their own initiative.

Sir Charles Middleton, later Lord Barham, was largely responsible for the creation of a navy capable of responding to the French challenge between 1793 and 1815.

Under the Consolidated Fund Act of 1787, most revenue collected was paid into a single Treasury fund account. Instead of having their own funds, government departments had to bid for money from a central fund. This gave the Treasury greater control over how the government spent its money. This marked a major step forward in efficient administration, and led to economies and reduction of confusion.

Commercial policies

Financial and administrative efficiency was paralleled by a commercial policy that encouraged growing trade. The value of Britain's imports doubled to £20 million between 1783 and 1790, increasing revenues from import taxes and duties, while exports rose from £12.5 million in 1782 to over £20 million by 1790. This was a major achievement. Economic recovery meant that British industries and trade were able to grow and flourish.

The United States of America

The United States was seen as a threat to Britain's commercial supremacy. Pitt's new Committee of Trade rejected the proposal that trade barriers should be reduced. Instead the Navigation Acts, which protected British shipping from foreign competition, were maintained with vigour. Imported and exported goods between Britain and the United States had to be transported in British ships. In 1783, American shipping was excluded from the West Indian islands, while trade with America for cheaper meat and fish via the French and Spanish islands was made illegal in 1787–88. This was done to protect British farmers and fishermen.

Although Britain had lost political control in America, it was able to retain commercial domination there by preventing America from challenging its merchant shipping. By 1787, British exports to America had returned to the levels achieved in the early 1770s.

India and the East

After the loss of the American colonies, the government focused its attention on India and the East, with their potentially large markets. As we have seen, Pitt had come to power because of the abortive Fox–North India bill (see page 13). He dealt with this issue quickly by introducing the East India Act of 1784. This Act set up joint control of India by the East India Company and a committee that sat in London and was answerable to parliament. The committee determined Britain's policy towards India, and the East India Company was allowed to continue ruling its conquered territories as well as conducting its commercial operations. Trade in the East improved under Pitt, though this was partly the result of the ending of tea smuggling.

Europe

In 1783, Britain was isolated in Europe. France and Spain, for example, had fought on the side of the American colonies against Britain. There were important commercial reasons for ending Britain's isolation in Europe as soon as possible. Negotiations were entered into with all the leading courts of Europe for reciprocally lowered tariff duties. These negotiations to enter into free trade agreements with Europe were a stark contrast to the protectionist policy Pitt adopted towards America.

The Eden trade treaty with France, signed in September 1786, was the only real – though temporary – achievement of this policy. French wines entered

Britain at the same rates as Portuguese wine, and France was opened to British goods through general tariff reductions of 10–15 per cent. Opposition from British manufacturers ensured that the silk markets were excluded from this agreement. Within three years, French manufacturers were complaining that the treaty was unfairly weighted in favour of British manufacturers. In reality, their complaint was a reflection of Britain's competitiveness in the early stages of industrialisation.

Commercial considerations played a part in Britain's challenge to French expansion into the Low Countries (Belgium and the Netherlands). Britain also wanted to stop France from using Dutch overseas bases like Cape Town. Britain's isolation in Europe was emphasised by the French alliance with the Dutch in 1785, which reduced the powers of the pro-English **House of Orange**.

The **House of Orange** ruled the United Provinces.

When the Prussians successfully invaded Holland in 1787, Orange fortunes were revived. This was followed by the Triple Alliance between Prussia, the United Provinces (the Netherlands) and Britain, which ended Britain's diplomatic isolation.

Conclusion

Pitt was an efficient rather than an innovative prime minister. He improved existing systems of government and taxation, building on the work of previous governments. His approach was cautious and responsive to opposition. Historians frequently argue that Pitt was committed to the principles of free trade – this may be true, but it did not divert him from the practicalities of politics. Diplomatic and commercial realities meant that his commitment to freer trade was always limited. Britain's commercial success was built on protection, and the move to freer trade resulted from British industry no longer needing protection. The outbreak of war in 1793 drove the British government back to protectionist policies.

How did Pitt: (a) restore national finances; (b) improve the operation of government; and (c) encourage the development of British trade between 1783 and 1793?

Pitt's achievement was to reduce the temperature of political debate in the Commons. Pitt was always willing to serve and this, rather than any desire to be popular, was the key to his political career.

How successfully did Pitt face the challenges of the French Revolution between 1789 and 1801?

In 1789, the fall of the **Bastille** foreshadowed revolution in France. Although reactions to the Revolution were mixed in Britain, many people were initially well disposed towards it. Pitt thought it might bring political advantages for Britain because the Revolution weakened France's colonial ambitions. Some

The **Bastille** was the royal palace and prison in the centre of Paris. Its capture on 14 July 1789 by a Parisian mob marked the beginnings of the French Revolution.

Tory populists emphasised the violence and brutality of the revolution in France. This cartoon entitled 'A family of sans culottes refreshing after the fatigues of the day' by James Gillray was published in Britain two weeks after the September massacres of 1792 when around 1,400 prisoners were slaughtered in Paris.

The 1688 **Glorious Revolution** occurred when the Catholic James II was replaced by the Protestant William III and Mary, so preserving constitutional monarchy and the powers of parliament.

What was the initial reaction in Britain to the outbreak of revolution in France in 1789?

Thomas Paine (1737–1809) worked as an excise officer, emigrating to America following a dispute over pay claims. He supported the independence of the American colonies, but returned to Britain in 1787. Indicted for treason, he fled to France in 1792. He died in America.

What were the main ideas expressed by Edmund Burke?

thought France should adopt the same constitutional system as Britain had; others thought the Revolution might lead to reform in Britain.

The British believed themselves to be the freest people in Europe, thanks to the 1688 **Glorious Revolution**, and many foreigners flatteringly took the same view. It is not surprising that, to many, the opening stages of the Revolution looked like a French attempt to copy Britain. Nevertheless, the French Revolution had a profound and ongoing effect on political life and on government in Britain. At the same time, it caused widespread debate in all sectors of British society and roused British reformers into action.

Reacting to revolution: the intellectual debate

In November 1790, Edmund Burke published his *Reflections on the revolution in France*. For him, religion lay at the heart of civil society. He celebrated aristocratic concepts of paternalism, loyalty and the hereditary principle in which the great social institutions – the church, the law, even the family – confirmed the aristocracy as the ruling class and the protectors of traditional values. He maintained that the government did not derive its authority from the consent of the governed, but from custom, practice and experience. However, Burke was no reactionary, arguing that any state that did not embrace change would lose the ability to conserve itself.

The response to Burke's book was immediate. **Thomas Paine** wrote the first part of *Rights of man*, published in February 1791, as a reply to Burke's

Reflections. Part Two was published in April 1792. It was only one of the 38 responses to Burke, but it was the most influential. It merged the debate about the revolution with a programme of practical and radical reform.

Paine put forward a simple message. He denounced Burke's idea of society as an association between past and present generations and his view of the role of the monarchy and the aristocracy. For him, power lay with the people and their rights. The impact of *Rights of man* was immediate: distributed in cheap editions, it was widely discussed.

To his supporters, Paine was a heroic figure. To his opponents, he was a symbol of the excesses of revolution. Between 1792 and 1795, the circulation of Paine's work was one of the main reasons given for the passing of repressive legislation.

The debate was not confined to a dialogue between Burke and Paine. Many of the radical authors knew each other and their work can be seen as a collective project. Between 1791 and early 1793 Paine, **William Godwin** and **Mary Wollstonecraft** produced a number of innovative and Utopian proposals concerning the establishment of a welfare state, the withering away of the centralised state and equality in relationships (they advocated removing the automatic obedience of employees to employers and women to men).

The government was concerned that 'informed opinion' was in the hands of this closely knit circle. While those individuals were addressing *each other*, they represented no threat to the established order. However, the combination of growing political organisation and a supply of radical writings to politicise the masses was another matter.

A loyalist backlash began in late 1792: the Association for Preserving Liberty and Property against Republicans and Levellers (see page 26 for more discussion on this organisation) commissioned and circulated popularly written anti-radical pamphlets to ensure the loyalty of the labouring population. The APLP maintained pressure on the radical writers, while the government took steps to control radical publishing.

This was helped by the patriotic reaction to the outbreak of war with France in early 1793. After the publication of Godwin's *Political justice* in February 1793, innovative radical thinking stopped. Fewer pamphlets were published and those that were, repeated old ideas and tried to reassure a moderate audience rather than develop new theories.

The objective of many radical thinkers had been to attract as much support as possible for an anti-government stance. By 1800, with European societies destabilised and Burke's fears about the effects of revolution apparently realised, the radical vision of communicating with a wide audience had been established.

William Godwin (1756–1836) was a political writer and novelist best known for his *Political justice*, published in 1793. He married **Mary Wollstonecraft** (1759–97), who died after giving birth to their daughter, Mary (later Mary Shelley, the author of *Frankenstein*). Mary Wollstonecraft was a radical feminist whose *A vindication of the rights of woman*, advocating equality between the sexes, was published in 1792.

Mary Wollstonecraft (1759–97).

What ideas did radical writers like Paine produce in response to Burke?

Reacting to revolution: radical demands for reform

Dissenters were Protestants (such as the Baptists) who refused to conform to the established church.

The **Corporation Act** of 1661 and **Test Acts** of 1673 and 1678 were passed during Charles II's reign to limit the power of Dissenters and Catholics respectively. The Corporation Act banned Dissenters from being members of a town council or corporation. The Test Acts required Catholics to take the Anglican sacraments before taking public office. Dissenters fought a long campaign, beginning in 1787, to have them repealed.

In what ways did economic conditions in the 1790s influence radical activity?

What were the corresponding societies? What were their aims?

Events in France stimulated the **Dissenters'** campaign for the repeal of the **Test and Corporation Acts**. At the same time, the Society for Constitutional Information (SCI), founded in 1780, began to circulate radical propaganda. And, as we have seen, in April 1792 Whig reformers formed the Society of the Friends of the People to campaign for parliamentary reform.

Economic conditions in Britain in the first half of the 1790s also played an important role in demands for reform. The disturbed state of Europe in 1792–93 led to economic depression in Britain, with widespread unemployment and lower wages. War interrupted trade and also placed increasing tax burdens on the middle and working classes. Following harvest failure in 1794, economic distress reached critical levels in 1795–96 as food prices increased at a time when the labouring population was already faced with higher taxation and lower wages.

It is important, however, not to see the reforming movement simply in terms of a response to economic conditions. Instead of being a forum for airing traditional economic grievances, movements such as the corresponding societies crossed the threshold into making demands for fundamental political change.

Corresponding societies

During the winter of 1791–92, popular radical societies were formed. The London Corresponding Society (LCS), founded in January 1792 by a shoemaker called Thomas Hardy, was the most important. Membership was open to all who were able to pay a penny at each weekly meeting. Although formed to discuss the poverty faced by many of the labouring population and the high prices of the day, the LCS quickly adopted a political programme for remedying their grievances: universal adult male suffrage, annually elected parliaments and redistribution of rotten boroughs to the large towns. The LCS grew rapidly and developed a sophisticated organisational structure of divisions, district committees and a general committee.

Two features characterised the LCS: its size and its social composition. By late 1794, its total active membership was 3,000, but after that government repression led to falling support. In the spring of 1796, membership had fallen to about 2,000 and to about 600 in 1797. Before it was banned in 1798, the LCS had only 400 active members. LCS membership was confined to a very small proportion of London's working population. It cannot be called a working-class organisation because of the extent to which its membership was made up of individuals from the middling and professional classes as well as artisans and tradesmen. There is no evidence that the LCS ever had much appeal to unskilled labourers or to the very poor.

Provincial radical societies had begun to spring up even before the LCS was founded. The Sheffield Society for Constitutional Information was formed in late 1791. Within a few months it had 2,500 members. In the autumn of 1792 it succeeded in bringing 5,000–6,000 people onto the streets to celebrate the French victory at Valmy and in February 1794 a similar number to press for peace abroad and liberty at home.

During 1792 the number of societies mushroomed and regional differences became more obvious. Manchester, for example, had been Tory since the 1750s and this may account for the slow initial development of the Manchester Constitutional Society. In 1788 a Revolution Society was established in Norwich. It was dominated by middle-class Dissenters, merchants and tradesmen and Norwich soon rivalled Sheffield in the vanguard of radicalism.

Weekly meetings and the spread of printed propaganda provided a focus for the activities of the radical societies. They corresponded regularly with each other and with groups in France. However, their attempt to reach a mass audience was limited. No attempt was made, for example, to organise a nationwide petitioning campaign.

The reformers overestimated the amount of mass support they had and dangerously underestimated the fears they would arouse in the authorities. On the whole, radical tactics were very restrained. In 1795 some radicals in Sheffield did try to incite food rioters to protest against the war and demand parliamentary reform, and similar tactics were used in the north-west in 1800. However, these were isolated examples and the radicals made no attempt to co-ordinate popular riots. Most radical leaders, with their middle-class backgrounds, were committed to non-violent action. When the governing class refused to concede reform, resorting instead to repression and persecution, most radicals lost heart or moderated their demands.

Reacting to revolution: the conservative response

The attack on popular radicalism came from three directions. There was an attack on its ideology, a populist and loyalist reaction, and a legislative attack by Pitt's government. The reform movement collapsed not simply because of the government's repressive actions, but also because the opponents of reform developed a defence of the existing political system that convinced those with property as well as large sections of the rest of British society.

Among conservatives, there was a tradition of resistance to constitutional change in the decades leading up to the French Revolution; events in France, especially after 1791, reinforced this tradition. Radicals at home were seen in the same light as revolutionaries abroad. French anarchy was contrasted unfavourably with British stability and prosperity. Conservative apologists and propagandists appealed to British hatred of France and exploited the public's fear of radical change.

Anti-radical propaganda, subsidised by the loyalist associations, the government and private individuals took many forms: pamphlets and tracts, pro-government newspapers, political caricatures and cartoons, and local newspapers. This concerted campaign was outstandingly successful and eventually the majority of English people became convinced that the French Revolution was a disaster.

How did the conservatives respond to radical ideas after 1792? How successful were their measures and why?

Loyalist associations

Loyalist associations emerged initially as a response to the Dissenter campaign for the repeal of the Test and Corporation Acts. By September 1792, 386 petitions expressing loyalty to the king had been received; by the end of 1793, the total number of Associations for the Preservation of Liberty and Property against Republicans and Levellers had reached about 2,000, making them the largest political organisation in the country. They spread from London into the neighbouring counties, then to the west, the Midlands and finally to the north. Active membership was largely confined to men of property, though they were able to enlist support from a cross-section of society. They can be seen as far more successful working-class organisations than the radical corresponding societies.

Loyalist associations adopted the organisational methods and some of the tactics of the reformers in that they produced a great deal of printed propaganda. They were not content to rely upon persuasion, however, and resorted to intimidation and persecution in order to defeat their opponents. Calls for loyalty and patriotism proved far more popular with the bulk of the population than demands for radical change.

Government repression

Pitt acted quickly against the threat posed by the radicals, inaugurating what has been called Pitt's 'reign of terror'. The government was convinced it faced a revolutionary conspiracy, a view reinforced by the information received from local magistrates and spies, and believed it was justified in taking firm action.

Seditious writings like those of radical writers such as Paine challenged the power of the state.

In May and December 1792, two royal proclamations were issued against **seditious writings**. These gave the Home Office the power to monitor the activities of the radical societies by using spies as well as more conventional methods like opening letters, receiving reports from local sources, watching the activities of radicals abroad and infiltrating radical groups. Its resources were very limited, with a staff of less than 25.

In 1794 Pitt moved against English radicals. Forty-one men, including Thomas Hardy of the LCS, were arrested and charged with high treason, but after he was acquitted further trials were abandoned. The government had more success against those publishing seditious material.

Parliament was prepared to pass legislation in support of the government though, in practice, this often turned out to be far less effective than anticipated. **Habeas Corpus** was suspended from May 1794 to July 1795 and from April 1798 to March 1801, but only a few were imprisoned without charge. The Treasonable Practices Act and the Seditious Meetings Act of 1795 proved less than effective weapons, despite the wide powers they gave to central and local government. The Treasonable Practices Act was designed to intimidate and no radical was ever prosecuted under it. The Seditious Meetings Act failed to prevent the increasing number of meetings organised by the LCS.

There was only one prosecution under the Unlawful Oaths Act of 1797, which was rushed through parliament following the Spithead and Nore mutinies over low pay and the appalling conditions on ships. It strengthened penalties against those who attempted to undermine allegiance to the authorities and administer unlawful oaths.

The banning of the leading radical societies in 1799 was unnecessary, largely because they were already in a state of collapse. The Combination Acts of 1799 and 1800 banned workers' organisations, thus completing the legislative armoury of repression.

Radicalism was increasingly driven underground. It did not re-emerge as a mass movement until 1812. Between 1794 and 1800, Pitt successfully drove radical politics to the margins of political life.

Government legislation was infrequently used, but it was a threat hanging over radicals, limiting their freedom of action. There were less than 200 convictions during the 1790s; whether this constitutes a government-inspired reign of terror is open to debate. The effect of the legislation was to intimidate and harass. It destroyed the leadership of the radical societies, silenced the ablest propagandists and frightened many into abandoning the reform movement. However, the collapse of the radical movement was not simply a matter of repression by government or magistrates. The war had revived deep-seated patriotism in most people for whom radicalism had lost its relevance.

> **Habeas Corpus** is a writ requiring that someone who has been arrested and imprisoned should be examined by the courts to see whether there are sufficient grounds for continued imprisonment. It is an effective means of protecting the individual against arbitrary arrest and detention.

> What methods did Pitt use to attack the radical societies after 1793? How successful were his policies?

Summary questions

1 Identify and explain any *two* factors that helped strengthen Pitt's hold on power between 1783 and 1793.

2 Compare the importance of at least *three* issues in ensuring Pitt's dominance of government in the period up to 1801.

3 Tory dominance and decline, 1812–30

Focus questions

◆ How and why was Lord Liverpool able to survive the radical challenges of 1812–22?

◆ How liberal were the Tory governments of 1822–30?

Significant dates

1812 Spencer Perceval assassinated; Liverpool becomes prime minister

1814 Napoleon abdicates and is exiled to Elba

1815 Corn Law passed; Napoleon defeated at Waterloo

1816 Income tax repealed against government's wishes; Spa Fields meetings

1817 Habeas Corpus suspended; Seditious Meetings Act passed; march of the blanketeers; Pentrich rising

1818 General election

1819 Peterloo massacre followed by the Six Acts

1820 George III dies, succeeded by George IV; general election; Queen Caroline affair

1821–22 Liverpool restructures his cabinet; beginnings of liberal Toryism

1826 General election

1827 Liverpool resigns; Canning becomes prime minister and chancellor of the exchequer; Canning dies; Goodrich becomes prime minister

1828 Goodrich resigns and Wellington becomes prime minister; Test and Corporation Acts repealed

1829 Catholic emancipation granted

1830 George IV dies; William IV succeeds to the throne; July Revolution in France; general election; Wellington rules out parliamentary reform; Wellington resigns

Overview

Between 1801 and 1812, Britain was ruled by five weak governments. Henry Addington succeeded Pitt and remained in office until 1804. Pitt then returned and was prime minister until his death in early 1806. The **Ministry of all the Talents** (1806–07) briefly took office, until they were dismissed by the king. Lord Portland was prime minister for two years after that and was succeeded by Spencer Perceval in 1809. After Perceval was assassinated in the lobby of the House of Commons in May 1812, Lord Liverpool became prime minister.

Between 1812 and 1822, Liverpool was faced with economic, political and radical challenges, caused by the war against France and the problems that resulted from returning Britain to peacetime conditions after 1815. Between 1822 and 1827, the government, still led by Liverpool, had considerable energy, largely because of the emergence of what has been called liberal Toryism.

Liverpool was a skilled politician: he was able to hold together a government of strong personalities with differing opinions, who were more prepared to serve under him than under each other. Liverpool's stroke and subsequent resignation in February 1827 released long-restrained tensions and rivalries. Three prime ministers followed in quick succession. Liverpool's successor, George Canning, died in August, within months of gaining office. His successor, Viscount Goodrich, was a disaster. Finally, the duke of Wellington took the helm in January 1828. During his ministry, the Test and Corporation Acts were repealed in 1828 and Catholic emancipation followed in 1829. Wellington's refusal to accept parliamentary reform led to the fall of his government in November 1830, after which the Whigs took power.

How and why was Lord Liverpool able to survive the radical challenges of 1812–22?

Liverpool became prime minister towards the end of Britain's protracted wars with France. For the first three years he was in power he was preoccupied with fighting the war against France and, after the French defeat, with ensuring peace and stability in Europe.

After the end of the war with France and the settlement of the terms of peace at Vienna in 1815, Liverpool was able to turn his attention to domestic matters and found himself faced with two major problems:

- the urgent need to reorganise government finances, and
- the revival of working-class radicalism.

How did Liverpool reorganise government finances?

The French Wars caused two trends in the British economy. The need for uniforms and weapons to feed the war stimulated demand in the increasingly mechanised manufacturing industry, especially in textiles and iron, and

> The **Ministry of all the Talents** was a coalition of politicians led by Grenville, with Fox as foreign secretary. Although it was Whig dominated, it included the group around Addington, later Viscount Sidmouth.

The **Luddites** were machine breakers who operated in Nottinghamshire, south Lancashire and Yorkshire between 1811 and 1813. The term Luddism is often applied more generally to any movement in which machines are smashed to protect existing technologies and employment.

production increased dramatically. Increasing mechanisation led to working-class resistance and **Luddism**.

During the war, large areas of England were enclosed (see Chapter 1). This made farming more efficient and allowed farmers to increase the amount of food they were producing. They borrowed money to pay for enclosing their land, but high profits meant that they could easily repay the banks. The war restricted the amount of wheat that was imported, thus pushing up its price until the early 1810s. As a result of this, landowners were able to charge tenant farmers high rents. This combination of circumstances – the expansion in the agriculture sector and restricted imports – meant that by 1815 Britain was less reliant on imported food, especially wheat.

By the end of the war, then, both industry and agriculture were in a strong position, but they were geared up to wartime production. The transition to peace proved difficult and posed a series of fundamental questions that would test government until the 1840s:

- What should the place of agriculture be in an industrialised society?
- How could the competing claims of farmers and industrialists be resolved?
- What was the relationship between consumers and producers?
- What role should government have in determining the overall direction of the economy?

Unemployment increased dramatically because it was not possible to absorb so many people into the labour force.

Up to a quarter of a million soldiers and sailors were **demobilised** in 1815 and 1816.

British governments in the late eighteenth century did not attempt to control change in the economy. After 1815, **unemployment** rose because of the **demobilisation** of the armed forces and because enclosure in farming and the mechanisation of the textile industry made it necessary to reduce the size of the labour force. This, combined with the necessity of returning the economy to peacetime conditions, forced the government to take a more active role in the economy. The issues of corn and finance dominated debates in the 1810s, while commerce (trade) became important in the 1820s. Each of these issues posed major political problems for the Tories.

Corn

For contemporaries **corn** meant wheat, barley and rye, though it was the cost of wheat that had the greatest effect on the public.

Despite the limitations the war placed on wheat imports, **corn** prices fell in 1813, 1814 and 1815 following good harvests in those years. In addition, the return to peace ended the embargo on widespread trade with Europe and resulted in a resumption of grain imports. Farmers found themselves under pressure: the combination of the lower corn prices and the higher taxation that was still in place in the aftermath of the war meant that they now found it difficult to repay bank loans. This had the following consequences for the farming sector:

- large numbers of bankruptcies;

'The blessings of peace or the curse of the corn bill' by George Cruikshank, 3 March 1815, a satire attacking the Corn Laws. Four landlords turn back a French boat with cheap corn, ready to see the poor starve rather than reduce the price of corn.

- rent reductions – falling prices led to some landowners reducing the rents they charged their tenants;
- wage reductions – falling prices and a surplus labour force (caused largely by the demobilisation of the armed forces) led to farmers reducing the wages they paid;
- distress in areas where farming was the main occupation.

Why did the landed interest call for agricultural protection in 1814 and 1815?

These events culminated in the passage of the Corn Law of 1815, which prohibited the import of grain until the domestic price reached 80 shillings a quarter (28 lb) for wheat. As prices rarely rose as high as 80 shillings, this measure effectively ensured that local farmers were able to charge a high price for their grain without the fear of being undercut by cheaper foreign imports.

Liverpool saw the legislation as a temporary measure to help farming return to normal after the war. The landed interest saw it as permanent or at least long term. Previous Corn Laws had tried to balance the interests of producers and consumers by maintaining prices at levels acceptable to both groups. The 1815 Act clearly favoured the interests of the producers. Manufacturers argued that parliament was interfering with the free market in their own narrow interests. Radicals saw the Corn Law as class legislation: keeping corn prices artificially high to help farmers penalised working people.

The reasons why Liverpool's government introduced legislation that was seen as unfair and favouring one sector of society were complex:

What justification was there for the introduction of the Corn Law in 1815?

- The protection of farming was not new: it originated in the Corn Laws passed in 1773 and 1804.
- Liverpool could not ignore the fate of one of the country's largest single economic interests, whose votes mattered in parliament.
- A Corn Law was justified on the grounds of national security. In the event of war, Britain would need a reliable domestic supply of food.
- Legislation was needed to maintain stability, as agriculture was the largest employer of labour. Higher corn prices were justified to protect jobs.
- Parliament was dominated by landowners and farmers and as they voted for this law the government had little option but to accept it.

Who protested against the introduction of the Corn Laws and why?

Reaction to the passage of the Corn Law was swift. Petitions were organised, and riots took place in London in March 1815, during which politicians' houses were attacked. Troops had to be brought to the capital to restore order. Higher food prices fuelled working-class distress, especially in rural England. Riots in 1816 and again in 1818 were, in part, a violent reaction to the Corn Laws. Even so, there were demands from tenant farmers for further protection of farming after 1815, especially during the agricultural crisis of 1821–23.

Political attitudes during this time were, however, changing. Liverpool was convinced, largely by the actions of radicals between 1815 and 1821, that governments that pandered to farmers at the expense of working-class consumers or tax-paying industrialists had a dangerously narrow political base. He made his own position clear in February 1822: 'The agricultural is not the only interest in Great Britain. It is not even the most numerous.' Farmers were being told bluntly that they could no longer expect to dictate government policies. Abolition of the Corn Laws was not practical, but their reform was. The government introduced minor changes in 1822, but price levels meant that they never came into operation. Liverpool regarded these as an interim measure while he considered a more permanent solution.

Rising wheat prices from 1823, the financial crisis in 1825 and growing depression in the manufacturing industry in 1826 brought fresh demands for the abolition of duties on foreign grain. Manufacturers lobbied parliament and anti-protectionists tried unsuccessfully to make the abolition of the Corn Laws an issue in the 1826 general election. Liverpool made it clear in 1826 that he intended to revise the 1815 Act the following year. The 1827 and 1828 Corn Laws, introduced by Canning and Huskisson respectively, completed the process begun in 1822. These two Acts introduced a 'sliding scale' that progressively reduced the amount of duty paid as the price of wheat rose. They were nevertheless a compromise because of disagreement in the cabinet on how best to handle this sensitive issue.

Finance

Britain's financial state in 1815 was not healthy: the French Wars had been expensive, taxation was high and unpopular, and 'cheap' paper money had been circulating since 1797. This was when Britain had gone off the **gold standard** and the Bank of England had suspended payments in gold and silver and had begun to issue paper currency (£1 and £2 notes). In 1814–15, government spending exceeded income from taxation by 45 per cent. The national debt had risen from £238 million in 1793 to £902 million in 1816. Roughly 80 per cent of government expenditure was spent on paying the interest on loans.

Reducing public spending and paying off debts was a major priority for Liverpool's government after 1815. Liverpool recognised that the transition to lower peacetime taxation would take time. What Liverpool and his chancellor Nicholas Vansittart needed was a period of financial stability.

Income tax was central to this stability. By 1815 it accounted for a fifth of all government income and, while it had never been popular, it had been tolerated. With the end of the war, demands for its abolition increased. In 1815 and 1816 the Whigs organised a successful national campaign against it. In 1816 Liverpool failed, by 37 votes, to continue the tax.

Abolishing income tax may have been popular, but it left government finances in chaos. To make up the lost income, Liverpool had to reduce government spending, borrow money and increase **indirect taxation**, which was unpopular with working-class radicals, who argued that indirect taxes like the Corn Laws and malt tax pushed food prices up and hit working people unfairly. £340,000 was trimmed from defence spending in 1816. Government departments were pruned and a 10 per cent cut was made in official salaries. Liverpool could do little to reduce spending further. By 1818, government income from indirect taxation covered the costs of government spending, thus achieving a balanced budget. However, Liverpool controlled only 9 per cent of spending. The rest was swallowed up by war pensions, servicing the interest on the national debt and interest on the loans that Liverpool had taken to meet the deficit between the cost of what Britain imported and what it exported, which amounted to £13 million. There was an overwhelming need for reform of the financial system.

Liverpool recognised that to achieve sustained economic growth he would have to return to a 'sound money' policy, by which he meant low levels of interest, and payments made in gold and silver rather than paper currency. Financial experts favoured the end of the wartime paper currency, arguing

The **gold standard** was the system under which a country's currency was exchangeable for a fixed weight of gold on demand at the central bank.

Why were national finances a problem for Liverpool in 1815?

Income tax was introduced in 1797 by William Pitt. Sir Robert Peel revived its use in 1842.

Indirect taxation is imposed on goods or services and is usually collected either when the goods move from one country to another (customs and excise duties, also called tariffs) or at the point of sale.

How important was income tax to government finance in 1815 and what were the consequences of its abolition in 1816?

that a return to a fixed gold standard was essential to a sound monetary policy. The landed interest also supported this – for them, it meant a return to 'proper' money and the end of a paper currency that to them represented financial speculation, industrialisation and uncontrolled urban development. Liverpool set up a select committee on currency, chaired by Sir Robert Peel. In May 1819, it recommended the gradual resumption of payments in gold and silver by 1823. This transition was achieved ahead of time and from 1821 Britain was back on the gold standard.

A second committee looked at government finance (taxation, spending and borrowing). The recommendations of this committee led to Vansittart's budget of 1819 which imposed £3 million of new taxes, including a new malt tax, and took £12 million out of **government reserves** to balance the budget. This was seen to herald a new system of finance. This committee laid down the basis of financial management which would dominate the remainder of the century: governments should aim for a surplus of income from taxation over government spending, which in turn would help to restore public confidence in government and allow the national debt to be further reduced.

Liverpool recognised that a revival in trade and manufacturing was essential if his financial policy was to work effectively. Trade was thus the third strand of his policies.

Trade

It was thought that moves towards **free trade** – such as removing tariffs on imports and loosening commercial regulations – would stimulate the sluggish economy, but Liverpool took a cautious approach towards this idea as it was unpopular among most sectors of society:

- The government derived much of its income from customs and excise.
- Farmers were suspicious of moves towards freer trade, as they believed this would inevitably lead to the repeal of the Corn Laws.
- Many merchants and manufacturers supported protection in markets in which they were weak and supported freer trade only where they had the competitive advantage.

Liverpool echoed these attitudes in a speech on trade in the House of Lords on 26 May 1820. Although he outlined the advantages of freer trade, he reassured his audience that absolute free trade was out of the question and that he was not considering abandoning agricultural protection.

Two committees were established to lay down strategies for implementing the move to freer trade. Thomas Wallace, vice-president of the Board of Trade, argued that freer trade would help industries out of depression, encourage the search for new markets and create employment. With Vansittart, he drew up

Despite the national debt, there were still **government reserves**, which were not used to eradicate the national debt.

How did Liverpool attempt to sort out government finances in 1819?

Free trade was shorthand for the policy of non-interference by the state in economic matters (or *laissez-faire*). It derived from the teachings of classical economists like Adam Smith, Malthus and David Ricardo.

Why were merchants and manufacturers unsure of the advantages of freeing trade?

the blueprints for the reforms that **Robinson** (Vansittart's successor as chancellor) and **William Huskisson** undertook after 1823.

In 1819 and 1820, Liverpool established clear guidelines for the development of new financial and commercial policies. Sound money policy, together with these reforms, led to a dramatic increase in government revenue. By 1822, Robinson's budget had excess revenue of £5 million. In 1823 Robinson was able to budget for a surplus of £7 million of which £5 million was used to repay debts, leaving £2 million for tax cuts. Surplus budgets in 1824 and 1825 allowed reductions in excise duties on a range of consumer goods and raw materials including coal, iron, wood, spirits, wine, rum, cider and coffee. In fact, there were budget surpluses until 1830 though they were insufficient to allow further tariff reductions.

The limits of tax reduction had been reached and Liverpool recognised, as early as 1824, that the only way out of this financial stalemate was the reintroduction of income tax. John Herries, chancellor of the exchequer under Goodrich, was preparing to reintroduce income tax when Goodrich's ministry collapsed in early 1828; Henry Goulburn, Wellington's chancellor, was only prevented from doing so in the 1830 budget because of the prime minister's opposition. It was eventually reintroduced in Peel's ministry in 1842.

Changes in commercial policy began in 1821 when Wallace reduced duties on timber imports. The following year he simplified the Navigation Acts by allowing the colonies to trade more freely with foreign countries, although trade between Britain and its colonies was still restricted to British ships. In 1823, Wallace resigned when William Huskisson became president of the Board of Trade, and he has not received the credit for developing the commercial policies that Huskisson then implemented. In 1823, he introduced the Reciprocity of Duties Act, which reduced tariffs if other countries would follow suit and, by 1827, most European countries and the United States had negotiated agreements for the mutual abolition or adjustment of discriminatory tariffs. Foreign ships were allowed freer access to British ports, especially London, which became the centre of world trade. As a result, the volume of goods traded increased. Even though tariffs had been reduced, the increase in the volume of trade meant that the income the government received from tariffs increased by 64 per cent between 1821 and 1827. The policies of Wallace and Huskisson had proved to be very successful.

Neither Liverpool nor Huskisson was a firm believer in free trade. Their policies were based on a belief that Britain would gain economically from free trade and that these policies would bring prosperity and political stability.

The commitment of Liverpool's government to free trade has been questioned by historians who have put forward many different reasons for his free trade policies. Some see the reduction in duties as the beginning of *laissez-*

Why did Liverpool's government adopt a policy of freer trade after 1820?

In what ways did the policies pursued by Robinson and Huskisson originate in 1819 and 1820?

Frederick **Robinson**, 1st Viscount Goodrich (1782–1859), was chancellor of the exchequer between 1823 and 1827. Ennobled in 1827, he was asked to serve as prime minister after the death of his friend Canning, but was unable to control his ministers. He resigned in January 1828. In 1833, he was created earl of Ripon and served as Whig lord privy seal (April 1833–May 1834). He later joined the Tories, serving as a minister between 1841 and 1843 in Peel's government.

William Huskisson (1770–1830) was president of the Board of Trade between 1823 and 1827 where he continued the work of William Pitt on financial reform.

How did Robinson and Huskisson develop financial and commercial policies after 1822?

faire economics, some see it as a practical measure to increase food imports into a country that was facing shortages, while others assert that the policy was principally social – economic expansion led to the creation of more jobs and consequently less poverty.

How did the government react to demands for radical political reform?

Attempts to increase the number of people who could elect MPs had been an ongoing political issue since the 1780s. William Pitt had tried, unsuccessfully, to reform parliament in 1785, and during the 1790s Charles Grey, a leading Whig, introduced several equally unsuccessful reform bills in the House of Commons. By the 1790s there was a clear division between the two main political parties over **parliamentary reform**, a division that lasted throughout the first thirty years of the nineteenth century. In broad terms, the Tories opposed all parliamentary reform, which they saw as a threat to the existing constitution and monarchy, and regarded calls for a wider democracy as little short of revolutionary. By contrast, the Whigs were broadly in favour of changes in the franchise. They saw the existing system as unfair and unrepresentative and recognised that the growing influence of the middle classes needed to be attached to the existing political structure to prevent revolution. Although neither party was committed to a democratic system of government in which the working classes had the vote, the case for middle-class enfranchisement was accepted by the Whigs by the 1810s and was taken up by them as a serious political issue in the 1820s.

Demands for parliamentary reform for the working classes took place beyond Westminster. The corresponding societies raised the issue in the 1790s, gaining considerable support across England especially from skilled artisans. Repressed by William Pitt in the late 1790s, working-class radicalism went into decline and did not re-emerge until almost the end of the French Wars. In 1812, Major John Cartwright, a radical leader who had campaigned for parliamentary reform since the 1780s, began the first of three tours of the Midlands and the north. His aim was to get the working and middle classes to work together to obtain parliamentary reform. The result was the creation of Hampden clubs, which were especially popular in the northern manufacturing districts hit by the slump in trade. Working class in composition, they demanded manhood suffrage (votes for all adult males) rather than the household or tax-payer suffrages demanded by middle-class reformers. When the Hampden clubs were finally banned in 1817, they were replaced by political unions, organised by northern working men, which helped to organise over 2,000 petitions for parliamentary reform between 1817 and 1818. These two radical organisations raised a series of questions that dogged radical activity until the 1850s:

Parliamentary reform describes attempts by middle- and working-class radicals to change the way in which MPs were elected either by increasing the number of property-owning voters or by allowing all men, irrespective of whether they owned property, to have the vote.

- Was parliamentary reform best achieved by class collaboration (middle and working classes working together) or by the working class acting alone?
- Should parliamentary reform be approached solely through demands for manhood suffrage or through achieving limited suffrage (household or tax-payer suffrage) and then moving on to demands for manhood suffrage after this? The problem with this approach and class collaboration was that, once the middle classes had achieved limited suffrage, their enthusiasm for further reform waned.
- What tactics should radicals use to achieve parliamentary reform? Should radicals rely on persuasion (the use of petitions and meetings) to achieve their aims or should they adopt a more revolutionary approach, using force if the government refused to respond to their demands?

It is easy to write off the revolutionaries as a failed minority and, in retrospect, their activities can be seen as naive and doomed to failure. However, there was a revolutionary underground in Britain that can be traced back to the late 1790s and it was prepared to confront the authorities with armed force. The problem that radicals faced was that attempts at mass action, when public order and property were threatened, increased public support for firm government action

The transition to a peacetime economy between 1815 and 1821 severely strained social and economic relationships. Falling demand for manufactured goods, especially textiles, and the flooding of the labour market with demobilised soldiers and sailors increased unemployment. In this climate of distress, the government found itself under pressure from two quarters. First, it faced protest that took traditional forms, like the Fenland riots of 1816 that aimed at restoring just wages and prices. Secondly, there were growing demands for political reform from the radical reformers like **Henry 'Orator' Hunt** and **William Cobbett**. Hunt built on the foundations of the Hampden clubs and mobilised people around demands for manhood suffrage, annual parliaments and the secret ballot.

Disturbances in 1815 and 1816 convinced **Lord Sidmouth** that the government faced a revolutionary challenge to its authority. The disorder at the Spa Field meetings in London, where calls were made for parliamentary reform, appeared to confirm his fears. The attack on the regent's coach in late January 1817 was followed later in the year by the **march of the blanketeers**. These events and the **Pentrich rising** in Derbyshire shifted middle-class public opinion, previously sympathetic to the radicals' demands, behind a government which was committed to preserving public order and defending property. In 1817, Habeas Corpus was suspended and the Seditious Meetings Act, which placed restrictions on meetings for 12 months, was passed. The opposition

Henry 'Orator' Hunt (1773–1835) was the major leader of the radical movement in the 1810s.

William Cobbett (1763–1835) was a radical working-class leader and journalist. He supported demands for parliamentary reform.

Henry Addington, 1st Viscount **Sidmouth** (1757–1844), was an able administrator, but a mediocre prime minister between 1801 and 1804. He was home secretary between 1812 and 1822.

The **march of the blanketeers** took place when unemployed textile workers from Lancashire and Cheshire decided to march to London to petition the regent for parliamentary reform. They were so called because they each carried a blanket. Few got beyond Stockport.

The **Pentrich rising** was led by Jeremiah Brandreth with little support and was easily put down.

Henry Hunt holds the Petition of Rights and urges the use of moral pressure not physical force, a reference to his speech at Spa Fields on 13 November 1816. This print by Robert Cruikshank (6 December 1816) is one of the very few prints not hostile to Hunt.

Whigs were as worried by events as the government and became more cautious in their approach to parliamentary reform.

Prompt action by the government only partly explains the decline in radical activities. The easing of economic conditions during 1817 and 1818 was an important factor. Habeas Corpus was revived early in 1818 and the Seditious Meetings Act lapsed in July that year.

Henry Hunt is shown presiding at a meeting of revolutionaries (Robert Cruikshank, 3 July 1818). How does Cruikshank show Hunt's respectability in the 1816 print but his revolutionary threat in this later one? What do these prints tell the historian about attitudes to radicalism between 1816 and 1818?

However, when economic conditions worsened in 1819, radicalism revived, reaching its peak in the **Peterloo massacre** in August 1819. Although Sidmouth had advised the Manchester magistrates against taking any hasty action, Liverpool's government had little choice but to support their actions. There was a wave of public support for the radical cause and even *The Times* attacked the actions of the Manchester magistrates. The problem that faced Hunt and the radical leadership was how to translate this support into practical action. It was clear that the government did not intend to give in to radical demands for parliamentary reform. They introduced the Six Acts of 1819, which reimposed repression by restricting meetings and what was printed in the press, preventing drilling, and allowing magistrates to seize weapons. The Acts also gave the government powers to deal harshly with even slight signs of discontent. The radical agitation faltered, despite the intense unpopularity of the government.

The **Peterloo massacre** took place on 16 August 1819 when a peaceful meeting was held at St Peter's Field, Manchester. Local magistrates decided to send the yeomanry to arrest Hunt, who was one of the speakers. In the ensuing chaos, large numbers of people were injured and 11 were killed.

The **Cato Street conspiracy** was an unsuccessful attempt to murder the cabinet in February 1820, led by the radical Arthur Thistlewood. He was hanged, along with four others.

What types of protest did Liverpool have to deal with between 1815 and 1821?

The **Cato Street conspiracy** had little impact on public opinion. Liverpool was able, however, to make political capital out of it during the election campaign resulting from the sudden death of George III in January 1820.

The government's unpopularity worsened over its handling of the Queen Caroline affair. When George IV became king on the death of his father, he had long lived apart from his wife. Queen Caroline had a long history of sexual indiscretions – but then, so had the new king, whose actions against her were seen by many as hypocritical. In June 1820, she returned from Italy to claim her rights as queen. George IV had no intention of allowing her to become queen and successfully managed to prevent her from attending his coronation in 1821. His attempts to divorce her were less successful. He instructed the government to dissolve the marriage, but it was forced to abandon its attempts to deprive Caroline of her title and dissolve the marriage in November 1820 after widespread popular and Whig opposition. Queen Caroline died suddenly in August 1821, three weeks after the coronation, and the London crowds forced the military to take her coffin through the City on its way to Harwich and to her family home in Brunswick. The queen's cause provided a rallying point for radical campaigners who used her plight to attack the corruption of the monarchy and its supporters.

As the economy revived in the early 1820s, radicalism declined once again. The public's energies were diverted into other forms of radical action. Some radical working men turned to religion and there were Methodist revivals in Lancashire and Cumberland. Others campaigned against the Combination Acts, which made trade unions illegal, a campaign which led to their repeal in 1824.

Two linked issues arise from the revival of radicalism after 1815: how revolutionary was it and how justifiable was the government's response?

The radicals posed a significant threat to the government in that they created a potential for revolution. This was a very real fear for central and local authorities, who feared a repeat of events in France 30 years earlier. In reality, however, radicals who advocated revolutionary action were never a leading force in the movement. Far more importantly, the radical platform's grievances challenged the whole direction of social development created by the industrial revolution. There was a growing belief that working-class grievances such as high levels of indirect taxation, the Corn Laws, the game laws that meted out harsh punishment to those convicted of poaching game, and the legal ban on trade unions could only be resolved by a parliament elected on more democratic principles.

Unrest and agitation, though they appeared to contemporaries to be part of a nationwide movement, are best seen in terms of responses to particular local conditions. In this situation, the local magistrates rather than central government were at the forefront of reaction. The problem that Liverpool faced was

The Peterloo massacre, 16 August 1819. The print was produced by George Cruikshank on the day of the incident and was designed to shock its audience. Cruikshank was not present at the Peterloo meeting. In what respect does this lessen the value of the print as a source for the Peterloo massacre?

that he had to formulate a national policy based on magistrates' reports about many different, localised incidents with particular, local causes, and reports from army officers and spies, who often exaggerated the nature of the radical threat for financial gain.

Liverpool was, therefore, responding to a perceived threat to public order that was based on inaccurate and, on occasions, deceptive information. Of course, the government did not wish to run any risk of revolution ever happening in Britain and, as a result, it often overreacted to events. Liverpool's approach was, in fact, relatively moderate. When legislation was passed, it was either, like the Seditious Meetings Act, given a time limit or, as the Six Acts demonstrated, largely ineffective in practice.

These radical demands challenged the political and economic power of the landed classes and industrialists, and it was this that added a potentially revolutionary dimension to the radical challenge. The reaction of the government, though criticised by contemporaries and historians as dictatorial, emphasised the need for public order and tried – not very successfully – to distinguish between genuine social grievances and deliberately disruptive radical activity. Despite this, little was done to try to alleviate social distress in the 1810s.

How liberal were the Tory governments of 1822–30?

Liberal Toryism

In the early 1820s, Liverpool made important changes to his cabinet. After **Castlereagh**'s suicide, **Canning** became foreign secretary and in 1822 Peel replaced Sidmouth at the Home Office. Robinson took Vansittart's place as chancellor of the exchequer and Huskisson became president of the Board of Trade in 1823.

In 1941 the historian W. R. Brock suggested that Liverpool's government went through a reactionary phase between 1815 and 1821 when anti-reforming or **ultra-Tory** ministers like Sidmouth suppressed liberties in defence of public order. In his opinion, this was followed by a liberal phase between 1822 and 1827 when liberal Tories like Huskisson, Peel and Robinson introduced reforms in financial policy, trade and the legal system. For Brock these changes to the cabinet represented a new style of politics: Castlereagh, Sidmouth and Vansittart supported repression abroad and high taxes at home, while Canning, Peel, Huskisson and Robinson championed liberal reforms at home and a liberal policy abroad by supporting countries like Spain, Portugal and Greece in their quest for more constitutional government. There are, however, several problems with this argument:

- The term liberal Toryism was not used by contemporaries, but was applied by historians. It implies that politicians such as Canning had a philosophical rather than a pragmatic approach to politics, which was not the case.
- Did liberals, in fact, dominate government? First, after 1823 the cabinet was one in which all shades of Tory opinion were represented. Liverpool provided continuity between 1815 and 1827, and he was certainly the only man who could hold together the cabinet between 1822 and 1827. Secondly, the new ministers of 1822–23 had already served in Liverpool's government and the ministers associated with the policy of repression, with the exception of Castlereagh, did not leave the political stage. Finally, the important division within the cabinet after 1822 was not between liberal and ultra-Tories, but between those who supported **Catholic emancipation** and those who opposed it. Liverpool sensibly made this an open question. On this issue, Peel and Canning, who Brock classified as liberals, stood at opposite poles.

If Brock's argument about Liverpool's cabinet can be challenged, what about changes in policy? Many of the liberal initiatives of the 1820s had been discussed or proposed between 1815 and 1821. Sidmouth had proposed some of the penal reforms later introduced by Peel (see below). Canning's foreign policy was a clear extension of that of his predecessor, Castlereagh. Robinson's financial and Huskisson's commercial policies owed much to the general economic strategy and incentives to trade agreed in 1819 and 1820 (see page 35). What was different in these years was the context. The revival of the economy from 1820–21 and the decline in mass radicalism meant that Peel, Huskisson and Robinson were operating in calmer times than Sidmouth and Vansittart. The government's focus after 1822 was less on maintaining public order, more on making Britain's economy prosperous. Economic prosperity led to political stability and a decline in radical activity.

Under Canning, Goodrich and **Wellington**, financial and commercial policies remained largely unchanged, and Peel continued his reforms of the legal system (see below) with the introduction of the Metropolitan Police in 1829. However, the repeal of the Test and Corporation Acts in 1828 and Catholic emancipation a year later represent a significant shift in government policy towards constitutional change.

In practice, Liverpool's administration was neither reactionary nor suddenly reformist in 1822. Any change of ministers, especially to those occupying key positions, will have an impact on the running of government. There was certainly an increase in the pace of reform, and the presentation of policy by the government was improved. However, this did not mean that the substance of government policy and the principles on which it was based underwent radical change. The similarities of the years before and after 1822–23 outweigh the differences.

Tory governments, 1827–30

Lord Liverpool's stroke in February 1827 and his resignation a month later released tensions over religion and constitutional reform which he had managed to hold in check. Within three years, his party was in tatters, divided and without effective leadership, leaving the Whigs in power.

When Canning became prime minister in April, leading Tories, including Wellington and Peel, refused to serve under him largely because he was a supporter of Catholic emancipation. However, the 1826 general election had strengthened the **Protestant Tories** in the House of Commons and Canning had no wish to weaken his position by pursuing a policy unpopular in his own party. Canning was also viewed with suspicion by right-wing Tories in two other areas. He wanted to restructure the Corn Laws and to pursue a foreign policy that improved Britain's global trading position. Both threatened protection, and moves towards freer trade at the expense of farmers threatened to split the Tory party.

monarchies of Europe. The Irish rising of 1798 and growing Irish immigration made matters worse. The issue of Catholic emancipation is considered from the Irish perspective in Chapter 6.

Arthur Wellesley, 1st duke of **Wellington** (1769–1852), rose to fame as a military leader in the French Wars, culminating in his victory over Napoleon at Waterloo in 1815. He was prime minister between 1828 and 1830. A sound military leader, he lacked the flexibility to be a good prime minister and party leader.

What was liberal Toryism?

Protestant Tories opposed Catholic emancipation.

When Canning died in August, he was succeeded by Frederick Robinson, Viscount Goodrich, who had been an able chancellor of the exchequer. However, he found it impossible to work with his ministers and resigned the following January. The king then turned to Wellington, Tory leader in the Lords, supported by Peel, who was leader in the Commons. To begin with, Wellington looked as if he could hold the Tories together. However, cracks soon began to appear.

In May 1828, Huskisson and his allies resigned from the government over internal disagreements with colleagues. Wellington's position was weakened by the need to give way over Catholic emancipation in 1829. Protestant opinion within the Tory party was outraged.

The death of George IV necessitated the 1830 election. Despite the fact that the government had granted Catholic emancipation, it was not a disaster for them. However, Wellington's opposition to parliamentary reform was. His statement on 2 November that the existing constitution was in need of no further reform was an attempt to unite his party, but it had disastrous consequences. It united all those opposed to Wellington – Whigs, radicals, as well as ultra- and liberal Tories. He no longer had the confidence of parliament and resigned on 16 November 1830. The Whigs returned to government, committed to parliamentary reform.

How liberal was the government's reaction to the need for legal reform?

From the 1770s, there were growing public concerns about the effectiveness of the legal system. In the civil courts, procedures were out of date and cases were frequently subject to long delays. The criminal law was seen as harsh and juries often preferred to find prisoners not guilty rather than sentence them to death for minor **capital crimes**. There were over 200 capital offences and a further 400 that could lead to **transportation**. There was no regular police force and the state of prisons had been subject to harsh criticism by reformers such as **John Howard** in the 1770s, Sir Frederick Eden in the 1790s and **Elizabeth Fry** after 1810.

This led to demands for reform of criminal justice from the first decade of the century. Campaigners like Sir Samuel Romilly protested at the 'lottery of justice': there was uncertainty about the appropriate punishment for different offences and, even when the death sentence was passed, it was far from certain that it would be carried out. Judges had too much discretionary power and responded to similar offences in different ways. Romilly and the other reformers were successful because they gained an increasing amount of parliamentary support from all the political parties.

The opponents of reform, however, insisted that justice was not a lottery, and that judicial discretion was sensible and conscientiously practised.

Capital crimes were those crimes that resulted in the death penalty.

Transportation was a type of punishment that led to convicted criminals being taken to Australia, sometimes for life.

John Howard (1726–1790) and **Elizabeth Fry** (1750–1845) were leading champions of prison reform. Howard was especially concerned with improving prison conditions, while Fry was concerned with the treatment of women prisoners.

Reformers could point to injustices, but anti-reformers were able to name many examples that showed the system working with mercy and moderation. The problem for the opponents of reform was that moderate and influential Tories, like Peel, were sympathetic to the reformers' aims.

Peel's reforms fell into two distinct types – reform of the legal system and more efficient policing. His appointment as home secretary in 1822 led to significant reform of the legal system. It is, however, important to recognise that he built on initiatives made by Liverpool's government, especially the recommendations of Sir James Mackintosh's 1819 committee. These recommendations were that the legal system was in need of reform to make it more acceptable, less archaic and fairer in its operation by removing outdated laws and reducing the number of capital crimes.

The prison system was reformed by the introduction of the Gaol Act of 1823, with amending legislation the following year. The Act tightened central control and tried to establish a degree of uniformity for the prisons of England and Wales. The legislation laid down health and religious regulations, required the categorisation of prisoners and the inspection of prisons by magistrates three times a year, and demanded that annual reports be sent from each gaol to the Home Office. Many local gaols ignored at least some of these regulations and Peel, reluctant to antagonise local sensibilities about independence, made no attempt to impose a national system of inspection.

The creation of the Metropolitan Police in 1829 represented a new way of thinking about policing. Full-time, professional and well organised, the police force was intended to be the impersonal agent of central policy. However, the new police often turned out to be very similar to the old, in personnel, efficiency and tactics. It was only later in the 1830s that legislation was introduced that would fulfil Peel's intentions.

How significant were the reforms Peel introduced? Compared to Lord John Russell, home secretary between 1835 and 1839, some historians argue that Peel merely 'tinkered' with the system by repealing statutes that were no longer used. Peel's reputation as a prison reformer is also suspect – in 1823 and 1824 he simply implemented legislation accepted by the government three years earlier. His introduction of the Metropolitan Police in 1829 built on his experience as chief secretary in Ireland where, in 1814, he had established an efficient police system. However, Peel established one important principle. He recognised that an effective legal system needed to operate within a framework of policies that were centrally determined and that, even if the administration of justice still lay largely at the local level, there needed to be central supervision of the process.

What reforms did Peel introduce?

How liberal was the government's reaction to the need for religious equality?

The **Corporation Act** prevented Nonconformists being elected to town councils, but they could be elected MPs under the Test Acts because there was no requirement to take the Anglican Communion. The two **Test Acts** prevented Catholics from membership of either the Commons or Lords unless they took the oath of supremacy and allegiance, and contained an anti-Catholic declaration condemning 'superstitious and idolatrous' Roman practices.

Catholics and Nonconformists had long been subjected to discrimination because of their beliefs. The **Corporation Act** of 1661 and the **Test Acts** of 1673 and 1678 meant that Nonconformists and Catholics had few political rights. The campaign by Nonconformists for the repeal of this legislation began in the 1780s. The issue of Catholic rights was more complex. As we have seen, the Catholic question remained unresolved throughout Liverpool's administration.

The formation of the Catholic Association in 1823, led by Daniel O'Connell, renewed Catholic agitation in Ireland and revived interest in emancipation. Bills giving varying concessions to Catholics passed the Commons in 1821, 1822 and 1825, but the Lords rejected them all. While Liverpool was prime minister, no discriminating legislation was repealed and he successfully contained differing opinions among his ministers. His resignation in early 1827 and the rapid succession of Canning and then Goodrich meant that the Catholic question could no longer be avoided. It is ironic that the duke of Wellington, the most Protestant of Tories, first repealed the Test and Corporation Acts in 1828 and the following year conceded Catholic emancipation.

Why was there little opposition to the repeal of the Test and Corporation Acts in 1828?

In 1828 and 1829, Wellington was faced by a stark dilemma. He was aware that, if he took any action that threatened the supremacy of the Church of England, he would face widespread opposition from his own MPs. However, he also knew that, if he failed to respond to the increasingly liberal attitudes held by MPs, then he might unite Whigs and Canningite Tories within parliament and encourage revolutionary activity outside parliament. A strong alliance of well-organised extra-parliamentary Nonconformists spearheaded the campaign for the repeal of the Test and Corporation Acts. Peel steered the legislation through the Commons and the Lords, where the bishops overwhelmingly supported the proposal. For them, however, Catholic emancipation was a different matter.

By 1828, resistance to Catholic emancipation was crumbling. The repeal of the Test and Corporation Acts had established the principle that the constitution could be changed. When Huskisson resigned from the Board of Trade in May 1828, he was replaced by Vesey Fitzgerald, an Irish Protestant MP. Newly appointed ministers had to seek re-election and in the subsequent County Clare by-election O'Connell stood against him and won.

As a Catholic, O'Connell could not take his seat in the Commons and Wellington and Peel were faced with two alternatives. They could use force to ban the Catholic Association who supported O'Connell (although there were insufficient troops in Ireland to do that) or they could concede emancipation.

Calling a general election on the issue would have solved nothing – the 1826 election showed the strength of anti-Catholicism on the mainland – but it was likely that British rule in Ireland would be challenged if large numbers of ineligible Irish Catholic MPs were elected. Wellington concluded that emancipation was necessary to prevent civil war in Ireland. Despite Tory opposition in both the Commons and the Lords, emancipation was easily achieved, largely because Wellington was able to count on the support of the Whigs. This undermined the Protestant basis of his government and split the Tories.

What alternatives faced Wellington and Peel over Catholic emancipation?

The cost for Wellington and Peel was high. They had betrayed their party and although Wellington's ministry limped on for over a year, it was barely supported by many Tories and vigorously opposed by the Whigs. Wellington hoped that things would improve before the next general election, scheduled for 1832–33, but the death of George IV at the end of June 1830 ended this hope.

What consequences did emancipation have for the Tory party?

Summary questions

1 Identify and explain any *two* factors that helped to strengthen the Tories hold on power between 1812 and 1822.

2 Compare the importance of at least *three* issues in ensuring Tory dominance of government between 1822 and 1830.

4

The Whig reforms, 1830–41

Focus question

◆ In what ways did the Whigs reform parliament and urban government?

Significant dates

1830 *November* Wellington speaks against the need for parliamentary reform; Wellington resigns; Whig administration formed under Earl Grey

1831 *March* First Reform bill introduced into parliament
April Government defeated on an amendment objecting to reduction in number of MPs for England and Wales at committee stage; parliament dissolved
June Whigs returned after general election; second Reform bill introduced into parliament
October House of Lords reject bill; widespread rioting in Nottingham and Derby and Bristol as a result of this
December Third Reform bill introduced into parliament and passes its second reading in the Commons before Christmas

1832 *January* William IV agrees to the creation of peers in order to ensure Reform bill can be passed
May Grey resigns because of opposition in the Lords; Wellington asked to form an administration, but is unable to do so; the king is compelled to recall Grey and confirms that peers will be created to ensure the passage of the bill
June Reform Act passed
July Scottish Reform Act passed
August Irish Reform Act passed
December Whigs win general election under the new franchise

1833 Abolition of slavery; Factory Act passed

1834 Poor Law Amendment Act passed

1835 Municipal Corporations Act passed

1837 Queen Victoria ascends the throne

1841 Whigs defeated in general election

Overview

The Whigs supported the idea of both parliamentary and social reform. When they came to power in late 1830, they placed parliamentary reform at the centre of their political agenda. This issue dominated debate until the Reform Acts were passed in 1832.

Parliamentary reform in 1832 and reform of towns and cities three years later characterised the 1830s as the decade of reform. This, together with important developments in dealing with the poor, factory conditions and education, marked the Whig governments as reforming administrations. The measures the Whigs introduced began a process of reform that was not completed until the 1870s.

In what ways did the Whigs reform parliament and urban government?

The political situation in 1830

The death of George IV and the accession of William IV in early 1830 had two important consequences:

- A general election had to be held within six months. This meant that Wellington was forced to fight an election at least two years before he expected to and while his party was still deeply divided over the issue of Catholic emancipation, which had been granted the previous year.
- George IV's long-standing veto on the Whig leader, **Earl Grey**, was removed as William IV was prepared to accept Grey as prime minister.

When Wellington conceded Catholic emancipation in 1829 he made himself very unpopular with his party and with the British people. His problems were made worse by the outbreak of **revolution in France** in July 1830 and by the Swing riots in August, both of which raised the threat of widespread public disorder in Britain. Despite Wellington's unpopularity, the Tories did well in the election and gained 21 seats. Parliamentary reform had been an important issue in some constituencies, but other important election issues included public concerns about economic conditions, the continuation of the Corn Laws, the effects of Catholic emancipation and the ending of slavery in the British empire.

On 2 November, Wellington gave a speech in which he ruled out further reform. The supporters of the liberal Huskisson and some ultra-Tories were prepared to vote against their party because of Wellington's attitude to further reform. He was consequently defeated on a crucial vote over the **civil list**. Wellington no longer had the confidence of the House of Commons and this

Charles Grey, 2nd **Earl Grey** (1764–1845), held office in 1806–07, but had to wait until 1830 to become prime minister, a position he held until 1834.

Earl Grey (1764–1845).

The **July Revolution in France** resulted in the removal of the last Bourbon king, Charles X, and his replacement by the more liberal Louis-Philippe.

The **civil list** is the money elected by parliament to support the royal family.

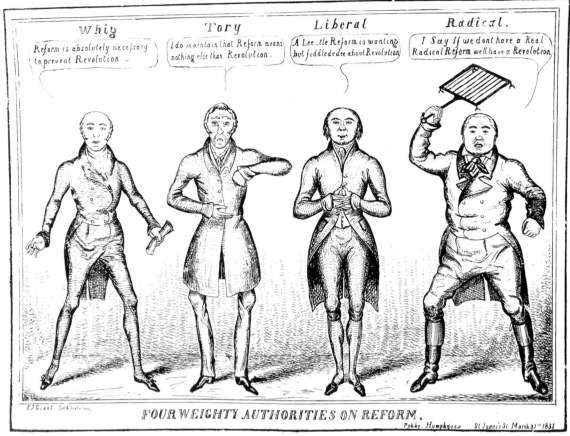

Four orators giving their views on the question of reform: Grey (Whig), Wellington (Tory), John Lee (Liberal) and William Cobbett (Radical) (Charles Grant, 31 March 1831).

led to the fall of his administration. He resigned the following day and the Whigs formed a government. This meant that the introduction of parliamentary reform was inevitable. The Whig's long-standing commitment to reform led to 18 months of frenetic activity inside and outside parliament, which culminated in the passage of the Reform Acts in mid-1832.

What factors led to the downfall of Wellington in 1830?

The Reform Acts of 1832

The Reform Acts redefined who had the right to vote in both counties and boroughs (see box below). The electorate of England and Wales increased by 78 per cent between 1831 and 1833, rising from 366,250 to 652,777. This still represented only 5 per cent of the population of England and Wales in the 1831 census.

Parliamentary seats were redistributed, especially in England, providing MPs for areas of growing population and economic influence. Fifty-six rotten boroughs lost both their MPs and 30 smaller boroughs lost one MP. These seats were then redistributed to towns previously without their own MPs.

While the Acts removed the most obvious defects of the unreformed system, they did not remove all the inequalities of representation: they did not introduce democracy, for example, nor did they give the middle classes control of the political system. Earl Grey observed that the Reform Acts were essentially 'aristocratic measures', aimed at preserving the power of the landowners by aligning them with the propertied middle classes.

The achievement lay in the fact that they established a new political climate in which questions about reforming the constitution and discussion of new political ideas were felt to be acceptable and were no longer considered to be revolutionary. Radical working-class opinion, however, was disappointed by the attitude of the Whigs to their demands. The working class was not united in its attitude to reform between 1830 and 1832: some radicals were prepared to accepted limited household suffrage and were prepared to work with middle-class reformers; others, led by Henry Hunt, demanded universal manhood suffrage and were not. Either way, working-class aspirations were not met by the Reform Acts and they were seen as the 'great betrayal'.

The Reform Acts of 1832

1 Disenfranchising clauses
- 56 rotten boroughs, returning 111 MPs, lost their representation.
- 30 boroughs with less than 4,000 inhabitants lost one MP each.
- Weymouth and Melcombe Regis gave up two of their four members.
- 143 seats were made available for redistribution.

2 Enfranchising clauses
- 65 seats were awarded to the counties.
- 44 seats were distributed to 22 large towns, including Manchester, Leeds, Birmingham and Sheffield, and to the new London metropolitan districts.
- 21 smaller towns were given one MP each.
- Scotland was given eight extra seats.
- Ireland gained five extra seats.

3 The franchise
- In the boroughs, the franchise was given to all householders who paid a yearly rent of £10 and, subject to a one-year residence qualification, to £10 lodgers (if they shared a house and the landlord was not in residence).
- In the counties, the franchise was given to 40-shilling **freeholders**; £10 **copyholders** and long-lease holders; and £50 short-lease holders or **tenants-at-will**. Borough freeholders could also vote in the counties where they held land if their freehold was between 40 shillings and £10, or if it was over £10 and occupied by a tenant.
- Electors in each constituency had to be registered.
- Those with **ancient rights** retained their vote until their death.
- There was to be no secret ballot.

Freeholders owned their own land.

Copyholders were tenants who had a lease for 20 to 25 years, giving them considerable security of tenure.

Tenants-at-will had short-term leases and were consequently more easily 'influenced' by their landlords to vote the way they wanted with the threat of eviction if the tenants did not.

Ancient rights applied to those who had the right to vote under the pre-1832 system.

Conclusion

Were the Reform Acts of 1832 an expression of change or continuity? Although contemporaries believed that the Reform Acts were middle-class

What were the
principal achievements
and shortcomings of
the Reform Acts?

measures, the composition of the 1833 parliament was not very different from the unreformed one. Between 70 and 80 per cent of MPs were still from the landed interest and no more than 100 were from the professional and industrial middle classes, a number comparable with elections before 1832. It would seem that the urban middle class were happy to elect MPs from the landed interest.

Municipal reform

Municipal reform was seen as a necessary part of parliamentary reform. In July 1833, a Royal Commission was set up to consider the question of municipal reform. Its report, published in 1835, formed the basis of the Municipal Corporations Act, which extended the principles of the Reform Acts of 1832.

The **county rate** was a
general tax. Local
government taxes were
raised either for specific
purposes (like building a
local bridge) or to cover
general spending.

Many towns were unincorporated (which means that they had no charter giving them independent rights), were under the control of the local magistrates and paid the **county rate**. Corporate towns, so called because they were run by a corporation, had charters, many of which dated back to the Middle Ages. The distribution of incorporated and unincorporated towns was an accident of history rather than a consequence of their size or importance. Many of the rapidly growing cities, like Birmingham, Manchester and Sheffield, were without corporations. Changes in population and the move from a rural economy to an industrial one meant that there were pressing arguments for reform:

- Law and order was a growing problem for both national and local government. Many feared that large towns were becoming increasingly ungovernable because of their undisciplined populations.
- The Whigs believed that reform would allow towns to compete equally for economic advantage.
- The corporations were generally self-electing. For radicals this meant that those in power could maintain themselves in power and exclude others, especially the middle classes.

In addition, the Royal Commission criticised the inefficiency and corruption of the existing corporations. The government accepted its proposals and the bill quickly passed the Commons. However, it met with substantial Tory opposition in the Lords. Its passage was eased when the Whigs compromised on some of the contentious issues: **aldermen** were retained and made up a quarter of a council, councillors had to have substantial property qualifications and in boroughs with over 6,000 inhabitants the town was to be divided into wards. The bill became law in September 1835. Twenty-two new boroughs were incorporated within 20 years, including Manchester and Birmingham in 1838.

Aldermen were, until
1974, the senior members
of a local council. They
were elected by other
councillors.

Why was municipal
reform necessary?

> **Municipal Corporations Act of 1835**
>
> - 178 corporations were abolished and replaced by elected councils.
> - A uniform household franchise was established by which all occupiers with a three-year residence qualification could vote for the first council and after that for one third of the council in every subsequent election.
> - Each council elected its own mayor and aldermen.
> - All debates would be open and accounts publicly audited.
> - Councils could take over the duties of local improvement commissions. Few councils took advantage of this permissive clause.
> - Councils could levy rates.
> - Councils had to form watch committees and could establish borough police forces.
> - The Act laid down procedures by which a town could petition for incorporation and so form a council.

Whig reforms, 1832–41

During the 1833 and 1834 parliamentary sessions Lord **Althorp**, leader of the House of Commons, showed that the Whig government's commitment to further reform remained strong. Nevertheless, legislation to improve the condition of the 'lower orders' such as factory, education and poor law reform (see Chapters 11 and 12) resulted partly from extra-parliamentary pressure and fact-finding commissions. Althorp's record suggests, however, that the Whig government did have political aims as well as humanitarian concerns, and they did not respond simply to extra-parliamentary pressures.

Melbourne led a government that was far less radical than Grey's and the pace of reform began to slow down. There were various reasons for this. Melbourne fought general elections in 1835 (called by the Tories after the minority government of Sir Robert Peel (see Chapter 5) was defeated) and in 1837 (after the death of William IV). After 1837, the Whig majority was reduced to 32, and Melbourne had to rely on the support of the Irish MPs or the agreement of the Tories to get legislation through parliament. By temperament Melbourne was not a radical reformer, preferring gradual to fundamental change. In addition, by 1835 Britain had experienced almost a decade of intense change and needed a period of stability. In the autumn of 1837, **Lord John Russell** offended radicals when he strongly defended the reform settlement and declared himself against further reform.

Melbourne's government did introduce important reforms in the church. The Ecclesiastical Revenues Commission, established in June 1832 to investigate the financial structure of the Church of England, had not been very effective. During Peel's minority administration in early 1835, a new commission was set up to 'consider the State of the Established Church'. Made permanent in 1836 as the Ecclesiastical Commission, it introduced a series of major reforms which reinforced state control over the Church.

John Charles Spencer, Viscount **Althorp**, 3rd Earl Spencer (1782–1845), played a central role in Grey's and Melbourne's ministries as chancellor of the exchequer and leader of the House of Commons. He succeeded his father as Earl Spencer in November 1834 and left political life. He was not an eloquent speaker, but had the confidence of the House of Commons because of his honesty.

William Lamb, 2nd Viscount **Melbourne** (1779–1848), was home secretary 1830–34 and prime minister in 1834 and again from 1835 to 1841. Though he led a Whig government, he was conservative in his attitudes. He holds the distinction of being the last prime minister to be dismissed by the monarch (William IV in 1834).

Lord John Russell, 1st Earl Russell (1792–1878), was a radical Whig politician, at least in his youth. He was postmaster general 1830–34, home secretary 1835–39 and colonial secretary 1839–41. He served as prime minister 1846–52 and again in 1865–66.

> What were the constraints on Melbourne's government which slowed the pace of reform?

Henry Brougham, 1st
Baron Brougham and Vaux
(1778–1868), was a
barrister and writer by
profession. He helped
found the *Edinburgh
Review* in 1802 and
London University in 1828.
He was lord chancellor
between 1830 and 1834,
introducing radical reform
of the legal system and
supervising the passage of
the Reform Acts.

Tithes were paid to the
Church of England and
consisted of a tenth part of
the main produce of the
land (corn, oats, wood etc.)
and a tenth part of the
profits of labour.

What major reforms
were passed between
1832 and 1841?

Reforming legislation passed between 1832 and 1841

1833

- Slavery was abolished throughout the British empire and £20 million was allocated as compensation for slave owners. The abolition of slavery was clearly influenced by the extra-parliamentary campaign. It also redeemed pledges given to the electorate by many Whig candidates in the 1830 and 1832 general elections. The measure disappointed humanitarians because it delayed the full emancipation of slaves until a period of apprenticeship in limited freedom had been served (seven years for slaves who worked on the land, five years for the rest).
- The Factory Act was passed, but it applied only to the textile industry. It restricted the employment of young children and established an inspectorate to enforce its requirements. This laid the foundation for later social and industrial legislation.
- £20,000 was granted to the voluntary societies that provided elementary education. This established the principle of state-assisted education.
- **Henry Brougham**, lord chancellor, reformed the law by establishing the central criminal court and the judicial committee of the privy council.
- The Irish Church Temporalities Act abolished ten Church of Ireland bishoprics and reduced the revenues of the remainder. Surplus revenues were to be used for purely church purposes.

1834

- The Poor Law Amendment Act reformed the existing system of poor relief. It introduced workhouses and stated that all relief should be provided in the workhouse. Parishes were grouped together into Poor Law unions to improve efficiency and reduce costs.

1835

- The Municipal Corporations Act was introduced.

1836

- The Commutation of Tithes Act legislated for **tithes** to be paid in money (known as a rent charge), based on the average price of corn in the previous seven years. They were very unpopular, especially with Nonconformists, and were often difficult for clergymen to collect.
- The Dissenters' Marriage Act allowed Nonconformists to be married outside the Anglican Church in a civil ceremony, in special circumstances.
- The registration of births, marriages and deaths was made compulsory with the introduction of civil registration. This ended the Anglican Church's monopoly of the registration of baptisms, marriages and burials.
- London University was given the right to grant degrees. This broke the monopoly of Oxford and Cambridge universities, where students had to be Anglicans to take a degree. London University was open to all Protestants.

1838

- The Pluralities Act placed restrictions on clergymen having more than one parish.
- Acts for building and enlarging churches were also passed.

1839

- The education grant was increased to £30,000 and government inspectors were appointed to supervise the schools receiving the grant.
- The Rural Police Act allowed magistrates to set up a paid county police force. In 1840, borough and county police forces were allowed to amalgamate if desired.

1840

- The excess revenues of cathedrals were distributed to parishes with the greatest needs.

Problems for the Whigs

The Whigs were a party of reform *and* reaction, especially when public order and property rights were threatened. When the Whigs came to power in November 1830, they faced many challenges to their authority:

- the Swing disturbances were taking place throughout southern England;
- there were campaigns against **stamp duty** on newspapers;
- the factory movement agitated for the reform of working conditions in factories;
- trade union activity took place on an unprecedented scale; and
- there were widespread demands for parliamentary reform.

The reforms introduced to address some of these grievances were not sufficient to appease the demands for change. As we have seen, radical working-class opinion was not satisfied with the reforms introduced by the Reform Acts of 1832, nor did the Factory Act of 1833 meet the aspirations of the extra-parliamentary factory reformers. The Poor Law Amendment Act of 1834 was widely opposed across the class spectrum. The government acted swiftly to repress opposition, culminating in the case of the **Tolpuddle Martyrs**.

Chartism posed a more serious challenge to the government. Russell, home secretary until late August 1839, initially behaved with restraint, assuming that its appeal was limited. By mid-1839, however, a harder policy had emerged as the Home Office recognised that local authorities could not manage without support. Drilling was banned, 6,000 regular troops were stationed in the north and leading Chartists were arrested.

The Tory party, defeated in the 1832 general election, revived and the Whigs found themselves under attack. Internal divisions made matters worse and gradually the Whigs saw their majority in the Commons eroded. The number of Tory MPs rose from 150 after the 1832 election to about 290 in 1835, and then 313 in 1837 and finally 370 when they won the election in 1841.

There was a long-running battle between **Edward Stanley**, the Irish secretary, and Lord John Russell over the direction of Irish policy. This dispute eventually led to the resignation of four cabinet ministers. Policies towards Ireland and others in favour of Nonconformists, largely initiated by Russell, led to the alienation of a number of the government's more moderate supporters in the House of Commons. Over 30 MPs who had voted for reform crossed to the Tory benches between 1833 and 1837.

In July 1834 the government was embarrassed by revelations that it had negotiated with Daniel O'Connell when deciding whether to renew the Irish Coercion Act, which gave the government extensive powers to deal with unrest in Ireland. This led to Grey's retirement and his replacement by Lord Melbourne. Melbourne proposed that Russell should become leader of the

There was a **stamp duty** on newspapers. This was very unpopular as it pushed up prices. Many believed it was a government device for keeping information out of the hands of the working class.

The **Tolpuddle Martyrs** were six farm labourers from Dorset who were transported to Australia for trade union activity. Their plight, seen by many as grossly unfair, proved an important focal point for radical activity in 1834 and 1835. Lord Melbourne refused to pardon them when he was home secretary, but when he became prime minister he allowed Lord John Russell, his home secretary, to do so.

Chartism is discussed in more detail in Chapter 14.

How did the Whigs deal with the threats posed by the Chartist movement?

Edward Stanley, 14th earl of Derby (1799–1869), was chief secretary for Ireland 1830–33 and colonial secretary 1833–34, but resigned over the question of lay appropriation. He was later prime minister of Tory governments in 1852, 1858–59 and 1866–68.

How did Peel's government's policy towards Ireland lead to its downfall?

House of Commons in November. William IV objected to this and Melbourne resigned. Peel formed a minority Tory administration and gained about 100 seats in the early 1835 general election, although this did not give him a parliamentary majority. He was defeated by an alliance between the Whigs and O'Connell's Irish MPs, who agreed to co-operate to remove him. He was forced to resign in April 1835, after which Melbourne returned with Russell as home secretary.

The Whigs' relations with the crown improved with the accession of Victoria to the throne in June 1837. A close personal relationship developed between Melbourne and Victoria. This was exploited in the 'Bedchamber crisis' of May 1839. When the Whig majority in the Commons was reduced to five, Melbourne decided to resign. The queen, however, refused to change any of the ladies of her bedchamber, who were all Whigs. Peel would not form a government under such circumstances and Melbourne returned to office. This gave the Whigs two more years in power, but Peel no longer supported them on moderate issues. Unemployment and manufacturing depression deepened after 1838 and the government appeared to have no answers to the economic and social problems facing Britain.

Why did the accession of Queen Victoria strengthen the Whigs' position in parliament?

Summary questions

1 Identify and explain any *two* factors that helped the Whig reform of parliament in 1832.

2 Compare the importance of at least *three* issues in determining Whig social reforms between 1833 and 1841.

5

Redefining Toryism

Focus questions

◆ How effective was Peel as a party political leader?

◆ Why is Peel's ministry of 1841–46 considered so successful?

◆ Why did Corn Law repeal lead to the collapse of Peel's government in 1846?

Significant dates

1829	Catholic emancipation granted
1832	Tories defeated in December general election; Reform Act passed
1834	Peel becomes prime minister of a minority Tory government; the Tamworth Manifesto
1835	Ecclesiastical Commission set up; the Tories gain seats in the general election, but Peel is defeated by an alliance of Whigs and Radicals; returns to opposition
1839	Bedchamber crisis
1841	Tories win general election and Peel becomes prime minister of a majority government
1842	Peel's first budget; Mines Act introduced
1844	Factory Act introduced; Bank Charter Act
1845	Irish famine begins and Peel commits cabinet to repeal Corn Laws in December
1846	Corn Laws repealed; Peel resigns after defeat on Irish Coercion bill in June
1850	Peel dies, following a horse-riding accident

Overview

Peel is generally recognised as the founder of modern Conservatism. He recognised that the Tory party needed to adapt itself after its disastrous showing in the **1832 general election**. In successive elections in the 1830s, the Tories increased their support in the House of Commons, eventually defeating Melbourne's Whig government in 1841.

In the **1832 general election**, 175 Tory MPs were elected out of the 658 MPs who sat in the House of Commons.

Peel was prepared to put the interests of the nation above those of the Tory party, and on two occasions he introduced policies that went against basic Tory beliefs. In 1829, he pushed through Catholic emancipation contrary to the wishes of the Protestant Tory majority; 17 years later, he went against the Tories' support for agricultural protection by repealing the Corn Laws.

How effective was Peel as a party political leader?

At this time, the leader of the opposition's role was very different from what we understand by the term today. In case of Peel in the 1830s:

- He was prepared to support government legislation when it was aimed at maintaining law and order.
- He was not the official leader of the Tories until the end of 1834. Wellington, the previous prime minister, who led the Tories in the House of Lords, was regarded by some as the Tory leader. Peel led the Tories in the Commons.
- Considerable distrust existed between Peel and the ultra-Tories. They feared that Peel would betray the party, as he had in 1829 over Catholic emancipation. Peel, on the other hand, did not believe that the ultras would act as part of a responsible opposition in parliament and rejected their view that politics should be determined largely by the interests of English landowners.

Who were the ultras and what did they believe in?

When William IV dismissed Melbourne's government in November 1834, he first turned to Wellington to form a new government. Wellington refused because he believed that prime ministers should carry authority in the House of Commons. The king then appointed Peel. Peel's minority administration lasted just 100 days, ending in April 1835, after which the Tories returned to opposition.

Peel did not become prime minister because he was leader of a party in the Commons; instead, his authority as leader of the Tories resulted from his appointment as prime minister by the king. This reinforced his view of the executive or administrative nature of government: he believed that strong government achieved more and was also preferred by the governed. This meant that efficient administration was necessary to maintain public order.

Peel's first loyalty was to the monarchy rather than to the Tory party. 'Party' as we understand it today was only just beginning to be important and Peel, like many of his contemporaries, saw the monarchy and the well-being of the country as his priority, with his party coming second. This was an important distinction and proved central to the decisions he made during the

Bedchamber crisis in 1839 and the crisis over the repeal of the Corn Laws in 1845–46.

Peel's attitude to parliamentary reform

In late 1832, the Tories were in a demoralised state. Although the party had opposed parliamentary reform, there were nevertheless those in the party who did not condemn reform entirely, but believed the Whigs had gone too far. Unquestionably, there were die-hard opponents of reform among the Tories: the ultra-Tories, in both the Lords and Commons, opposed parliamentary reform, municipal reform, church reform, factory reform and Poor Law reform.

At the opening of parliament in early 1833 Peel made it clear that although he was not against further reform, he believed that it should be undertaken slowly and deliberately. He believed that if change was necessary it should reinforce, not undermine, the constitution and Britain's governing elite. This policy was not designed to pacify the opponents of change in the party.

Peel was dedicated to good government by men of integrity. He believed that power should be held by an elite with the education and expertise necessary to act in the national interest. Public opinion had its place, but Peel wanted to re-establish the proper balance between executive government and public opinion, which he believed had been altered by the crisis over reform. Like most of his contemporaries, Peel was not a democrat. He believed that the people did not have the necessary education or judgement to make central decisions and that, if parliament surrendered to outside pressure, the quality of its judgements would be weakened and the interests of the nation would be jeopardised.

Reconstructing the Tory party

Peel's achievement in the 1830s was to make the Tory party more relevant to a changing society. He recognised that in order to restore the fortunes of the Tories it would be necessary to alter the widely held view that the Tory party was opposed to change and was supported by only a small part of the population. To do this, Peel needed to increase support for the party among the newly enfranchised urban middle classes (see Chapter 4) and to rekindle support among the landed interest who had voted Whig in the 1832 general election. He did this by linking the interests of all property owners (whether landed, industrial or commercial) to the need for public order, while maintaining the existing constitution.

His appointment as prime minister in 1834–35 gave him the opportunity to make his position clear to the new electorate. In the **Tamworth Manifesto** of December 1834 Peel outlined his position on three issues:

A close relationship developed between the young Victoria and Lord Melbourne after she became queen in 1837. This was exploited in the **Bedchamber crisis** of 1839. In May 1839 the Whig majority was reduced to five and Melbourne decided to resign. The queen, however, refused to accept Tory ladies-in-waiting to replace her existing Whig ladies. Peel refused to form a government under such circumstances. As a result, Melbourne returned to office for a further two years.

What was Peel's attitude to reform?

The **Tamworth Manifesto** was an address by Peel to his constituents at Tamworth.

- First, to further his aim of broadening the appeal of the Tory party, the Manifesto contained a direct bid for uncommitted middle-class voters by appealing to 'that class which is much less interested in the contentions of party, than in the maintenance of order and the cause of good government'.
- Secondly, Peel was anxious to emphasise that he accepted the Reform Acts as 'a final and irrevocable settlement of a great Constitutional question' and that he would make no attempt to reverse the changes already made by the Whigs. He committed himself and his party to moderate reform ('a careful review of institutions, civil and ecclesiastical, undertaken in a friendly temper, combining, with the firm maintenance of established rights, the correction of proved abuses and the redress of real grievances') where there was a strong case for it. This was designed to gain the support of the middle classes who wanted further reforms.
- Finally, he made his support for the Church of England clear, which was essential if he wanted the co-operation of the ultras. However, he also made it clear that he was prepared to support reform of the church's abuses and 'to extend the sphere of its usefulness and to strengthen and confirm its just claims upon the respect and affections of the people'.

On what issues did Peel make his position clear in the Tamworth Manifesto?

The Manifesto was seen as too liberal by some, but the majority of the ultras went along with Peel.

Sir Robert Peel (1788–1850).

Throughout the 1830s, Peel sought to broaden Tory support in the country and convince dissidents within the party that he had taken account of their interests. This was accompanied by the gradual introduction of the term 'Conservative' in place of 'Tory'. Tories believed in the uncompromising defence of the privileges enjoyed by institutions connected to the Anglican landed interest, while Conservatives accepted the need for gradual and cautious change designed to reconcile those institutions with the needs of the modern world. Peel's strategy of reform in order to conserve the Tories effectively prevented radical reformers from eroding, or even destroying, the traditional ruling institutions of the country. Conservatism may be seen as an extension of the work of the liberal Tory reformers of the 1820s.

In what ways is it possible to distinguish between 'Tories' and 'Conservatives' in the 1830s?

The 1841 election

Peel is credited with the election victory in 1841: without his leadership, many contemporaries believed that the Tories would have been assigned to permanent opposition. Peel's parliamentary performance during the 1830s was an important element in the Tories' revival. His grasp of economics had allowed him to capitalise on the growing economic problems faced by the Whigs after 1838. These problems were caused by the widespread economic depression in the manufacturing industries that lasted until the early 1840s. There were also other factors at work over which Peel had little or no control.

After the 1832 election, the dominance of the Whigs began to be eroded. Forty Whig MPs who had supported the Reform Acts moved to the Conservative benches between 1832 and 1837. In June 1834, four Whig cabinet ministers resigned over Irish appropriation (see Chapter 6) – by the late 1830s two had become Conservative supporters and, in the 1840s, cabinet ministers. In addition, the Whigs were perceived to be unable to control the radicals, a situation that Tory propaganda exploited.

The unexpected frequency of general elections after 1832 also aided the Conservative cause. Peel used William IV's invitation to form a government in late 1834 to call an election in 1835. Another election was held on the death of William IV in 1837. These gave the opportunity of voting Tory to those voters who were concerned that the Whigs wished to push reform further and threaten their position as property-owners. The Conservatives increased their MPs by about 100 in the 1835 election and added 40 more in the election two years later. By-election successes between 1837 and 1841 further improved their position. Between 1837 and 1841, they were only 30 votes short of the Whigs and their normal voting allies. The electoral tide was running in their favour.

The emergence of a party organisational structure also played an important part in reviving Tory fortunes. Peel played little part in organisational changes

Francis Bonham was largely responsible for reorganising the Conservative party in the 1830s.

in the Tory party in the 1830s – the initiative came from individuals like **Francis Bonham**. The Reform Acts required voters to register and this provided opportunities for local supporters to organise and consolidate their party's voting strength. Peel recognised the need for party organisation, but he was, at least initially, ambivalent in his attitude. He was suspicious of extra-parliamentary pressure, which meant that his relations with many local Tory organisations were not particularly close. By 1837, however, Peel was urging his supporters to register. The fact that the Conservatives were a much better organised party than the Whigs in 1841 was an important factor in their victory.

During the 1830s, Peel turned the Conservatives into a viable party of government and established a sense of direction and leadership. However, there were important divisions of principle between Peel and the right wing of the Conservative party that were to re-emerge after 1841, with disastrous consequences.

Why is Peel's ministry of 1841–46 considered so successful?

When Peel took office in 1841, he recognised that the major problem facing Britain was economic and his priority was to make the country debt-free and affluent. He set about establishing a government based on administrative effectiveness. Before the Corn Law crisis, the focus of his administration was on financial and economic reform. Peel believed that a prosperous country was one in which social distress and disorder would be reduced.

Protectionist Tories argued for continuing the Corn Laws to protect British farming.

Although Peel had attempted to broaden the base of the Conservative party in the 1830s, the election was a triumph for **protectionist Toryism**. The party did best in the English and Welsh counties and in those boroughs little changed by the Reform Acts. The MPs elected were largely from the section of the party that had no interest in change and little sympathy for reform. Above all, many were ardent protectionists. Tory votes had been cast in favour of a party that was most likely to protect landowners and defend the established church. Their perspective was far narrower than Peel's. Nevertheless, Peel appointed to important positions those in the party who supported his policies and beliefs. His only concession to party feeling was the appointment of the **duke of Buckingham**, a leading protectionist, to the post of lord privy seal.

Richard Grenville, 2nd **duke of Buckingham** (1797–1861), was known as the 'farmers' friend'. He served briefly in Peel's government until January 1842 when he resigned over the Corn Laws.

Peel increasingly adopted policies out of sympathy with the majority of his MPs. Public duty on behalf of the monarch and in the interests of the nation was his priority; party came a poor second. This proved to be a problem, particularly as the election had been fought largely on the question of protection.

The route from the electoral triumph of 1841 to the political disaster of 1846 was, in retrospect, a logical one.

Economic and financial reform

Peel's financial and commercial reforms in the 1840s were designed to promote public order as much as to relieve the economic complaints of manufacturers and consumers.

In the late 1830s the economy slumped and, consequently, Peel inherited a budget deficit in 1841. He recognised that the only way he could remedy this was to build on the work undertaken by Huskisson in the 1820s, and introduce tariff reform and reintroduce **income tax**. Parallel to his budgetary programme, Peel reformed the business practices of banks and companies. The 1842 budget also sought to restore prosperity to the manufacturing sector and so promote social stability.

Income tax was reintroduced at 7d (3 per cent) in the pound on annual incomes above £150 (which excluded most of the working classes); this was expected to raise £3.7 million. Peel assured MPs that income tax would not be made permanent and would only be retained for three years. This significantly reduced opposition from the Whigs and from within the Conservative party.

Customs duties were reduced on about 750 items and maximum duties on imported raw materials, partially manufactured goods and manufactured items were set at 5 per cent, 12 per cent and 20 per cent respectively. Duties on imported timber were completely cut. All export duties on manufactured goods were abolished. Peel argued that reduced import duties would both encourage trade and provide cheaper goods for British consumers. The level of tax paid on corn was reduced; as a result, Buckingham resigned from the cabinet.

These proposals were controversial, especially to the protectionists, who saw them as the abandonment of protection for farming, and to free traders, who did not think Peel had gone far enough. They were, however, generally popular and certainly politically astute. This was particularly the case with the electorally important middle classes, who recognised that Peel had gone as far as he could at this stage without completely alienating his own party.

The 1842 budget did not produce immediate improvements in trade or employment. The economy remained sluggish throughout 1842 and trade did not revive until late 1843. By 1844, however, there was clear evidence that the economy was recovering, helped by good harvests in 1843 and 1844 and by a boom in railway investment. Government finance moved into surplus in 1844 and further changes took place in the 1845 budget. The estimated budget surplus of £3.4 million for 1845–46 was sufficient for Peel to dispense with income tax, but he argued in his 1845 budget that it should be renewed for a

Income tax had previously been introduced by William Pitt during the French Wars as a wartime tax. In 1816, against the wishes of the Tory government of Lord Liverpool, parliament had voted against its continuance.

William Gladstone (1809–98).

further three years to allow further reductions in tariffs. Peel argued that this would result in greater economic prosperity.

Peel's economic liberalism had its origins in the 1820s. At its heart was the 'sound money' policy with its low levels of taxation and freeing of trade in order to produce a balanced budget. Peel argued that, without political and economic stability or control of the amount of money in circulation, there would be inflation and this would limit economic growth. He thought it was necessary to restrict the Bank of England's power to issue money 'to inspire just confidence in the medium of exchange'. Finally, Peel suggested that, if businessmen and industrialists were given the freedom to exploit the market, the result would be increased profitability, improved employment and economic growth for everyone's benefit.

Peel considered the Bank Charter Act of 1844 to be one of his most important achievements. Its aim was to establish a more stable banking system by preventing the excessive issuing of paper money that had led to some crises in the past. Between 1826 and 1844, overissue by provincial banks had caused the failure of a quarter of all the banks entitled to issue their own notes. The Act defined the position of the Bank of England in the British economy very carefully:

- The Bank was allowed to issue notes to the value of its gold reserves, to a limit of £14 million.
- No new English provincial bank was allowed to issue its own notes. The Act recognised 279 banks with note-issuing powers.

Peel's ultimate aim was to reduce the provincial banks' rights of issue and to concentrate this function within the Bank of England. The effect of the 1844 Act might have limited the scope of banks to finance economic growth had it not been for the new gold discoveries in California and Australia from the late 1840s. These increased the Bank of England's reserves and enabled them to increase the issue of notes. Without this, the economic expansion of the 1850s and 1860s, for which Peel is often credited, would not have occurred.

When the Bubble Act was repealed in 1825, **joint-stock companies** were freed from the regulations that had prohibited their growth for over a century. The result was increased investment in projects of every sort: docks, gas and water companies and, especially after 1830, railways. However, many of these companies collapsed because they were poorly organised or fraudulent and large numbers of people lost their savings. As a result, **William Gladstone**, president of the Board of Trade, introduced the Joint Stock Companies Act in 1844. This Act established the registrar of companies, with which all companies with more than 25 members and freely transferable shares were required to register. In addition, company directors had to submit fully audited accounts to the registrar. This Act helped to protect the public from unscrupulous companies and created a more responsible climate for company development.

Poor law and factory reform, 1842 and 1844

Peel believed that social reform and successful economic conditions were linked: economic growth would lead to the creation of new jobs which would reduce distress and also stimulate consumption. Support for social reform was lukewarm within the Tory government and Peel was sceptical of the value of direct government intervention in solving social problems. He recognised that his government could not abdicate all social responsibility but, like many contemporaries, he believed that its role should be limited and cost-effective. For example, Peel had supported the passing of the Poor Law Amendment Act in 1834 and the further amendments in 1842, when the operation of the Poor Law was tightened further to reduce costs. Peel argued Britain's welfare provision was still generous and fair compared to other countries.

Although Peel's government was not known for its support for social reform, publication of reports from committees originally set up by the Whigs in the late 1830s, and extra-parliamentary pressure from radicals, as well as some Tory politicians, led to two important acts being passed:

- The Mines Act of 1842, which banned women and most children from working below ground, was introduced by the opposition Whigs.
- The first Factory Act was passed in 1833. In 1843, Sir James Graham, the home secretary (who had defected from the Whigs in 1834) introduced a Factory bill which sought to reduce the hours worked by women and children. It also proposed that more hours of compulsory schooling be provided, largely by the Church of England, for children aged 9–13. There was widespread opposition from Nonconformists, who did not intend to allow the Church of England to take control of factory schools, and the bill was withdrawn. The following year it was reintroduced without its education clauses and passed.

Why did Corn Law repeal lead to the collapse of Peel's government in 1846?

Deteriorating relationships

Relations between Peel and his backbenchers were strained from the early days of his ministry. Peel was insensitive to the interests of many Conservative MPs and made little attempt to win backbench support. He took the loyalty of Conservatives in parliament for granted and was irritated when it was withheld.

What legislation was passed by Peel's government between 1841 and 1845 to deal with the economy?

Why was legislation passed by Peel's government between 1841 and 1845 to deal with social problems?

Conservative whips warned Peel of the unpopularity of his 1842 budget among protectionists (in the event, 85 Conservatives failed to support it), while Poor Law and factory reform also led to backbench discontent. These rebellions did not threaten Peel's position in 1842 and 1843, but they did widen the divisions between Peel's government and his protectionist MPs.

In March 1844, 95 Tories voted against Peel for an amendment to the Factory Act and, in June, 61 Tories supported an amendment to a government proposal to reduce the duty on foreign sugar. Both amendments were carried and, although Peel had little difficulty in reversing them, the way in which he did this caused considerable annoyance: he threatened to resign if the Tory MPs refused to support him. Reluctantly they fell into line. In early 1845 party morale was low and party unity was strained. On the issue of Corn Law repeal, Peel pushed his party too far.

In what ways did Peel and the remainder of the Conservative party have different attitudes towards protection?

The Anti-Corn Law League

In September 1838 the Manchester Anti-Corn Law Association was formed by a group of local businessmen. Their aim was the total abolition of the Corn Laws. Lecture tours in the north of England encouraged the formation of other local associations and links were established with London free traders. In February 1839 a delegate meeting of all the Anti-Corn Law Associations was held in London. When the House of Commons rejected a motion against the Corn Laws in March 1839, the delegates set up the Anti-Corn Law League (ACLL) as a national organisation, with its headquarters in Manchester.

The ACLL was an economic pressure group with a very specific objective. The League based its appeal on the economic advantages of free trade – cheaper food, more employment, higher exports and greater prosperity – and the first phase of its work aimed to persuade the public of the case against the Corn Laws.

Lord John Russell had hinted in 1839 that the Whigs might support repeal, but Peel remained silent on the issue. **Cobden** saw that repeal would only be achieved through electoral activity. This marked the beginning of a new phase in the League's activities. In the 1841 general election, eight Leaguers (including Cobden) were elected, thus giving the League an important parliamentary base.

The election of Peel and the protectionist Conservatives in 1841 put the ACLL in an awkward position. Peel's majority meant that the League's arguments were not given much of a hearing in parliament. This led to a crisis of confidence for Cobden, **Bright** and the other leaders of the ACLL. This crisis was heightened by deepening distress in the northern manufacturing districts during the winter of 1841–42. The League was at its lowest ebb in the summer of 1842, with few policies and an increasing lack of confidence.

Richard Cobden (1804–65) was a manufacturer of calico in Manchester who, with John Bright, led the Anti-Corn Law League after 1839.

John Bright (1811–89) was a cotton manufacturer from Rochdale in Lancashire.

The ACLL's capacity for intensive agitation was increased by an overhaul of its organisation. In March 1842, the League divided the country up into 12 areas, each with its own organisation. This improved both the collection of money and the enrolment of new members. The League's propaganda machine was also expanded. From December 1842 its newspaper, *The Circular*, began to appear weekly and in 1843 *The Economist*, acting as the forum for free-trade ideas, was founded. Cobden and Bright undertook widespread lecture tours and anti-Corn Law tracts were sent to every elector.

From 1842 to 1845, the League directed its energies towards preparing for a decisive struggle at the expected 1848 general election. Attempts were made to win over tenant farmers. These failed because many tenant farmers supported protection and may even have influenced their landlords to take a protectionist stance. The League also used indirect methods. It tried to create new free trade votes by buying up freeholds in key constituencies, with some success in south Lancashire and the West Riding. By the summer of 1846 only a small number of seats had been made safe in this way. Peel was not intimidated into repealing the Corn Laws to avoid an anti-Tory landslide in the counties.

The stimulus for repeal came from inside the cabinet and parliament because of the Irish crisis of 1845–46 (see Chapter 6). The League can perhaps take credit for the conversion of Lord John Russell, the Whig leader. The same cannot be said of Peel's decision. He had concluded that the Corn Laws had to go, long before the Irish crisis. Repeal in 1846 was an ordered retreat, made by a prime minister and parliament; it was not as the result of an electoral contest or pressure by the Anti-Corn Law League.

Why did the Conservative election victory in 1841 cause problems for the Anti-Corn Law League?

Arguments for the repeal of the Corn Laws

By 1845, it was increasingly recognised that repealing the Corn Laws was in the national interest. The Corn Laws were designed to protect farmers against cheap corn imports from Europe. By the mid-1840s, however, there was a widespread shortage of corn in Europe and Peel reasoned that, as there were no surpluses available to flood the British market, British farmers had nothing to fear from repeal.

As early as 1841 Peel had, in fact, recognised that the Corn Laws would eventually have to be repealed. The moves to free trade in the 1842 and 1845 budgets were part of this process. He argued that tariff reform did not mean abandoning protection for farming, but called instead for fair, rather than excessive, protection. In 1842, Peel reduced the levels of duty paid on imported wheat from 28s 8d to 13s per quarter when the domestic price of wheat was between 59s and 60s. The expected protectionist Tory rebellion did not occur. Yet Peel did not announce his intention to repeal the Corn

Laws until late in 1845. There are different possible explanations for his decision:

- Peel had accepted the intellectual arguments for free trade in the 1820s and supported the commercial policies put forward by Huskisson. His thinking was influenced by Huskisson's view that British farmers would eventually be unable to supply the food needed by Britain's growing population and, therefore, it would be essential to import foreign grain. This would mean that repealing the Corn Laws would be inevitable. Peel may have accepted this, but he was the leader of a protectionist party. The protectionists were convinced that Peel intended to abandon the party's commitment to agricultural protection and so he was compelled to wait for the right time to introduce the idea of repeal.

- Historians have argued that time ran out for Peel with the Irish Great Famine of 1845–46. By October 1845, at least half of the Irish potato crop had been ruined by blight. This led to a major subsistence crisis since large numbers of people depended entirely on the potato crop for food. If the government was to reduce the worst effects of famine, every barrier to the efficient transport of food needed to be removed. The most obvious barrier was the Corn Laws: in order to open Irish ports to unrestricted grain imports, the Corn Laws would have to be either suspended or abolished. Peel maintained that suspending the Corn Laws was not a viable option as it would be impossible to reconcile public opinion to their reimposition later. Other historians have a problem with this argument. The failure of the potato crop meant that many Irish people did not have any way of earning the money they would need to pay for imported corn, even if it was sold more cheaply. The £750,000 spent by Peel's government on public work projects, cheap maize from the United States and other relief measures were of far more practical value to the Irish people than the repeal of the Corn Laws. These historians maintain that Peel used the opportunity provided by the Famine to introduce a policy on which he had already made up his mind; the crisis in Ireland merely accelerated this process.

- As we have seen, Peel disapproved of extra-parliamentary pressure and viewed the lobbying of the Anti-Corn Law League with considerable suspicion. The success of the League, especially between 1841 and 1844, may have persuaded Peel *not* to move quickly to repeal. He saw it as his duty to act in the national interest and did not want to be accused of acting under pressure. The activities of the League threatened to divide landed interests. Peel's belief that social stability was essential for economic growth meant that giving in to the League was an unacceptable political option. Peel was also critical of the League's propaganda, especially its language of class warfare. The strident, anti-aristocratic attacks by the League and the creation of a protectionist Anti-League raised the possibility of commercial and industrial interests being pitted against agricultural interests. Peel recognised that the Anti-Corn Law League might exploit the crisis in Ireland and repeal was therefore a pre-emptive strike designed to take the initiative away from middle-class radicals, while helping the landed interest to maintain their control of the political system.

Can the Anti-Corn Law League take credit for the repeal of the Corn Laws?

The politics of repeal

Peel told his cabinet in late 1845 that he proposed repealing the Corn Laws, maintaining that it was in the national interest to do so. His argument was too sophisticated for the protectionists. For small landowners and tenant farmers, the most vocal supporters of protection, repeal meant ruin. Peel's belief that free trade would offer new opportunities for efficient farmers had little impact. Although only Viscount Stanley and the duke of Buccleuch resigned on the issue, Peel nonetheless felt that this was sufficient for him to resign as well.

He hoped that Lord John Russell and the Whigs would form a government and repeal the Corn Laws. This might have allowed him to keep the Conservative party together. Although Russell had recently announced his conversion to repeal in his 'Edinburgh Letter' in December 1845, he was unwilling to form a minority administration. This meant that Peel had to return to office. Predictably, repeal of the Corn Laws passed its third reading in the Commons in May 1846. The Whigs voted solidly for the bill, but only 106 Tories voted in favour of repeal compared to 222 against. The great Tory landowners voted for repeal as they recognised that it did not threaten their economic position; the bulk of the opposition came from the MPs who represented the small landowners. Retribution was swift: in June 1846, enough protectionists voted with the Whigs on an Irish coercion bill to engineer Peel's resignation. He did not hold office again, and died in 1850.

What were the factors that contributed to Peel's decision to repeal the Corn Laws?

Summary questions

1   Identify and explain any *two* factors that affected the strength of the Tories from 1829 to 1841.

2   Compare the importance of at least *three* issues that influenced Peel's relations with his party between 1841 and 1846.

6

Peel and Ireland

Focus questions

◆ Why was Catholic emancipation such a controversial issue?

◆ How did Peel deal with Ireland?

◆ What were the social and economic effects of the Great Famine?

Significant dates

1798   Irish rising

1800   Act of Union between England and Ireland

1823   The Catholic Association founded by Daniel O'Connell

1829   Catholic emancipation is granted

1841   Peel becomes prime minister

1845   The Great Famine begins in Ireland

Overview

Ireland was a problem for successive English governments. This was largely because a Protestant minority in Ireland ruled a Roman Catholic majority whose political and economic rights were severely restricted. Until 1829 Catholics were discriminated against because of their religion and, although they were given some legal and political rights in the 1790s, Catholics were denied access to parliament, both in Dublin and, after 1800, in Westminster. Economically, Catholics formed the poorest sections of a predominantly rural and agricultural society. They were also seen as a potential source of revolution and, therefore, as a threat to Britain's security. Politicians like William Pitt and Sir Robert Peel tried to improve the position and status of Catholics, but they met with considerable opposition from Irish Protestants and an anti-Catholic British public. It is not surprising that to some Catholics the Great Famine of 1845 was seen as an attempt to resolve the Irish problem through starvation.

Why was Catholic emancipation such a controversial issue?

Pitt's legacy

In the early 1780s, Ireland had a rapidly growing population of around 4 million people, most of whom were Roman Catholic tenant farmers. However, Anglo-Irish Protestants, who were often absentee landlords, owned about 80 per cent of the land. They were bitterly resented by their poverty-stricken Catholic tenants. This Protestant elite governed Ireland in Dublin, largely for their own benefit, and they resented interference from Britain. **Catholics** had been deprived of their political rights in the late seventeenth century and their Protestant rulers were unwilling to change this.

In the 1770s and 1780s, the Irish parliament supported the Americans in their fight for independence. This turned Ireland into a dangerous, pro-American country on England's doorstep. Politicians in Westminster agreed on two things, both designed to prevent Ireland from following the American colonies into independence:

- First, Ireland should have a significant amount of self-government. As a result, parliamentary reform, introduced in 1782–83, gave the Dublin parliament legislative independence. (This did not prevent parliament at Westminster passing laws that affected Ireland.) This did little to solve the Catholic problem as Catholics still could not become MPs in the new parliament because of the restrictions imposed on them by the late-seventeenth-century Test Acts. Only a few Dissenters were elected and no **Presbyterians** sat in the Dublin parliament. The control of the Anglican landowners over parliament and parliamentary seats increased dramatically after 1782.

- Secondly, Ireland should have greater access to British markets. Pitt saw this as a way of strengthening the British empire as well as creating political stability. In 1785, he proposed free trade between England and Ireland, which he thought would benefit Irish trade. British manufacturers organised a vigorous campaign against the threat from Ireland, especially to the woollen trade. Pitt had little choice but to withdraw his proposals. Despite this, Ireland's trade with Britain increased significantly in the 1780s with Irish linen exports, for example, trebling between 1781 and 1792.

Pitt's control over Irish politics during the 1780s was severely limited by the independent actions of the Dublin parliament. The French Revolution led to renewed demands among Irish Catholics for political and parliamentary reform. The Dublin parliament responded by insisting that Ireland's security could be guaranteed only by continued Catholic oppression.

Pitt did not accept this and he attempted to win over the Catholic gentry by extending their rights. In 1792, an Irish Catholic Relief Act allowed Catholics

Catholics were denied access to public office, to ownership of land and to full involvement in the running of their country. The existence of legal restrictions was used by the minority Protestants to maintain their political dominance.

Presbyterians were Protestants; the Presbyterian Church is the established church in Scotland.

What was the impact of American independence on Ireland?

to enter into mixed-faith marriages and gave them access to education and legal training. The following year they were given the same municipal and parliamentary franchise as Protestants. However, these concessions did little to improve their status as they remained disbarred from membership of the Irish parliament. Pitt's reforms raised the expectations of the more radical Irishmen but satisfied few, and resulted in heightened Protestant fears of eventual Catholic domination.

In late 1791, two societies of United Irishmen were formed: in Belfast the society's supporters were mostly Presbyterian and middle class, while in Dublin they were mostly Catholics. As they became increasingly nationalistic, they began to extend their appeal to all Irishmen. Freedom from English rule appealed to both Protestant and Catholic middle-class radicals, who had been denied access to political power, as well as to the Catholic peasantry, who had grievances against the Protestant landowners and the Anglican Church. In 1794, they went underground and their leadership sought French assistance to bring about revolution in Ireland.

However, the French did not support their rebellion in 1798 and this, combined with British repression, led to its failure. The rising was badly planned and poorly carried out, and it was defeated by the end of the year.

What were the arguments for union?

However, the 1798 rising convinced Pitt that the Dublin government could not keep Ireland loyal. Constitutional union of the two kingdoms seemed to him to be the solution. Pitt believed that he would have to remove the remaining disabilities against Catholics before they would support the idea of union with England. In this, he faced opposition not only from the Protestant minority in Ireland and politicians in Westminster, but also from George III. He decided that he would concentrate on getting the support of the Irish parliament for union and would work for Catholic emancipation once union had been achieved.

The **Act of Union** meant that the separate Irish parliament disappeared and 100 Irish MPs were added to the House of Commons. Twenty-eight Irish peers were elected for life to the House of Lords. One archbishop and three bishops represented the Irish Anglican Church. The Anglican Churches of England and Ireland were united.

The inability of those opposed to union to come up with any real alternative ensured the passage of the **Act of Union** in 1800, and constitutional union between England and Ireland took place on 1 January 1801.

Committed as Pitt and some of his colleagues were to Catholic emancipation, they were unable to win over the king. In March 1801 Pitt resigned over the policy that he saw as necessary. The Catholic community felt betrayed by the British government and soon became increasingly anti-unionist in attitude; at the same time they began to develop a strong sense of their own separate religious and national identity.

How did the Act of Union fail to deliver what Pitt expected?

The Catholic Association

By the early 1820s, the Catholic cause in Ireland was divided and bankrupt. In England the Catholic question was a major problem for Lord Liverpool's

Daniel O'Connell at a monster meeting at Clifden, County Galway, 20 September 1843.

government. The electorate voted overwhelmingly against emancipation in the general elections of 1818, 1820 and especially 1826. The cabinet was divided on the issue: between 1815 and 1822 they had agreed that emancipation would not be raised as a matter of government business but that when it was raised independently ministers could vote as their consciences dictated. Emancipation bills passed the Commons in 1821, 1822 and 1825, but they were all rejected in the Lords.

Then in the spring of 1823 **Daniel O'Connell** formed the Catholic Association; its main aim was that of Catholic emancipation. O'Connell recognised that, even with a majority in the House of Commons in favour of emancipation, the House of Lords and the king could stand in the way of change.

O'Connell, however, took a broader view of the Catholic problem and his campaign also included demands for electoral reform (to increase the number of Catholics who could vote), reform of the Church of Ireland and tenants' rights. This allowed him to appeal to the interests of the whole Catholic community and helped him to raise the money he needed to fund his campaign. He persuaded supporters to pay one penny a month to support his fight for Catholic emancipation – this was known as Catholic rent. Parish priests were made members of the Association and they collected the money. About £20,000 was raised in the first nine months of collection in 1824–25 and a further £35,000 was collected between 1826 and 1829. This enabled the Association to become a truly national organisation, run from Dublin, that was supported by the vast majority of the Catholic community.

O'Connell had realised that it was essential to make the Irish Catholic

Daniel O'Connell (1775–1847), whose father was a small landowner and shopkeeper, came from the Irish Catholic gentry. Educated in France, he studied law at Lincoln's Inn in London between 1794 and 1796, qualifying as a barrister at the Irish Bar in 1798. He was known as the Liberator because of his success in achieving emancipation. He was much less successful in his campaign for repeal of the Act of Union in the 1840s.

Church an integral part of the movement. Parish priests could mobilise the mass of the Catholic population, which was something the Establishment viewed with alarm.

The great open-air meetings often addressed by O'Connell also played a central part in the work of the Association. They gave O'Connell a platform from which to demand justice for Ireland and to make veiled threats to the British government: mass support could lead to mass disobedience, the possibility of violence and growing demands for separation from Britain.

O'Connell's growing support across Ireland allowed him to call on voters in the 1826 election to vote for candidates who supported emancipation. Previously, landlords had taken it for granted that their tenants would vote as they dictated. In the election, many Catholics voted for candidates favoured by local Catholic agitators and consequently four pro-emancipation candidates were returned to parliament.

On the mainland, in contrast, many of the Tory MPs elected in the 1826 general election were opposed to Catholic emancipation. This reflected public opinion and attitudes, which were not improved by the steady influx of Irish immigrants after 1800 and especially after the 1821 famine. Irish immigrants, with their alien religion and language, were seen by many working-class people as a threat to their jobs because the Irish were prepared to work for lower wages. Irish Catholics were concentrated in London and other cities, where they were seen as a political threat. For much of the nineteenth century the government was deeply concerned about the possibility of union between Irish nationalists and radical agitators.

What was the Catholic Association and what methods did it use to achieve its aims?

Emancipation achieved, 1828–29

In early 1828 parliament repealed the Test and Corporation Acts, thereby ending all legal restrictions on the civil rights of Dissenters. This made it extremely difficult for Wellington and Peel to ignore the issue of Catholic emancipation, especially since resistance to Catholic emancipation inside parliament had been weakening since 1812.

When O'Connell decided to contest a by-election in County Clare in July 1828, the issue was brought to a head. This placed the government in an awkward position: if O'Connell won, he would not be able take his seat in the House of Commons because he was a Catholic.

With the support of the Catholic Association and the local priests, O'Connell easily won the by-election. Wellington and Peel, both of whom had previously opposed emancipation, were now faced with two contradictory pressures. O'Connell's victory brought the prospect of civil war in Ireland much closer, yet English public opinion remained overwhelmingly opposed to emancipation.

Why was the by-election held in County Clare in July 1828 significant?

As it turned out, the County Clare by-election was a fortunate accident because it allowed Wellington and Peel to introduce emancipation on the basis that it would prevent widespread disturbances in Ireland. Their decision was entirely political: the choice was between emancipation or revolution in Ireland. Emancipation was easily achieved, despite opposition in the Commons (142 Tory MPs voted against it) and in the Lords, where Wellington was able to rely on Whig support. The cost for Wellington and Peel was high – both were criticised as betrayers of the ancient constitution and of the Church. More important was the legacy of bitterness that was left within the Tory party.

What convinced Wellington and Peel that emancipation could be delayed no longer?

The Roman Catholic Emancipation Act of 1829 gave full civil and political rights to Roman Catholics. They could now become MPs and occupy public offices (with a few minor exceptions, such as the office of lord chancellor). O'Connell believed that Catholic advancement in politics, government service and the professions would eventually lead to the end of Protestant dominance in Ireland. The Act did, however, introduce a change in the voting qualification: that was raised from a 40-shilling freeholder to a £10 householder. This cut the Irish electorate to a sixth of its former size. Despite this, emancipation was seen as a victory for Catholicism.

How did Peel deal with Ireland?

The Conservative victory in 1841 brought to a head the conflict that had festered for 30 years between Peel and O'Connell. Peel was not prepared to repeal the Act of Union. Nevertheless, he recognised that there was a need to convince the Irish of the benefits of union. Peel's Irish policy combined strong opposition to O'Connell and the Repeal Association with legislation that addressed some of Ireland's problems.

Calls for repeal

In the 1841 election the number of Irish MPs who supported O'Connell was reduced to 18. As a result, O'Connell decided to concentrate on agitating for repeal of the Act of Union through extra-parliamentary pressure in the form of the Repeal Association.

The repeal campaign was closely based on the emancipation movement of the 1820s, though it was waged on a much larger scale. It was financed by the **repeal rent** and used **monster meetings** to get its message across and put pressure on the British government. Support came from the Catholic peasantry, who believed that repeal would lead to the loosening of landlord control, and the Catholic Church. It also had the support of **Young Ireland**, a small group of more extreme nationalists. However, the Catholic middle

Repeal rent was the 1840s equivalent of the Catholic rent.

Monster meetings were large-scale demonstrations.

Young Ireland was a nationalist Irish group formed in 1840. In 1846 its leaders came out in favour of the use of force in support of repeal and they were expelled from the Repeal Association.

THE MODERN SISYPHUS.

"Sisyphus is said to be doomed for ever to roll to the top of a great mountain a stone which continually falls down again."

SISYPHUS . . SIR R. P— L.   THE STONE . . D. O'C——L.   THE FURIES . . LORD J. R——L. S——L, &c.

Sir Robert Peel, 1838, portrayed as 'The Modern Sisyphus'. How does the artist convey the enormity of Peel's task in Ireland? Why did Ireland prove to be fatal to Peel's political career?

What methods did O'Connell employ to achieve repeal?

classes were less committed to repeal than they had been to emancipation. They were far more concerned with retaining what they had gained as a result of union and were suspicious of the apparent advantages of repeal.

There was, however, an important difference between the repeal campaign in the 1840s and the successful emancipation campaign. In 1828–29 Wellington had led a divided and, to some degree, demoralised party. In this period, by contrast, Peel had the support of his party, which had a large majority in the House of Commons. Peel was prepared to tolerate the repeal campaign as long as it remained within the law. The monster meetings and O'Connell's claim that 1843 would be the 'Year of Repeal' worried Peel's administration.

In October 1843, a mass meeting to be held at Clontarf was banned. Although O'Connell accepted the decision, he was arrested, tried, imprisoned and then released. Clontarf marked the end of an effective repeal campaign: O'Connell simply did not have the united support he had had in 1828–29. The Catholic middle classes were worried by the mass agitation and Young Ireland differed sharply with O'Connell over long-term aims and tactics.

Peel's reforms (see below) and then the Famine robbed the repeal campaign of its momentum. O'Connell could do little to alleviate conditions during the Famine and his parliamentary party was eclipsed after his death in 1847. O'Connell's enduring achievement was to make it clear that the grievances and claims of Ireland had become an intrinsic part of British domestic politics.

What were the major reasons for the failure of the repeal campaign?

Peel's reforms

Peel had considerable first-hand experience of Ireland, as he had been chief secretary for Ireland between 1812 and 1818. As chief secretary he had established the Peace Preservation Force in 1814 to counter widespread rural unrest. The first 'peelers' were appointed by the government and could be sent to any area where disturbances were taking place. Local rate-payers had to pay for the Force whether they had requested its presence or not. This made it very unpopular with landowners. Although the Force was used in 16 counties up to 1822, it did not have a major impact on rural crime. In 1836 it was amalgamated with the Irish Constabulary, which had been established in 1822. Peel also co-ordinated relief efforts during the famine in 1816–17, which was caused by the failure of the potato crop. A narrowly averted duel with O'Connell in August 1815 laid the foundations of a lifelong mutual hostility.

The six years Peel spent in Ireland played a central role in determining his later attitudes to Ireland. When he was chief secretary, he had criticised the corruption of Irish MPs and the attitudes of the Protestant minority, while continuing to defend the system. He also saw first hand the effects of the famine; this determined his attitudes in 1845–46.

Peel recognised that there were two main obstacles to good government in Ireland:
- poor relations between tenant and landlord, and
- bad relations between the British government on the one side and the Catholic middle class and moderate clergy on the other.

Responsibility for the first problem was delegated to a Royal Commission set up in 1843 and headed by the earl of Devon. Its report appeared in 1845. It made suggestions for reform in areas such as land reclamation, public works to provide employment, and the extension throughout the rest of the country of the Ulster custom of paying outgoing tenants compensation for any improvements they made to the land during their occupancy. The report had no significant impact on Peel's government, apart from a compensation bill that was dropped because of opposition from the Lords.

In tackling the second problem, Peel argued that if the moderate Catholic clergy could be persuaded away from the repeal movement, the Church of Ireland would be able to retain its privileges. But a policy of religious concessions had its difficulties. Irish Protestant Conservatives were unwilling to give political posts to Roman Catholics. In addition, anti-Catholic feeling had hardened even further since 1829 because of the violence of O'Connell's repeal campaign in the 1840s and because of increasing numbers of Irish Catholics in mainland Britain.

Peel identified charitable endowments as an area of reform that would benefit Irish Catholics and he subsequently introduced the Charitable Bequests Act of 1844, which aimed to remove legal obstacles to endowments made to the Catholic Church. Many Catholic bishops and clergy did not immediately welcome the Act, but they soon recognised that it was a gesture of conciliation.

In 1845 Peel turned to Irish education. He looked first at the better training of Catholic priests at **Maynooth College** near Dublin and then at the creation of improved higher educational facilities. Each proposal ran into strong opposition. The state had supported Maynooth since 1795, but its grant of less than £9,000 per year was inadequate. Peel wanted it increased to £26,000 and also wanted to make a special building grant of £30,000. His aim was to raise the social and intellectual level of the Catholic priesthood, in the hope that this would make priests more moderate.

For Peel's opponents **Maynooth College** was yet another example of his 'flexibility'. They pointed out that in 1829 he had argued that Maynooth's charter should be revoked and Irish priests brought under government control.

With the support of his government, Peel introduced his Maynooth bill in April 1845. He did not fully appreciate the nationwide hostility to this bill: Anglicans saw it as implicit official recognition of the Catholic Church and as a challenge to the position of the Anglican Church of Ireland, while Nonconformists opposed it because they disliked any link between the church and state. A joint central Anti-Maynooth Committee was set up and over 10,000 petitions poured into parliament between February and May 1845.

Nevertheless, Peel pressed ahead with his bill. Despite the widespread extra-parliamentary opposition from the Anti-Maynooth Committee, the bill went through, with the support of the Whigs and some Conservatives. Peel was subject to bitter criticism from his party – once again, it was believed, he had betrayed them.

How did Peel seek to improve conditions in Ireland during his period as prime minister?

Peel's policies for Ireland in 1844 and 1845 attempted to suppress demands for repeal, and to detach moderate Catholic clergy and the Irish middle class from the repeal movement. The price of concessions to Ireland was the break-up of Peel's own party. It never recovered from the shock administered by the Maynooth grant. The Great Famine administered the final blow.

What were the social and economic effects of the Great Famine?

By the summer of 1845 the press and many politicians were predicting the repeal of the Corn Laws. The news of the potato blight in Ireland in September 1845 and imminent, widespread famine merely brought matters to a head. Peel had no illusions about the effects of blight. As Irish secretary, he had lived through the famine of 1817 and he knew that a scheme of national relief at the tax-payers' expense would have to be organised before the full effects of famine were felt the following spring.

Peel did not think that the tax-payer could be asked to contribute to the feeding of Ireland and still tolerate the existence of the Corn Laws. He had three options open to him: he could leave the law intact, suspend it until the Irish problem was resolved or abolish it. Leaving the law intact while the Irish starved was out of the question, while suspending the Corn Laws posed political problems. It was unclear how long suspension would last, but it was likely to be for more than a year. This meant that an unpopular resumption of the Corn Laws would occur in 1847 when a general election was due. The problem with abolishing the Corn Laws was that the Conservatives were committed to protection. Peel also recognised that repeal alone would not alleviate the problems facing Ireland, as the Irish most affected by the Famine would not be able to afford to buy cheap grain from Europe.

How did the beginnings of the Famine in 1845 make repeal of the Corn Laws more likely?

The Great Famine, 1845–46

The Great Famine began unexpectedly in the late summer of 1845. By September, potatoes were rotting in the ground and, within a month, blight was spreading rapidly. Three-quarters of the country's crop, the major source of

Bridget O'Donnel of West Cork, starving during the Famine.

food for about three million people, was wiped out. The following year, blight caused a total crop failure.

Famine caused by potato blight was nothing new in Ireland. There had been failures in 1739, 1741, 1801, 1817 and 1821. In 1741, for example, perhaps 400,000 people died as a result of famine. The Great Famine was only one demographic crisis among many, but most historians regard it as a real turning point in Irish history: it was simply a disaster beyond all expectations and imagination.

Contemporaries and historians have considerable difficulty in explaining why the Famine took place. It is generally agreed, however, that the structure of the Irish economy, and especially its system of land tenure, played a significant part. Most of the cultivated land in Ireland in the 1840s was in the hands of Protestant landowners. Estates were regarded as sources of income for these landowners, many of whom lived in England, rather than as long-term investments. They failed to invest in Irish farming and tenants were unable to afford to invest in their land because of the high rents they had to pay.

There was insufficient land available to satisfy demand, which led to the division of land into smaller farms by landowners. By 1845 a quarter of all holdings were between 1 and 5 acres, 40 per cent were between 5 and 15 acres and only 7 per cent were over 30 acres. This created underemployment and forced many labourers to become migrant workers in England for part of the year. They became navvies for road building, canal digging and railway construction. Many turned seasonal migration into permanent settlement. There was little other work for them in Ireland: inadequate investment meant that Ireland's industrialisation was not progressing fast enough to provide the employment necessary to absorb its growing population.

The potato made the division and subdivision of land possible. It was easy to grow, even in poor soil, and produced high yields. Two acres of land could provide enough potatoes for a family of five or six to survive on for a year. Potatoes could also be used to feed pigs and poultry. Subsistence on the potato allowed tenants to grow wheat and oats to pay their rent.

What were the major causes of the Great Famine?

How did the British government react?

Peel's response was rapid and, within limits, imaginative. The crisis finally convinced him of the need to dismantle the Corn Laws, but he realised that this would, because of its contentious nature, take time. Immediate solutions were needed. In November 1845 a special commission was established to co-ordinate relief efforts. It did two things:

- Labourers needed work so that they could afford to buy food. The government established public work schemes on a large scale. These became the boom years of Irish railway construction.

- Food had to be kept at a level that prevented profiteering. £185,000 was spent on supplies, chiefly Indian meal.

These measures, however, only met the immediate crisis. Lord John Russell succeeded Peel in mid-1846 and he lacked Peel's Irish experience. Economy and efficiency replaced Peel's more humane policy. The full extent of the Famine was seriously underestimated in official circles. The government also experienced problems ensuring that those in need had access to the food that was provided.

How did Peel try to alleviate the problems caused by the Famine?

What were the consequences of the Famine?

Between 1841 and 1851 the population of Ireland fell from over 8.2 million to 6.5 million. Emigration accounted for perhaps 0.8 million and became an accepted part of Irish life. This meant that about a million people lost their lives as a result of the Famine. Actual starvation rarely caused death, but it weakened people sufficiently for fever and diseases, like typhus, to take their toll. In early 1849 a serious outbreak of cholera added to the problem. The impact of the Famine was felt differently in both regional and social terms. Western and south-western counties were hardest hit. Counties on the east coast, where food could be more easily imported, were least affected. The north-east did not suffer a crisis, despite its high density of population, because of the more industrial nature of its economy. But it was not unaffected – many disease-ridden migrants crowded into Belfast, where poor living conditions helped to spread disease.

Labourers and small farmers were the chief victims of the Famine. The numbers of those who farmed less than 15 acres were decimated by death, disease, emigration and the workhouse. This meant that many of the smaller farms disappeared: in 1841, 71.5 per cent of holdings fell into this category, but by 1851 this figure was 49.1 per cent. There was a consequent increase in the number of holdings over 15 acres. Livestock farming expanded on these larger farms, encouraged by attractive prices in Britain and by reductions in transport costs.

In 1851 the agricultural economy was apparently still in a state of crisis: the potato had lost its appeal, low agricultural prices gave little promise of recovery to those who had survived and the Poor Law rates were increased to cope with larger numbers applying for relief. But from the mid-1850s change was rapid. Livestock increased in value and numbers, arable farming declined slowly and tenant farmers, whose numbers remained relatively stable for the next 50 years, enjoyed a prosperous stability.

The Famine, with its deep social, economic and psychological effects, marked a watershed in the political history of modern Ireland. The Repeal

Association of O'Connell was dead. Under O'Connell, Ireland had been generally loyal and pacifist. That loyalty and pacifism perished in the Famine. Whether English rule was, in fact, to blame for the Famine mattered less than the widespread belief that it was. Young Ireland made an attempt at independence from Britain in the abortive rising of 1848. A sense of desolation, growing sectarian divisions, the rhetoric of genocide and the re-emergence of some form of national consciousness eventually led to the emergence of a movement dedicated to the independence of Ireland from English rule.

What were the major results of the Famine?

Summary questions

1 Identify and explain any *two* factors that caused Ireland to be a problem for Westminster politicians between 1780 and 1830.

2 Compare the importance of at least *three* issues that influenced Peel's attitudes to Ireland between 1829 and 1846.

Britain at war, 1793–1815

Focus questions

- What were British interests between 1793 and 1841?
- How and why was Britain able to win the war with France between 1793 and 1815?

Significant dates

1789   The French Revolution begins

1793   War with France declared

1802   War ends with Treaty of Amiens

1804   War resumes

1805   Battle of Trafalgar takes place

1808   Peninsular War begins

1814   Napoleon defeated and sent into exile

1815   Battle of Waterloo takes place and Napoleon is defeated

Overview

Between 1793 and 1815, except for a short interlude between 1802 and 1804, Britain was at war with France and its allies. The French Revolution posed a major threat to Britain's interests in that it challenged stability in Europe, which was important to Britain's trade and political security. The expansion of the French Revolution also raised the possibility of revolution in Britain.

This chapter considers two major issues. First, it considers the nature of Britain's foreign policy interests between 1793 and 1841. This discussion provides the background for an examination of Britain at war and for the discussion of foreign policy after 1815 in Chapter 8. Secondly, it examines the problems faced by successive prime ministers – from William Pitt to Lord Liverpool – in fighting a maritime and land war against France with allies whose support was bought and could be unreliable.

A. STOPPAGE to a STRIDE over the GLOBE

A satirical cartoon from the late 1790s hostile to the young Napoleon's victories in the Italian campaigns. 'Little Johnny Bull' is there to check French expansion.

The final defeat of Napoleon at Waterloo in June 1815 marked the end of two decades of political instability in Europe and the beginning of a Europe in which large-scale war was absent for almost a century.

What were British interests between 1793 and 1841?

Throughout the late eighteenth and nineteenth centuries, British foreign policy was based on two general principles: security and trade. These issues tended to underline and sometimes determine the action that was taken. Pitt, Castlereagh, Canning and Palmerston all accepted that their responsibility was to ensure that British trade could be carried on throughout the world without interference. For them, free trade was not simply an economic policy, it was seen as a means of achieving international peace. They believed that the major cause of war was economic competition between countries and that, if competition could be reduced by introducing freer trade, then the prospect of expensive and often fruitless European and colonial wars might be removed.

There were two areas in which these two general principles (security and trade) manifested themselves in British foreign policy between 1793 and 1841: relations with its colonies on the one hand, and with its continental neighbours on the other:

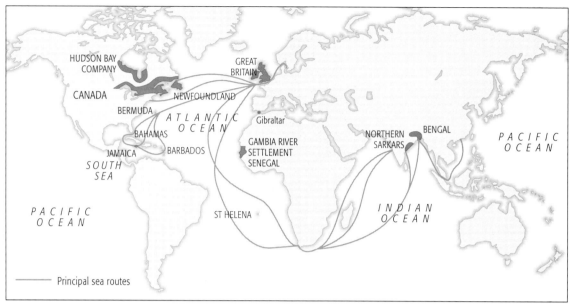

The British empire, 1784.

- Colonial expansion was in Britain's economic interest, and colonial wars were fought largely for wealth, raw materials and to gain new markets. Although Britain had lost its American colonies in 1783, by then it had already gained Canada and Newfoundland, with their furs and fisheries. Britain was also dominant in the Caribbean and in India, which had sugar and cotton, and it was opening trade links with China.

- However, the key to Britain's security lay in its continental policies. A **balance of power** in Europe was central to British foreign policy; it made overseas expansion and trade in Europe possible, and allowed for security at home (including security from subversive ideas).

Britain needed allies in Europe to protect it against invasion and to secure its continental markets. It had to be prepared to aid its allies with **subsidies** and with military support. For example, Britain had important interests in the **Low Countries**, which provided routes and markets for Britain's exports. The Low Countries also had the potential to offer enemies a base (such as the harbours of the Scheldt estuary) from which an invasion into Britain could be launched. French expansion into the Low Countries was seen by Pitt as a threat both to Britain's markets and to its security. It was to secure Holland against this expansion that the British government entered into war with France in January 1793.

By the 1790s, Britain was already well advanced industrially and commercially. Its economic and population growth meant that Britain was increasingly dependent on international trade for both food and industrial raw

balance of power: contemporaries believed that if the power of the leading states in Europe was 'balanced', with no one power dominating another, then expensive and unnecessary wars could be avoided and peace maintained.

What were the major considerations on which Britain's foreign policy was based after 1793?

Subsidies were sums of money paid by Britain to its European allies to help their military action against France.

The **Low Countries** are modern-day Belgium and the Netherlands.

materials. Britain's efforts to pursue a strong trading position were often seen as aggressive by foreigners: for example, it resulted in Britain becoming involved in the politics of the New World in the 1820s and of China in the 1840s.

Although contemporaries believed Britain to be the greatest power in the world in the first half of the nineteenth century, it was, in fact, in terms of the continent, only one of five **great powers**: Britain, France, Austria, Prussia and Russia. It was the balance between these five powers that dominated much of Britain's foreign policy. Pitt planned a 'Concert of Europe' among the five great powers which would ensure a more effective system of European security, with a new distribution of power in order to contain future French aggression and a guarantee between the powers to maintain the balance of power. This would be achieved through discussion at congresses or conferences, in an attempt to avoid war.

The **great powers** were Britain and France (the 'western powers', with systems of government based on constitutional monarchies) and Russia, Austria and Prussia (the 'eastern powers', with systems of government based on the absolute power of the ruler).

Austria, Russia and Prussia, unlike Britain, believed that the Concert should be more interventionist. They wished to use its powers to defend the existing structure of society and of legitimate – by which they meant conservative – authority. Britain agreed with this position when it came to the containment of France and was quite prepared to support the restoration of the Bourbons (the French royal family) in 1814, even though the principle of legitimacy did not have the same ideological appeal to the British government as it did to the other European powers. But all the great powers were prepared to abandon the principle when it conflicted with their national interests or ambitions.

British statesmen believed that the Congress of Vienna of 1814–15 (see Chapter 8) had created a desirable balance of power in Europe and that peace could be preserved as long as no power threatened to upset this balance. Consequently, there were no permanent alliances in Europe between 1815 and 1841. British governments at the time preferred to support a balance of power policy in Europe and become involved only when that balance seemed threatened by one of the great powers. After Waterloo in 1815, pragmatism and the specific interests of the great powers, rather than a particular ideology, characterised foreign relations.

As far as Britain was concerned, the Congress of Vienna defined British continental ambition to maintain stability in Europe; as long as a general peace was kept, British trade could expand unhindered. Nevertheless, Britain was quite prepared to see the Vienna settlement altered as long as its basic aims were still fulfilled. For example, in the 1830s Britain was prepared to see Belgium become independent from Holland as long as its neutrality was guaranteed. By 1841 Palmerston regarded some parts of the Vienna settlement as obsolete, but he was nevertheless disinclined to make any changes in Britain's approach to European affairs.

There was continuity between Britain's foreign policy before and after 1815. The French Revolution and Napoleonic Wars reinforced Britain's belief in the need for a balance of power in Europe. Castlereagh and Canning put into practice the plans that William Pitt had made for peace. Pitt, Castlereagh, Canning and Palmerston all promoted a policy of free trade. This meant having a powerful navy to protect trade routes from attack by colonial rivals and to prevent rival European powers from blockading Britain.

How and why was Britain able to win the war with France between 1793 and 1815?

The outbreak of the French Revolution in 1789 was welcomed initially by most politicians in Britain. The Whigs, especially, saw it as the dawn of liberty. Pitt believed that the Revolution would be a useful distraction for France, Britain's major rival: it would weaken France's control over its colonies, thus providing greater trading opportunities for Britain.

In his 1792 budget, Pitt planned to reduce defence spending as part of his desire to reduce levels of taxation – evidently he did not intend to interfere in France's internal affairs. This was in keeping with Britain's tradition of non-interference in European affairs unless its interests were directly threatened.

In Britain, attitudes to the Revolution were slow to change. No action was taken, for example, when Prussia and then Austria declared war on revolutionary France in 1792. The French victory over the Austrian and Prussian invasion of France at Valmy in September 1792 and over Austrian forces at Jemappes in November 1792 led to the fall of the Austrian Netherlands. This was followed by the fall of Antwerp and the opening of the Scheldt estuary to all shipping. It was this event that forced Britain into action. The French had also made it clear that they were willing to assist all those who wanted to break the yoke of monarchy and tyranny, which threatened security in Europe.

Pitt and his foreign secretary, Lord Grenville, were willing to let France resolve its own internal problems if it withdrew its forces from Belgium and renounced interference with the internal government of other countries. Pitt's objective was to restore the balance of power in the **United Provinces** and remove the French threat from this region.

In what ways did France pose a threat to Britain in the early 1790s?

The **United Provinces** was the area corresponding to modern-day Belgium and the Netherlands. They were ruled by Austria.

Fighting France, 1793–1802

Pitt and Henry Dundas, his secretary of war, approached the war with a three-pronged strategy. The first two strategies had been used against France earlier in the century, but the third strategy was something new.

- First, a naval strategy was employed: the Royal Navy blockaded the French coast and attacked enemy colonies, especially in the Caribbean. This not only weakened France's commercial base, but also ensured that the colonies could be used as bargaining counters in subsequent peace negotiations.

- Secondly, a war was fought on the continent, using small units of British forces, paid mercenaries and subsidised allies.
- Finally, Pitt supported opponents of the Revolution inside France, especially in the west (Brittany and the Vendeé), where there was considerable opposition to revolutionary change.

The first part of this strategy was successful, the others less so. The major problem facing Pitt in the summer of 1793 was which of the conflicting war aims to pursue:

- Should he concentrate his energies in securing the Low Countries against French aggression?
- Should the main thrust of his campaign be against France's colonies?
- Should he aid counter-revolutionary forces within France to destabilise the revolutionary regime?

The first and second options reflected the approach that had been used throughout the century; it was the third option that was different and brought an ideological element to the war. Both sides saw their actions in crusading terms: for or against revolutionary and republican ideals.

The First Coalition, 1793–97

Britain alone could not defeat revolutionary France, with its superior armies, generals and tactics. The British army was too small and poorly trained to be an effective force, the British commanders of the 1790s were not particularly competent and the British army was in no position to sustain a long continental campaign. Of the 50,000-strong army, half were needed for police and **garrison** duties in Britain and Ireland and the rest were scattered abroad. This weakness led to the formation of the First Coalition in February 1793, consisting of Britain, Austria, Prussia and Holland. Spain and Sardinia also entered the coalition, strengthening Pitt's belief that the war would not last long.

Pitt had hoped that he could successfully defeat the Revolution from within France. But Britain's support of French royalists was both inadequate and too late, and a plan to land French **émigré troops** in southern Brittany in mid-1795 was also unsuccessful. The revolutionary forces were better prepared than the British had expected and their earlier successes had given them higher morale than the British troops. In addition, Pitt failed to grasp the power of French patriotism in the 1790s – many people in France preferred the revolutionary to the Bourbon government and they certainly favoured any French government over the restoration of the monarchy engineered by Britain, the national enemy.

Pitt adopted three strategies in the war with France. What were they and what was the motivation behind each?

Garrison troops were based in Britain to prevent invasion from the continent and revolution at home.

Emigré troops were royalist troops who supported the Bourbon monarchy.

The anti-French coalition proved very fragile and between 1795 and 1797 it collapsed. Holland, which had a strong pro-French party, was conquered by the French army in January 1795 and declared war on Britain in May that year. Prussia made peace at Basle in April 1795. Spain followed suit in July and entered into an alliance with France. The defeat of Austria in 1796 and 1797 led to them making peace with France. Belgium was in French hands. This left Britain to fight on alone.

Colonial and naval success, 1793–1801

The gains Britain made between 1793 and 1801 were either colonial conquests or naval victories. The British navy cut the French off from their overseas empire as first French, and later Spanish and Dutch, colonies were occupied. French settlements in India were seized in 1793, though French influence and military support remained, especially in Mysore. In the West Indies, Britain took Tobago in 1793 and supported a rebellion in Santo Domingo. Control was extended over the French islands of Martinique, St Lucia and Guadeloupe in 1794, though Britain had abandoned the last two by the end of the year because of disease which left 40,000 dead and 40,000 incapacitated. Haiti, rich in coffee, sugar and cotton, seemed to have been wrested from France and Spain when its coastal towns were captured in 1794, but it was never secured. The Franco-Dutch alliance of 1795 led to Britain's seizure of Dutch colonies at the Cape of Good Hope, in Ceylon and in the West Indies. British trade and empire had been maintained and extended through military operations, backed by Britain's naval supremacy.

But in Europe French dominance seemed complete. In 1796–97 two attempts were made at achieving peace: in October 1796 Lord Malmesbury, a diplomat, was sent to Paris; this initiative was followed by a second series of negotiations the following July at Lille. Negotiations collapsed over demands that Britain should surrender all its conquests while France should keep everything it had gained.

Events became increasingly unfavourable to Britain. From late 1796, Pitt faced the possibility of an invasion – historians have seen this as the greatest threat to British national security between 1588 and 1940. The external threat of invasion was made worse by problems in Ireland (which France was willing to exploit), naval mutinies, and high prices and inflation at home. However, naval victories over the Spanish at Cape St Vincent and the Dutch at Camperdown in February and October 1797 ended France's hopes of invading Britain.

In early 1798, Napoleon began an attack on British power in India. French agents began to intrigue with **Tipu of Mysore**, who was the East India Company's greatest enemy in southern India. Tipu was eventually defeated and

How did Britain try to defeat France between 1793 and 1797? Why was it unsuccessful?

Tipu 'the Lion' of Mysore was the cruel, yet enlightened ruler of Mysore. He was strongly pro-French.

Lord Nelson (1758–1805).

killed in 1799, after which the territorial power of the East India Company was extended.

Napoleon invaded Rome and Switzerland and, using his naval control of the Mediterranean, took Malta and defeated the rulers of Egypt. However, he lost his military advantage when the French fleet was destroyed by Nelson at the Battle of the Nile in August 1798. The implications of Nelson's victory were far-reaching. The French lost their naval supremacy in the Mediterranean and their army was stranded in Egypt, although it was not actually defeated until 1801. In Europe, the failure of Napoleon's Egyptian expedition encouraged those states with grievances against him to band together. This led to the formation of the short-lived Second Coalition against France.

In what ways were colonial and naval strategies successful between 1793 and 1801?

The Second Coalition, 1798–1801

It was clear that coalition warfare was the only way to achieve outright victory and end French expansionism, but the experience of the First Coalition showed how difficult this was going to be. The Second Coalition against France, consisting of Britain, Russia, Austria, Turkey, Portugal and Naples, proved to have even fewer unifying features than the first.

Early, limited success was followed by disunity and defeat. Austria was defeated in 1800 and made peace with France in 1801. France cultivated good relations with Russia, Prussia and Denmark, with a view to closing northern Europe to British trade. This caused Russia to withdraw her support from the coalition during 1800. These moves threatened Britain's domestic stability, since poor harvests made it necessary for it to import grain from the Baltic region.

Then Russia, Prussia, Denmark and Sweden formed an alliance, largely because Tsar Paul was irritated by Britain's seizure of Malta, which was a blow to Russia's Mediterranean ambitions. Britain acted swiftly: after Hanover was invaded by pro-French Danish and Prussian troops, Nelson destroyed the Danish fleet in Copenhagen in March 1801 and consequently the invading troops were withdrawn from Hanover. After the assassination of Tsar Paul and the succession of Alexander I, relations between Britain and Russia improved slightly.

Why did the Second Coalition fail and with what results?

The consequences of the formation of the First and Second Coalitions were similar. In both 1797 and 1801, Britain was left isolated after France successfully defeated the coalition armies. France's grip on Europe had been gradually tightened. But the British navy had saved Britain from invasion in 1797 and had successfully defeated the navies of France, Spain, Holland and Denmark. It had secured Britain's colonial possessions and enabled Britain to seize enemy colonies in the West Indies, Africa, India and Ceylon. The success of the British navy encouraged France to concentrate on its army, rather than its navy, which increased the pressure on Britain's allies in Europe. Sea power and land power fought each other to a standstill, each dominant in its own sphere. The only solution was a compromise peace, declared in 1801–02, which gave both sides breathing space.

Why was a compromise peace signed in 1801?

The cost of war

The war was expensive for Britain and ended Pitt's economic reforms in Britain. He was hesitant about pushing up taxes and relied heavily on borrowing to finance the war (borrowing increased from £4.5 million in 1793 to £44 million by 1797). The effect of heavy borrowing was inflationary and in 1797, following a run on the banks caused by the abortive and ill-planned French landing at Fishguard in Wales, the government authorised the Bank of England to suspend cash payments (in gold and silver coins) and to issue paper notes for small denominations (£1 and £2) instead. By introducing paper money, Pitt had inadvertently stumbled upon one aspect of a successful wartime financial policy.

It was not until Pitt announced his intention to impose income tax in 1798 that he began to explore other aspects of wartime financial policy. Income tax was a logical, if unpopular, solution to the expense of war and it was only accepted on the understanding that it was a temporary wartime measure. Although it only raised about half of the £10 million Pitt had hoped to raise annually, it made a significant contribution to funding the war.

Pitt has been criticised for indiscriminate and poor use of subsidies for Britain's European allies, which were funded by borrowing. It is important to see these subsidies in the context of the whole war: of the £66 million paid in subsidies between 1793 and 1815, only £9.2 million was provided before 1802, which suggests that criticism of Pitt might be unjustified. However, criticism of Pitt is more acceptable when Britain's lack of military success, paid for by these subsidies, is considered. This was a consequence of several things. Pitt's concern to keep the Low Countries out of French control was not shared by other members of the two coalitions, both of which were loose alliances between distrusting states. Prussia, for example, was more interested in the Baltic than the North Sea and hoped that the partition of Poland would give it more territory, while Austria's priority was to sever its connections with Belgium and consolidate its position in central Europe.

How did Pitt pay for the war?

Amiens to Waterloo, 1802–15

The Peace of Amiens, negotiated by Hawkesbury (later Lord Liverpool) and Cornwallis and ratified by parliament in May 1802, received a poor press from contemporaries and subsequently from historians.

When Austria surrendered to France, Britain lost any leverage it had in Europe. Consequently Addington (prime minister between 1801 and 1804) accepted terms which recognised French predominance on the continent and agreed to the return of all overseas conquests. Viewed simply in territorial terms, Amiens was disastrous, but Addington and his ministers saw it as a truce, not as a final solution. Britain had been at war for nine years and Addington was fully aware of growing pressure for peace from both MPs and the nation. Canning, one of the most vehement critics of the peace agreement, admitted that MPs were in no mood to subject its terms to detailed scrutiny and that they would have consented to almost any terms.

Why did parliament support the unsatisfactory treaty of Amiens in 1802?

Amiens to Trafalgar, 1802–05

In the year between the Peace of Amiens and the inevitable renewal of the war, Addington made military and financial preparations that placed Britain in a far stronger position than it had been in 1793.

British naval and military strength was not allowed to run down. In 1803, the fleet was remobilised. Addington retained a regular army of over 130,000 men: 50,000 were left in the West Indies (given back to France in 1802) to allow for the prompt reoccupation of the islands when the need arose. This left 81,000 men in Britain which, together with a **militia** of about 50,000, provided an army far larger than anything Napoleon could mount for the invasion he planned for 1805. The Army of Reserve Act of 1803 produced an additional 30,000 men. Addington also revived the Volunteers, which raised

The **militia** was made up of part-time soldiers.

380,000 men in Britain and 70,000 in Ireland; by 1804, they were an effective auxiliary force. The final step was to improve the quality of the officers; this was achieved by reforms introduced by the duke of York and the establishment of the Royal Military College in 1802.

Addington improved on Pitt's financial management of the war in his budgets of 1803 and 1804 by deducting income tax at source. Once war was renewed in 1804, Addington adopted the simple strategy of blockading French ports. By keeping French merchant and navy ships in port, the British navy eliminated French commerce from the seas. Colonies that had been recently returned to France and its allies were reoccupied and Addington sought allies on the continent who were willing to resist French expansion.

In what respects was Britain better prepared for war in 1803 than in 1793?

Continuity of strategy

Napoleon recognised that final victory depended on conquering Britain and so, during early 1805, he prepared for invasion. To succeed, he needed to control the Channel and prevent the formation of another European coalition against France. He failed on both counts. In October 1805 the defeat of the combined Franco-Spanish fleet at Trafalgar denied Napoleon naval supremacy. In addition, he was forced to divert troops he had intended to use to invade Britain to fight against Russia and Austria.

Between 1805 and 1807, however, France confirmed its military control of mainland Europe. The Third Coalition, consisting of Britain, Russia and Austria, was formed in August 1805 and defeated in 1806 and 1807. Once again, Britain stood alone.

Economic warfare

When Napoleon realised that a successful invasion of Britain was unlikely, he turned instead to economic warfare. The Berlin Decree of November 1807 threatened to close all Europe to British trade – this became known as the Continental System. This was not a new tactic, but France's unprecedented control of Europe meant that British shipping could now be excluded from the continent.

However, it was impossible to seal off Europe completely from British shipping. Parts of the Baltic and Portugal remained open, and Russian ports were reopened to British commerce in 1810 when Alexander I finally recognised the threat posed by France.

Napoleon also did not ban the export of French wines and brandies to Britain, and during the harvest shortages in Britain of 1808–10 he allowed French and German wheat to be exported. Most importantly, he had no control over Britain's trade with the rest of the world and it was here that Britain focused its attention.

Napoleon Bonaparte (1769–1821).

The Battle of Trafalgar, 1805.

The British response to the creation of the Continental System came in the form of Orders in Council. In January 1807, the Ministry of all the Talents banned all trade from those French-controlled ports from which British shipping was excluded. To avoid antagonising the United States, this decree did not affect shipping between the New World and French-controlled ports.

The Portland ministry took a harder line: far stricter Orders were issued in November and December 1807. Naval blockades extended the exclusion of shipping (including the United States) from all French-controlled ports. The major purpose of the Orders was to disrupt European commerce and create dissatisfaction with the Napoleonic regime. Although this strategy was successful, it caused a deterioration of relations between Britain and the United States.

What was the Continental System and how did Britain respond to it?

In the end, Napoleon failed to achieve an economic stranglehold on Britain because he did not have naval supremacy and because Britain's economic expansion was directed at non-European markets. The British blockade of France inflicted far more harm on France than exclusion from Europe ever did to Britain.

Total victory, 1808–15

The final phase of the war began in 1808 when Napoleon attempted to exchange influence in return for control in the Iberian Peninsula. When he

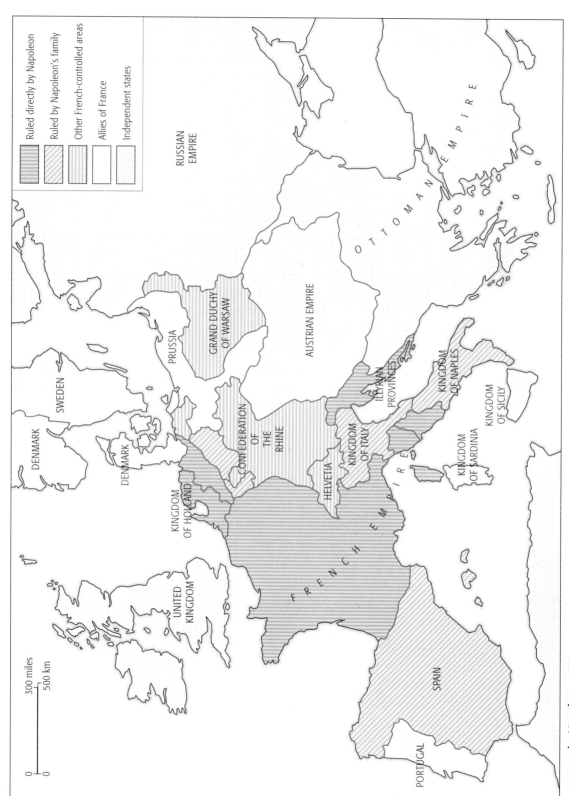

Europe under Napoleon, 1810.

installed his brother, Josef, as king, the nationalists there rose against Napoleon. Anti-French hostility in Portugal (which had been annexed the previous autumn) persuaded Castlereagh, secretary of war, to send 15,000 troops to support the Portuguese. This was the same strategy that had been used since 1793 – offering limited armed support to the opponents of France.

In the next five years British troops, at no time more than 60,000 strong, led by **Arthur Wellesley** and his Portuguese and Spanish allies, fought a tenacious war (known as the Peninsular War) with limited resources. Fighting in Spain and Portugal (the Peninsula) provided Britain with the opportunity of undertaking offensive operations against Napoleon on a scale that was not, before 1813, possible elsewhere in Europe. Surrounded on three sides by water, the Peninsula was an area where Britain's superior naval power could be used to good effect by harassing French communications, supporting guerrillas and allowing military landings on different parts of the long coastline. Unable to support their troops locally, Napoleon's commanders found it difficult to concentrate their superior forces into large armies, or at least concentrate them for any length of time. The result was five years of skirmish, small battles and sieges as Wellington gradually wore down French resolve. By campaigning

Arthur Wellesley was created Viscount Wellington in 1809.

Duke of Wellington (1769–1852).

with and for Spain and Portugal, Britain demonstrated to the rest of Europe that any enemy of Napoleon became, in Canning's phrase, 'instantly our ally'. This stance was excellent propaganda in dealing with countries like Russia, clearly showing as it did Britain's determination to fight, and this in turn made France insecure all over Europe. Wellington's victory at Vimeiro in August 1808 was followed by the Convention of Cintra, which repatriated the French troops and set Portugal free. His decisive victory over the French at Vitoria in Spain in August 1813 allowed him to cross the Pyrenees and invade France.

How did the Peninsular War contribute to the final defeat of France?

Napoleon's position in Europe was weakened by his unsuccessful and costly Russian campaign of 1812. In the spring of 1813, the British government created the Fourth Coalition, consisting of Britain, Austria, Russia and Prussia. Now foreign secretary, Castlereagh's first objective was to keep the allies together long enough to achieve the total defeat of France. He knew that a general European settlement was impossible without total defeat of France. When Castlereagh arrived in Basle in February 1814, French troops were in retreat: Napoleon had been defeated in the three-day Battle of the Nations at Leipzig the previous October and Wellington had invaded south-west France. As a result of this, Napoleon was forced to abdicate in 1814.

Despite the mistrust that existed between the allies, Castlereagh achieved the Treaty of Chaumont in March. The allies each agreed to keep 150,000 men armed and not to enter into a separate peace with France. Napoleon's abdication and exile to Elba in 1814 allowed Castlereagh to implement his second objective: the redrawing of the European map to satisfy all nations, including France. This was achieved at the Congress of Vienna in 1814–15. In March 1815 Napoleon returned to France with the intention of regaining power, but he was defeated at the battle of Waterloo in June. His campaign made no real difference to the peace process, however.

Napoleon was exiled to the southern Atlantic island of St Helena, where he died in 1821.

Summary questions

1   Identify and explain any *two* factors that affected British foreign policy between 1793 and 1815.

2   Compare the importance of at least *three* issues that determined the conduct of British foreign policy in this period.

8 Foreign policy, 1814–41

Focus questions

- How successful was Castlereagh in securing an effective peace at Vienna, and from 1814 to 1822?
- How effectively did Canning secure British interests between 1822 and 1830?
- How effectively did Palmerston secure British interests between 1830 and 1841?

Significant dates

1814–15	Congress of Vienna
1818	Congress at Aix-la-Chapelle
1820	Congress at Troppau
1821	Congress at Laibach
1822	Castlereagh commits suicide; Canning becomes foreign secretary; Congress at Verona
1823	Munroe Doctrine
1827	Battle of Navarino; Canning's death
1830	Palmerston becomes foreign secretary
1833	Treaty of Unkiar Skelessi
1839	Treaty of London
1842	Treaty of Nanking

Overview

Castlereagh, Britain's foreign secretary from 1812 until his suicide in 1822, wanted to ensure peace and stability in Europe. This would leave Britain free to pursue its international commercial and colonial interests. He believed peace and stability could be achieved by maintaining a balance of power between the great powers in Europe – Austria, Russia, France, Britain and Prussia. At the Congress of Vienna, the great powers agreed that they would co-operate to resolve disputes in Europe and would hold regular congresses to achieve this.

The problem **Castlereagh**, and subsequently **Canning and Palmerston**, faced was that each of the great powers was prepared to intervene, both diplomatically and militarily, in the affairs of other nations to support their own interests. Any action of this kind would upset the existing balance of power. This meant that Britain would also have to intervene to support its interest in European stability. This was especially the case in the Low Countries (Belgium and Holland), the Iberian Peninsula (Portugal and Spain) and in the Near East (the **Ottoman Empire**), where Britain had either commercial or **strategic interests**.

How successful was Castlereagh in securing an effective peace at Vienna, and from 1814 to 1822?

The Vienna settlement, 1814–15

Napoleon's failure in Russia in 1812, Wellington's victories in Spain and Portugal (see Chapter 7), and the creation of the Fourth Coalition (consisting of Britain, Austria, Prussia and Russia) in 1813 resulted in defeat for France. Napoleon abdicated in 1814 and the Bourbon monarchy was restored. The **Hundred Days** in 1815, which culminated in the final French defeat at Waterloo, ended the threat from Napoleon.

What the great powers feared was a repeat of French domination of Europe: this was the reason for creating a balance of power between them. For Castlereagh, this meant a settlement that would satisfy each of the mainland powers so that they were unlikely to dispute it in the future. He believed that it was in Britain's interests to ensure peace in Europe and to remain free from European commitments. This would enable Britain to pursue the development of its colonial empire and increase its wealth through overseas trade.

The Vienna settlement evolved over more than a year. The territorial settlement of the Congress of Vienna consisted of three agreements signed in 1814 and 1815. The first Treaty of Paris (30 May 1814) was the peace treaty with France after Napoleon's abdication. The Final Act of the Congress of Vienna (9 June 1815) contained most of the post-war settlement, negotiated in Vienna between October 1814 and June 1815. The second Treaty of Paris (20 November 1815) revised the peace terms with France, making them slightly harsher after Napoleon's Hundred Days.

The terms of the post-war settlement

Britain, Austria, Prussia and Russia had fought against France to ensure their own survival and independence. As victors, they expected to strengthen their

Castlereagh, Canning and Palmerston were foreign secretaries between 1812 and 1822, 1822 and 1827, and 1830 and 1841 respectively.

The **Ottoman Empire** consisted of large parts of the Balkans controlled by the Turks throughout the nineteenth century.

Britain's **strategic interests** were, in the case of the Low Countries, access to the River Rhine and preventing an enemy power from controlling the Channel; the Iberian Peninsula was important because it controlled entry to the Mediterranean and to the Atlantic shipping routes; and threats to the Near East from Russia posed problems for Britain's control of India.

What were Castlereagh's main aims at the Congress of Vienna?

The **Hundred Days** was a three-month period in 1815 during which Napoleon escaped from his exile on the Mediterranean island of Elba, returned to France, took back power for himself and relaunched the war.

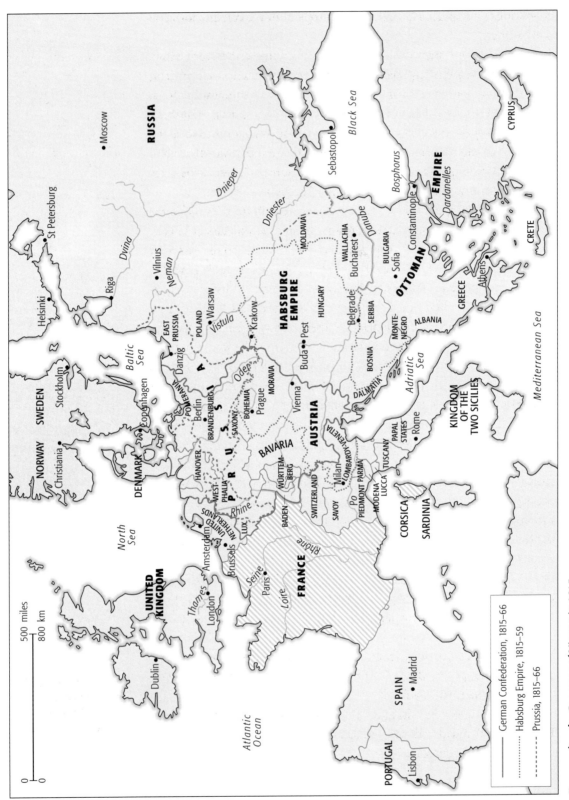

Europe after the Congress of Vienna in 1815.

Legend:
German Confederation, 1815–66
Habsburg Empire, 1815–59
Prussia, 1815–66

500 miles
800 km

Places and regions:
RUSSIA
Moscow
St Petersburg
Helsinki
Riga
Vilnius
Dvina
Neman
Dnieper
Dniester
Black Sea
Sebastopol
OTTOMAN EMPIRE
Bosphorus
Dardanelles
Constantinople
CYPRUS
CRETE
Athens
GREECE
ALBANIA
MONTE-NEGRO
Adriatic Sea
Mediterranean Sea
MOLDAVIA
WALLACHIA
Bucharest
Danube
BULGARIA
Sofia
SERBIA
Belgrade
BOSNIA
DALMATIA
HABSBURG EMPIRE
HUNGARY
Buda
Pest
Vienna
AUSTRIA
Krakow
Vistula
POLAND
Warsaw
Oder
EAST PRUSSIA
Danzig
POMERANIA
Baltic Sea
Stockholm
SWEDEN
NORWAY
Christiania
DENMARK
Copenhagen
North Sea
BERLIN
BRANDENBURG
P R U S S I A
SAXONY
BOHEMIA
Prague
MORAVIA
BAVARIA
WÜRTTEM-BERG
HANOVER
WEST-PHALIA
UNITED NETHERLANDS
Amsterdam
Brussels
LUX.
Rhine
BADEN
SWITZERLAND
SAVOY
PIEDMONT
Milan
LOMBARDY-VENETIA
Po
MODENA
PARMA
LUCCA
TUSCANY
PAPAL STATES
Rome
KINGDOM OF THE TWO SICILIES
CORSICA
SARDINIA
FRANCE
Rhône
Seine
Paris
Loire
UNITED KINGDOM
London
Thames
Dublin
Atlantic Ocean
SPAIN
Madrid
PORTUGAL
Lisbon

own positions by acquiring land either in Europe or in the colonies formerly owned by France.

Castlereagh did not want to gain any territory on mainland Europe. However, he wanted Belgium (especially the port of Antwerp) to be independent, to protect the British coastline and to guarantee access to European markets. He also wanted to see Spain and Portugal free from French influence. Castlereagh accepted that Italy should be an area of Austrian influence and that Prussia should be expanded. This would allow Austria and Prussia to guard against further Russian expansion into Europe. These aims were reflected in the territorial changes made at the Congress of Vienna.

The centre of Europe was bolstered against aggression from Russia in the east and France in the west by strengthening the position of Austria in Germany and Italy. Austria gained Venetia in Italy and Dalmatia on the east coast of the Adriatic Sea and kept the northern Italian state of Lombardy as well as lands in Germany and in Galicia (which was part of Poland). Russia's territorial gains were limited to northern Europe: Russia gained Poland (apart from Posen, Thorn and Galicia) and Finland. Prussia, the most successful of the great powers in 1815, doubled its population by gaining the Rhineland as a buffer state with France, over half of Saxony, Posen and Thorn from Poland, and Swedish Pomerania on the Baltic Sea. Although the territorial settlement agreed was inevitably a compromise, it satisfied the great powers.

The Vienna settlement brought Britain few territorial gains though what it did acquire supported its major interests:

- Britain gained the Cape of Good Hope (South Africa) and Ceylon (now Sri Lanka) from Holland and Mauritius from France; these territories were of strategic and commercial importance in relation to India.
- Britain's special interest in the Low Countries (modern-day Belgium and the Netherlands) was central to its trade with Europe. Most British exports entered Europe through the Scheldt estuary, which was safeguarded by Britain's possession of Heligoland and by Austria's decision not to take back the old Austrian Netherlands (later Belgium), which was united with the United Provinces (the Netherlands). As a result, no great power controlled the Low Countries.
- Britain gained Malta from France and the Ionian Islands from Venetia; these territories provided Britain with bases in the Mediterranean to guard against the advance of Russia.
- The British West Indian islands of St Lucia and Tobago (gained from France) and Trinidad (gained from Spain) reinforced Britain's commercial control over the Caribbean.

What did Britain gain from the Congress of Vienna? Why were these gains important to Britain?

The **Bourbons** were the royal family of France. Louis XVI was executed in 1793 and his brother Louis XVIII was restored in 1814. He died in 1824 and was succeeded by Charles X. Louis-Philippe of Orléans finally replaced the Bourbons in the revolution of 1830.

Other terms of the agreement were:

- France was not treated too harshly: as well as losing territory in Europe and some colonies, France had to pay compensation of 700 million francs to the allies and endure an army of occupation for between three and five years. In addition, the **Bourbons** were restored.

- Castlereagh was also eager to encourage liberal economic ideas (by which he meant free trade) in Europe, but this was seen by the other great powers as a ploy to help Britain gain commercial advantage. Political liberalism and the creation of constitutional monarchies were viewed with even more suspicion by the other great powers and Castlereagh approached these issues with great care. He was ready to accept other countries adopting more liberal constitutions, but only where he considered it appropriate and in Britain's interest.

  Castlereagh had only limited success in each of these areas and in the end, neither was included in the treaty. Free trade was increasingly acceptable to Britain with its vibrant and expanding industrial economy, but the other great powers lacked Britain's industrial base and so relied far more on protecting their own economies from competition. As far as political liberalism was concerned, Castlereagh held the view that other countries should be free to make their own decisions as to whether this was appropriate for their own governments. It was a far from popular position and the Holy Alliance of 1815 (see page 103) reflected the more widely held view among the European powers that revolutionary change should be resisted at all costs.

The abolition of the **slave trade** took place in 1807. Britain paid off other countries that practised the trade. Spain was given £400,000 in 1820 and Portugal followed Spain's lead by accepting £300,000. The Dutch were not paid cash but ended the trade in their colonies in 1815 in return for keeping most of their colonies in the East Indies, such as Java, that Britain had captured during the war.

- Britain also pressed for the abolition of the **slave trade**, but Castlereagh was only able to obtain vague promises of action by the other powers like Spain, Portugal and the United Provinces.

- Monarchies were restored in Spain and Naples. This led to instability later as countries did not always want to go back to the system of government that existed before the war.

- The Kingdom of the Netherlands was created by uniting Holland and Belgium, Austria voluntarily giving up its rule over this area. This was a change that favoured Britain's commercial interests.

The congress system

The main aim of the great powers at the Congress of Vienna was to ensure political stability in Europe. The congress system was set up to enable them to meet to resolve problems when necessary.

Article VI, drawn up by Castlereagh, was a crucial element in organising the congresses. It stated that the four victorious powers had 'agreed to renew their meetings at fixed periods – for the purpose of consulting on their common interests'. The vagueness of its terms was deliberate: Castlereagh recognised that, although there was an advantage in keeping the allies together as long as possible, a more specific commitment would have been overruled by those of his cabinet colleagues who were opposed to further involvement in Europe.

In practice, there was no system. The congresses met in different places: Aix-la-Chapelle, Troppau, Laibach and Verona, and meetings were held at irregular intervals, in 1818, 1820, 1821 and 1822, with the middle two congresses almost merging. There was no permanent staff to support the congresses.

The first congress was called to deal with outstanding problems arising from the allies' treatment of France. There was no clear reason for calling any of the other three, other than to discuss the revolutions that broke out across Europe between 1820 and 1822.

Holy and Quadruple Alliances

By the end of 1815, two further alliances had been signed: the Holy Alliance of Austria, Russia and Prussia in September, and the Quadruple Alliance of Britain, Russia, Austria and Prussia in November.

The Holy Alliance was **Tsar Alexander I**'s idea. He wanted to establish an alliance of Christian kings who would work together to maintain order, peace and friendly relations between the states of Europe. Britain did not sign this alliance because Castlereagh considered it to be both unnecessary and vague. The Holy Alliance was a reactionary move which reflected anxieties about all revolutionary movements on the part of the great continental powers. It was used in the 1820s to justify intervention by the great powers in the affairs of smaller states where a revolutionary change seemed likely.

The Quadruple Alliance was largely concerned with the future running of Europe. Its aims were more specific and practical than the rather vague notions of 'justice, Christian charity and peace' of the Holy Alliance. The Quadruple Alliance against France was to be preserved for 20 years, an army of occupation was to remain in France for between three and five years and Napoleon was never to be allowed to return to France.

Britain and the four congresses

- At the first congress held at Aix-la-Chapelle in 1818, France was brought back as one of the great powers in the so-called Quintuple Alliance, in part to balance the growing power of Russia.

  Tsar Alexander proposed that the Alliance should guarantee existing rulers their thrones and frontiers. He also argued for regular congresses to be held to direct the use of troops to restore deposed leaders. Castlereagh vigorously opposed this proposal because he did not agree with

Viscount Castlereagh (1769–1822).

What was the congress system and how was it intended to operate?

Tsar Alexander I, tsar of Russia from 1801 to 1825, played a leading part in the defeat of Napoleon in 1815. His approach to foreign policy after 1815 was motivated by a belief in Christian brotherhood.

intervention by the great powers and it was, for the moment, dropped. The congress at Aix-la-Chapelle was the most successful of the four.

- The second congress was called because the rebellions in Spain, Naples and Portugal threatened the rulers there. Held at Troppau in 1820, its main concern was to maintain the balance of power in Europe. The terms of the Vienna Settlement were unclear about whether the balance of power created at Vienna in 1815 was to be maintained indefinitely or whether it should be open to limited change. Castlereagh made his position clear in the State Paper of 5 May 1820: 'it [the Quadruple Alliance] never was intended as a Union for the government of the world, or the superintendence of the internal affairs of other states'. Castlereagh was prepared to support change in the balance of power as long as it did not threaten the overall peace of the continent.

  Russia, Prussia and Austria took the opposite view and signed the Troppau Protocol, which committed them to intervention if revolutionary changes in any state threatened other states or international peace.

- The State Paper of May 1820 has been recognised as one of the fundamental statements of British foreign policy, in which Castlereagh established a general set of principles about British attitudes to intervention. It was a secret document that was initially only circulated to British ambassadors and the governments of the great powers. In it, Castlereagh set out his understanding of the nature of the Quadruple Alliance and firmly rejected the right of the powers of Europe to interfere in the internal affairs of their neighbours. He was determined to prevent any great power intervention in Spain for two reasons. First, British public opinion overwhelmingly supported the revolt. Second, Spain was seen as a neutral buffer state on important British trade routes. He therefore rejected the idea of a congress, stressing that intervention in Spain would be resisted by the Spanish and would be unlikely to succeed.

- The congress reassembled at Laibach in January 1821. Lord Stewart, the British ambassador in Vienna, represented Britain. Ferdinand of Naples appealed to the congress for help in dealing with the rebels in his country. Although Britain could not object to Austria dispatching an army in view of Austria's treaty arrangements with Naples, it opposed the use of international force.

  The outbreak of a revolt in Wallachia and Moldavia in the Ottoman Empire was followed by the Greek revolt (see page 107). This united Britain and Austria, as both countries were anxious that the Russians should not profit from the situation by expanding at the expense of Turkey. Little was settled at Laibach and a new congress was arranged to meet at Verona in 1822.

- The threat to British interests in the Near East (see page 99) obliged Castlereagh to consider attending the congress at Verona in person. However, his death threw British policy into some confusion. Canning, his successor, did not go to Verona and quickly withdrew Wellington, who had gone in his place, because he was needed in case Russia intervened in Greece.

  The Verona congress maintained the facade of unity, but it was increasingly clear that the interests of the great powers had diverged.

This was as far as the congress system reached. Verona was the last formal gathering of the great powers. There was an attempt, at St Petersburg in 1825, to deal with the Greek rebellion, but it did not attract all the great powers and failed to reach any decisions because of the different attitudes of the states involved.

Castlereagh's policies between 1814 and 1822 were based on his belief in a balance of power between the great European powers as a way of securing Britain's defence. It was in Britain's interests to have a peaceful Europe so as to avoid being drawn into future continental wars. This would leave the country free to develop its colonial empire and increase its wealth through overseas trade. In this, Castlereagh was very successful.

> Why did Castlereagh take a different stance from the major European countries on intervention?

How effectively did Canning secure British interests between 1822 and 1830?

Canning joined the cabinet in 1816. It is possible that he had a hand in drafting the 1820 State Paper and he certainly accepted it as the basis for his own policies. Canning ruthlessly pursued British interests and gained a reputation as a crusader for liberalism and nationalism.

Canning was well aware of the limitations of British power and was pragmatic in his approach to foreign affairs. He did not want Britain deeply involved in the politics of the continent and sought to regain the freedom of action that would allow Britain to pursue its proper interests: security, trade and support for liberal causes. Both Canning and **Palmerston** were competitive and belligerent in their approach to foreign affairs.

Canning and the Americas

In Spanish America, demands for change had led to revolution. Britain feared that the European great powers would intervene and this posed a problem for its important economic interests in both North and South America. The United States had already recognised the rebel governments in Latin America and was also concerned about the possibility of European intervention.

> Henry John Temple, Lord **Palmerston**, (1784–1865) became the Whig foreign secretary in late 1830. Palmerston entered parliament in 1807 and in 1809 he became secretary of war, without a seat in the cabinet. He remained at the war office until 1828.

Canning had little choice but to be cautious for two reasons. First, he was opposed by the king and Wellington, who were both reluctant to recognise countries in revolt against their lawful rulers. Despite this opposition, Canning was able to exert sufficient diplomatic pressure on France so that it agreed not to intervene in the rebel Spanish colonies. Secondly, he recognised that the United States was suspicious of British motives in South America. In December 1823, President Munroe issued his famous Munroe Doctrine, in which he banned all European countries from assisting Spain in its struggle against the rebels. He also made it clear that any extension of European colonisation to the New World was unacceptable to the United States. The Munroe Doctrine maintained that the New World was the United States' sphere of interest, just as the great powers considered Europe their sphere of influence. Canning was faced by a United States no longer willing to accept intervention by European powers in areas it now saw as part of its sphere of interest.

Canning supported the rebel colonies for two reasons. First, he was motivated by Britain's economic interests. Latin and South America had great potential as markets for Britain's manufactured goods and as sources of raw materials like wood (even though this potential was not realised until the 1830s). Supporting rebel leaders who might later become rulers of independent countries made sound economic sense. Secondly, it proved popular with his supporters inside and outside parliament. Canning was seen to be standing up for the rights of oppressed peoples who were trying to break free from oppressive European regimes. This helped to reinforce his political credibility as a supporter of liberal political movements. In reality, however, support was given to movements for political reform when it was in Britain's interest to do so and denied when it was not.

George Canning (1770–1827).

Canning and Portugal

Between 1823 and 1826, revolutionaries were struggling for power in Portugal. Canning wanted to maintain the special relationship that existed between Britain and Portugal, so in 1824 he sent the British fleet to Lisbon to support King Juan VI. He also helped to arrange the peaceful separation of Brazil from direct Portuguese rule. This was important for Britain as it opened Brazilian markets to British trade, although was not directly relevant to the struggle within Portugal.

King Juan's death in 1826 led to the accession of the eight-year-old Donna Maria to the throne, although she was not finally crowned until 1834. Her father, Pedro, had renounced the throne in her favour, preferring to remain as emperor of Brazil. This led to a revival of the claims of her uncle Miguel, who was supported by Spain. Direct British action resulted: Canning rushed 5,000 troops to Lisbon and threatened Spain with war. This ensured Maria's succession and the acceptance of the 1826 liberal constitution by the Portuguese parliament. British naval power played a major role in the success of Canning's actions and a naval presence at Lisbon maintained British influence.

How and why did Canning intervene in Portugal?

Canning and Greece

As long as the conservative alliance of Russia, Austria and Prussia was united, Britain remained isolated in Europe. Disagreement between Austria and Russia over the Greek revolt against the Turks after 1821 permitted Canning to take a leading role in establishing an independent Greece.

Russia wanted to expand its influence into the Ottoman Empire and into the Mediterranean. It was in Britain's interest to prevent Russia from becoming a Mediterranean naval power and to secure the stability of the Ottoman Empire and open it to British trade.

The Greek revolt roused mixed feelings in Britain. British policy-makers faced a dilemma. Canning believed that preserving the Ottoman Empire offered the best hope of stability in the Mediterranean. Then in 1822, 25,000 Christians were massacred by the Turks on the island of Chios and 47,000 were sold into slavery. This outraged the British public, already influenced by the departure of about 1,000 people, such as the poet Lord Byron, to Greece to support the Greek rebellion. There was also a great deal of sympathy for the Greeks among Britain's ruling class who were educated on the history and literature of classical civilisations.

The Greek crisis threatened both European security and British trade. There was a danger of British banks, which had invested in Turkey, suffering losses. Canning needed to find a solution that satisfied both the need to preserve the Ottoman Empire and the demands of the Greeks for independence. He had to find a way to restore stability in the area.

Russia was sympathetic to the Greek struggle because of its interest in eroding the boundaries of the Ottoman Empire, even though its support for the Greek rebels broke up its conservative alliance with Austria. Canning recognised the Greeks as a lawful country pursuing a lawful war in March 1823, after which Tsar Alexander tried to get the British to agree to joint intervention. By the end of 1824, Alexander had abandoned this strategy because he could not get Britain and the other great powers to support it.

The Greeks, experiencing Ottoman military victories, appealed to Britain in July 1825 for protection and mediation. Canning's response was to seek a solution through negotiation. However, his priority was to avoid a Russo-Turkish war over Greece and the possibility of Russian territorial expansion. He concluded the St Petersburg Protocol of April 1826 with **Nicholas I**, in which they agreed that Greece should become an autonomous state, nominally under the sovereignty of the sultan of Turkey. Austria and Prussia

Nicholas I succeeded Tsar Alexander in late 1825.

refused to accept this. Nevertheless, the Protocol was formalised in the Treaty of London in 1827.

When the Turks, strengthened by further victories over the Greeks, refused to accept the Protocol, British, French and Russian ships were sent to the eastern Mediterranean. On 20 October 1827, a combined Turkish and **Egyptian** fleet was annihilated within two hours at the Battle of Navarino. This was followed by the outbreak of war between Russia and Turkey in April 1828 over Greece.

The outbreak of war between Russia and Turkey marked an end to the policy of mediation pursued since 1826. Canning did not live to see the breakdown of his Greek policy. Under Wellington it simply drifted. Domestic issues, rather than foreign policy, dominated parliament. Russia made small territorial gains from the war with Turkey that ended with the Treaty of Adrianople in September 1829. The Greeks achieved independence from Turkey the following year.

Egypt was part of Turkey's empire.

How did Canning seek to resolve the problem of Greek demands for independence from the Ottoman Empire?

Conclusion

Canning was generally regarded as a successful foreign secretary. This view was helped by his ability as a self-publicist, in stark contrast to Castlereagh. Yet both Canning and Castlereagh pursued the same basic aims abroad: security, trade and liberal causes, in that order. Castlereagh did so through negotiation and co-operation with the great powers. Canning's style was more abrasive and competitive; he sought wider European support only if it was absolutely necessary. In reality, Canning's achievements were far more limited than he liked to believe. His policy in the Americas, where he maintained that 'he called the New World into existence to redress the balance of the Old' was marked more by rhetoric than by concrete achievement. His attempt to restore stability in Greece and the Ottoman Empire, in alliance with Russia, broke down soon after his death. Portugal alone represented success in achieving his aims.

How effectively did Palmerston secure British interests between 1830 and 1841?

Although Palmerston saw himself as Canning's true successor, his approach to foreign policy was different. Palmerston was more prepared to intervene in the affairs of other countries to support Britain's interests. He believed that Britain stood for the defence of constitutional rights in other countries and for the extension of 'liberty and civilisation'.

In the 1830s, Palmerston was faced with the results of a series of challenges to the Vienna settlement. The July Revolution of 1830 in France was seen by

Lord Palmerston (1784–1865).

Palmerston as a limited political revolution which the Bourbon king had brought upon himself by failing to recognise demands for reform. He also recognised that the new government of Louis-Philippe was not aggressive and that the best way of maintaining stability in Europe was to recognise his new government. Revolution had, however, spread from France into Belgium, where riots broke out in August.

The Belgian problem

The decision taken at Vienna in 1815 to unite Belgium and Holland under the Dutch House of Orange was intended to be a barrier to French expansion. Although the two countries had complementary economies, there were religious and linguistic divisions between the two. As a result, it was a difficult union – the Belgians felt increasingly repressed by the Dutch and began demanding independence.

In early 1830, Wellington established an ambassadorial conference in London to discuss the problem of Belgian aspirations. As a result, William I of Holland reluctantly accepted Belgian independence in January 1831. The Belgians drew up a new constitution and in February 1831 elected the duke of Nemours, the son of Louis-Philippe, as their king. Knowing this would prove unacceptable to the other powers, Louis-Philippe vetoed it and Leopold of Saxe-Coburg became Leopold I of the Belgians. The Dutch invaded Belgium in August 1831 because they refused to accept the new king. Leopold appealed for aid to Britain and France, who co-operated: while the British fleet blockaded the coast, the French army forced the Dutch to withdraw.

The great powers agreed that Belgium should become an independent state and that they should guarantee its neutrality. The terms of this agreement were acceptable to the Belgians, but not to the Dutch. Antwerp in Belgium was still controlled by William; he refused to withdraw until France intervened in 1832, forcing his hand.

Palmerston was prepared to accept limited French military intervention in Belgium, but he had considerable difficulty in persuading both the king and parliament to support this policy, which seemed a complete reversal of the 'containment' of France, agreed in 1815. A new armistice was agreed in 1833 between Belgium and Holland, but a final settlement was delayed until the Treaty of London of 1839 because of Palmerston's involvement in the Near East (see page 110).

In what ways was Belgium a problem in the 1830s? How did Palmerston seek to resolve this?

The Iberian Peninsula

Palmerston's reputation was improved by his handling of problems in Portugal and Spain where, as in the Low Countries, Britain had long-established strategic and commercial interests. British support for Maria (see page 106) had collapsed with Canning's death and by November 1830 Miguel was in control of almost the whole of the country. Maria's supporters held only Terceira in the Azores.

Palmerston, like Canning, believed that Britain's interests were better served by having the **liberal** Maria on the throne rather than the **absolutist** Miguel. In 1831, the French, with British approval, sent a fleet to Lisbon to put pressure on Miguel. Again Palmerston came under attack from the Tory opposition because of the co-operation he received from France. British opinion, which supported Maria, was better pleased when he extended British support to Pedro, who abdicated his Brazilian throne to come to the assistance of his daughter. He landed at Oporto in July 1832 and Palmerston made little attempt to stop British volunteers, notably Charles Napier, from enlisting under Pedro. Napier defeated Miguel's fleet off Cape St Vincent in July 1833 and took possession of Lisbon three weeks later, thus securing Maria's throne. She was finally crowned the following year.

Spain, like Portugal, was also divided between liberals and absolutists in the 1830s. After King Ferdinand VII died in September 1833, succession was disputed between the supporters of his young daughter Isabella and her mother Christina, who had been proclaimed regent, and the supporters of Ferdinand's younger brother, Carlos, who argued that the Salic Law forbade the accession of women to the throne. Carlos had the support of conservatives and the Catholic Church, while Isabella was supported by the liberals.

For Palmerston, the attitude of Russia, Prussia and Austria was more disturbing. They had signed an agreement at Münchengrätz in September 1833 pledging to uphold conservative causes – one effect of this was that they provided financial assistance to Carlos. In April 1834, Palmerston countered this by establishing a Quadruple Treaty between Britain, France and the queens of Portugal and Spain. This prevented either the eastern powers or France (acting alone) from intervening in Spain. It also established, in an embryonic form, the idea of two balancing power blocs, a western bloc of Britain and France and an eastern bloc of Russia, Prussia and Austria. The conflict between Christina and Carlos continued until late 1839 when Carlos was finally defeated. Palmerston's influence in Spain was less than it had been in Portugal, but in both countries he had prevented unilateral intervention by France.

The Eastern Question

Palmerston took a decisive stand on the **Eastern Question** and here his influence on events was considerable. He hoped that the Turks would leave Europe, but he recognised that this would leave a political vacuum that would benefit Russia. As a result, he adopted a policy of support for the Ottoman Empire,

Liberals wanted a more democratic constitution, while the **absolutists** called for a return to complete or absolute control by the monarch. In the longer term, the liberals were in the ascendant.

What part did Palmerston play in the political problems of the Iberian Peninsula in the 1830s?

The **Eastern Question** reflected concerns about the future of the Ottoman Empire. Britain was concerned about Russian expansion into the Balkans and had often supported Turkey against Russian aggression.

which in the 1830s was under attack from the rebellious pasha of Egypt, Mehemet Ali, who had been its ruler since 1805.

Mehemet Ali had aided Turkey against Greece in the 1820s, aid that would probably have been successful but for the intervention of the great powers. In return, the sultan had promised him Syria and Crete. After the Greek settlement, Mehemet Ali demanded his reward but, in view of his limited success, the sultan refused to give him Syria as well as Crete. In 1831, Mehemet Ali invaded Syria and the following year defeated the Turkish army.

Constantinople was threatened and the sultan of Turkey appealed to Britain for assistance to try to limit Mehemet Ali's advance. Palmerston would have been willing to provide aid, but the cabinet overruled him. The cabinet also rejected French offers of joint intervention.

In desperation, the sultan turned to Russia. As the Russian naval squadron entered the **Bosphorus**, Mehemet Ali's forces retreated. The British and the French, worried by Russia's intervention, urged the sultan to compromise. Peace was made in May 1833, and it gave the Egyptians what they wanted in Syria. The Treaty of Unkiar Skelessi in July 1833 formalised Russian influence in Constantinople. It was an agreement that aroused considerable suspicion in Britain and France because it contained secret clauses, the most important of which was an Ottoman undertaking to close the western end of the Bosphorus to foreign warships if Russia requested it. The three eastern powers agreed publicly to maintain the integrity of the sultan's dominions and secretly to oppose any further advance by Mehemet Ali.

The **Bosphorus** is the strait separating the Black Sea from the Mediterranean.

An uneasy peace prevailed in the Near East until 1839, but neither the sultan of Turkey nor Mehemet Ali was content to leave things as they were. The former wanted revenge against an ambitious subject, while Mehemet Ali wanted, if not complete independence, at least hereditary possession of Egypt under nominal Ottoman rule.

By 1839, the sultan's army had been reorganised and he invaded Syria to drive the Egyptians out. Mehemet Ali's son, Ibrahim, had little difficulty defeating the sultan's army and, once again, the road to Constantinople lay open. On 1 July 1839, the sultan died. He was succeeded by the 16-year-old Abdul Mejid. The Ottoman Empire seemed on the point of total collapse and the great powers were seriously alarmed, as this would have led to instability in the Balkans and encouraged Russian expansion.

Palmerston was in a difficult position. He recognised that the crisis gave Russia further opportunities to strengthen its position, but by this time he was more suspicious of France's presence in the Mediterranean. France had interests in north Africa and was prepared to weaken the Ottoman Empire. The Quadruple Treaty, reached between Britain and France in 1834 (see page 110), had gradually been eroded. The French had consolidated their hold over

Algeria after 1830 and favoured giving considerable concessions to Mehemet Ali. This made him a real threat to British economic and strategic interests. He directly threatened British routes to the River Euphrates and the Persian Gulf. At the same time, the Red Sea route to India was under Egyptian control. France's growing support for Mehemet Ali posed a threat to British interests in India, where in the eighteenth century France had fought with Britain for control.

Palmerston did not hesitate to join with Russia, the other eastern powers and Turkey in an agreement to which France was not a party. The Convention of London was signed on 15 July 1840. Mehemet Ali was offered the hereditary possession of Egypt and the possession of Syria during his lifetime only. He failed to respond in the 20 days given him and, on 3 November, a British fleet bombarded Acre (in present-day Lebanon).

The French, angered by the attack on Acre, began to speak in warlike terms. However, the French cabinet was equally divided between peace and war parties and so nothing came of their threats. Once Mehemet Ali had submitted in early 1841, in part as a result of the bombardment of Acre, Palmerston allowed the French to rejoin the **Concert of Europe**. The 1840 Convention of London was superseded by the Straits Convention of 13 July 1841. It forbade the passage of foreign warships through the Straits while the Ottoman Empire was at peace and ended the advantages that Russia had gained in 1833 with the Treaty of Unkiar Skelessi. Palmerston's policy had achieved stability in the Near East using only limited military action. He also ensured the preservation of the Concert of Europe through his co-operation with Russia.

The **Concert of Europe** was established as a result of the Congress of Vienna. It aimed to prevent the danger of revolution as much as the threat of France. It was based on the principle that if representatives of the great powers of Europe could meet (in congresses) then European problems could be resolved without the expensive need for war.

What was the Eastern Question? How successful was British policy in this area?

China and opium

Trade between Britain and China had always been difficult. It had been under the control of the East India Company until the abolition of its monopoly in 1833. After 1833, the protection of British trade and British citizens became the responsibility of the British government. Britain was determined to open up the Chinese trade and to compel Peking to adopt western diplomatic conventions.

There was a considerable demand for opium in China, and the East India Company had made good profits by growing it in India and exporting it to China in return for Chinese merchandise. The Chinese authorities in the 1830s hesitated between banning opium imports or regulating them. In the late 1830s, those calling for a ban won the argument.

When British ships refused to allow the Chinese authorities in southern China to board to search for opium, the Chinese placed the small British trading community at Canton under virtual house arrest. They then attacked a British warship and ordered the suspension of all trade with Britain. Banning trade was one thing, but the arrest of British citizens and attacks on British shipping was another matter altogether. The British government in India sent naval assistance to Canton. A clash between Chinese and British warships escalated into naval war by June 1840. In 1841, a major battle took place in which the Chinese fleet was sunk and shore batteries captured.

For Palmerston the issue was not whether Britain should protect opium smugglers; he did not question the Chinese government's right to ban the trade. The issue was that British interests in the peaceable trading community in Canton, not implicated in the opium trade, were under attack. The Chinese maintained that the community to which criminals belonged should be held accountable for their actions, but this notion of collective responsibility was alien to the British concept of individual innocence or guilt. Palmerston did not accept that this gave the Chinese the right to interfere with British subjects.

The war was still in progress when the Whigs were defeated in the 1841 election and the incoming Conservative government made no significant change in policy. The war continued until the Chinese made concessions in the Treaty of Nanking of 1842. Five ports were opened up to foreign trade, not merely to the British, though they gained an advantage in China by the annexation of Hong Kong in 1842.

What were the consequences for Britain of the war with China?

Britain and the United States

In 1830, Britain had a number of outstanding disputes with the United States of America, one of which was slavery and the slave trade.

Both Britain and the United States had declared the slave trade illegal in 1807. In 1815 the Congress of Vienna, under pressure from Castlereagh, also outlawed it. Enforcing the ban proved to be a problem. Britain had signed a number of 'right of search' treaties with the smaller nations of Europe, which permitted British ships to arrest slavers flying their flags. Larger nations were more difficult to convince. Palmerston negotiated treaties of this type with France in 1831 and 1833, and in 1838 he almost secured the agreement of all the great powers of Europe to one treaty that would have allowed a common right of search over all slavers. French anger at Palmerston's handling of the Eastern Question led them to withhold ratification and the treaty was never put into practice.

The United States had consistently refused to enter any right of search agreement with Britain. This was partly the result of Britain's action against American shipping during the Napoleonic Wars, but had more to do with the powerful lobby of the slave-owning southern American states. Palmerston accepted that Britain could not, in the absence of a treaty, stop and search American shipping, but he was concerned that slavers of other nations hoisted the American flag to escape capture. He therefore argued for a more limited 'right of visit' to check whether a suspected ship was entitled to the flag she was flying. Eventually in 1840, Palmerston came to an agreement with the United States and they signed a treaty that agreed to a mutual 'right of search'.

Conclusion

Canning and Palmerston dominated British foreign policy between 1822 and 1841. Their approaches were different and the degree to which their policies were effective and successful in promoting British interests varied. Both foreign secretaries had to deal with the interests of France, Russia, Austria and, to a lesser extent, Prussia, especially when those interests threatened the stability of Europe. Britain's direct influence in Europe was restricted to those areas where its naval power could exert pressure – on Belgium, the Iberian Peninsula and in Greece. Outside Europe, both foreign secretaries were committed to promoting Britain's commercial interests in the global economy, especially in South America and in the Far East. Here Britain was more successful in asserting its authority.

Summary questions

1   Identify and explain any *two* factors that affected British foreign policy between 1815 and 1827.

2   Compare the importance of at least *three* issues that determined the conduct of British foreign policy under Palmerston between 1830 and 1841.

9

The first industrial nation

Focus questions

◆ Why was Britain the first industrial nation?

◆ What was the nature and extent of change?

Significant dates

1761	The Bridgewater Canal opens
1764	Hargreaves invents the jenny
1769	Arkwright invents the water frame
1779	Crompton invents the mule
1783	Cort invents the puddling and rolling process
1785	Cartwright invents the power loom
1793	War breaks out with France
1801	First national census undertaken
1815	French Wars end
1830	Liverpool–Manchester railway opens

Overview

In the latter part of the eighteenth and the first half of the nineteenth century, Britain underwent what has become known as the **Industrial Revolution**, with factories pouring out goods, chimneys polluting the air, exports escalating and productivity spiralling upwards. But industrial change did not happen suddenly after 1780; it had been taking place throughout the eighteenth century. There was revolutionary growth in the textiles, coal and iron industries and substantial growth in a whole range of traditional industries. New technology led to increasing mechanisation, but **handworking** was also more widely used and the division of labour was introduced.

Change resulted from combining old and new processes. Steam power, for example, was used alongside water power for decades. Work organisation varied: in 1850, factories co-existed with domestic production, artisan

Historians disagree on a number of issues concerning the **Industrial Revolution**. It is, however, increasingly clear that the traditional view of the Revolution as simply dynamic and relatively short-lived provides an incomplete picture.

Traditional, unmechanised manufacturing techniques are known as **handworking**.

workshops and large-scale mining and metal production. The extent of change also varied across industries and regions.

Why was Britain the first industrial nation?

Answers to this question usually focus on why industries like cotton, iron and coal expanded, and what influence the spread of steam power had. These issues are important, but too much emphasis on them neglects the broader economic experiences of Britain in this period.

Similarly, the question 'Why did the Industrial Revolution take place in Britain?' misses the crucial point that economic change did not occur in the whole of Britain. Growth was regional: **industrialisation** took place in particular areas such as Lancashire, the central lowlands of Scotland, south Wales and around Belfast. In other parts of the country, such as Norfolk and Suffolk, deindustrialisation occurred as the woollen industry declined as a result of competition from Yorkshire.

Nevertheless, economic change had an effect, however small, on all aspects of British society. Particular circumstances that were present in Britain made change possible and, in that sense, can be said to be causal. Others circumstances held back progress, but change occurred despite them. This section will look at the importance of key factors to explain growth in the economy between 1780 and 1850.

Population

If it is possible to identify a single cause for the Industrial Revolution, then a strong case can be made for **population growth**. Between 1780 and 1850, the population of England and Wales increased from around 7.5 million to nearly 18 million. This resulted in a greater demand for goods like food and housing.

Nevertheless, the increase in demand for other goods – such as more manufactured goods or a more efficient means of communication – did not necessarily follow from population expansion. The problem is one of timing. When did population growth occur? When did economic growth occur? Did they correspond? Although historians broadly accept that Britain's population increased rapidly from the mid eighteenth century, they are less certain when the economy began to grow. The beginnings of economic growth can be seen in every decade between the 1750s and 1790s, though increasingly historians agree that the best case can be made for the 1770s and 1780s.

If population growth stimulated demand, you would expect economic and population growth to coincide. However, they did not. Economic growth began to accelerate in the last quarter of the eighteenth century, while the maximum rate of population growth on mainland Britain did not happen

Industrialisation is the process of change in the eighteenth and early nineteenth centuries when Britain developed from an agricultural to an industrial economy.

Population growth in mainland Britain stimulated an already growing economy. However, in Ireland population growth in the eighteenth century was followed by stagnation in the first half of the nineteenth century and by famine.

until after 1810. Nevertheless, some historians argue that when the population began to expand after 1750, it provided the critical ingredient necessary to trigger off industrialisation.

Historians agree that population growth had favourable effects on economic growth in three important respects:

- It provided Britain with an abundant and cheap supply of labour.
- It stimulated investment in industry and agriculture because of increased demand for goods and services.
- Urbanisation, caused by the movement of people into towns, made it profitable to create or improve services. For example, the building of the canal from the Bridgewater coalmines at Worsley to Manchester took advantage of the growing demand for cheap domestic coal.

The nature of population growth, the reasons why it increased, its chronology and its relationship to economic growth are issues that historians have debated with some intensity in the last 30 years. Some of the conclusions they have reached – such as whether population growth was the result of rising births or falling deaths – remain tentative; others – like the impact of growth on the economy – are more definite.

> In what ways did population growth contribute to economic growth after 1780?

Trade

In 1750, Britain was already a well-established trading nation. Colonies provided raw materials as well as markets for manufactured goods. London was a major centre for the **re-export trade**, while the slave trade played a major role in the development of Liverpool and Bristol and its profits provided an important source of capital for early industrialisation.

> The **re-export trade** took place when goods were imported from Europe and Britain's colonies and then re-exported to other colonies or foreign countries.

By the 1780s, the export trade was expanding annually by 2.6 per cent. Cotton accounted for just over half Britain's exports by 1830 and three-quarters of all exports were associated with textiles such as cotton, woollens and silk. This represented a narrow trading base and helps to explain why the British economy experienced depression in the 1830s and early 1840s. British factories were overproducing for European and global markets that were already saturated with textile goods. This meant that some changes took place in the type of goods exported: iron exports grew from 6 per cent in the 1810s to 20 per cent by 1850, and coal became a more important export.

In the 1780s, Europe was a major market for British goods and this remained the case in 1850. However, there were important new markets for British goods during this time:

- The United States increasingly became a destination for exports of manufactured goods. This process of change was helped by the opening-up of Latin American markets in the early nineteenth century.

The port of London in the early nineteenth century.

- India was a huge market for cotton goods. Similar possibilities existed in the Middle East and in South America. Britain increasingly shifted trade towards less developed economies that were able to provide it with imports of tropical products.

The increase in overseas trade has been highlighted by some historians as a primary cause of economic growth, based on the fact that export industries grew at a faster rate than other industries. This growth in trade between 1780 and 1850 was an important factor in Britain's economic development for the following reasons:
- It stimulated domestic demand for British products.
- International trade gave Britain access to raw materials that both widened the range and reduced the cost of British products.
- Those countries that were exporting goods to Britain had, as a result, the purchasing power to buy British goods.
- Profits from trade were used to finance industrial expansion and agricultural improvements.
- It was a major cause of the growth of large towns and industrial centres.

The role of British trade must, however, be put into perspective. Changes in the pattern of British trade between 1780 and 1850 – the export or re-export of manufactured goods in return for imports of foodstuffs and raw materials – were relatively small and developments in industry from the 1780s consolidated already existing trends. Exports may have helped the textiles and iron

industries to expand, but they made little impact on the unmodernised, traditional manufacturing sectors.

Inventions

Britain's claim to be the 'first industrial nation' was largely based on its ability
to produce manufactured goods more cheaply and in greater quantities than
its foreign competitors. This was, in large part, the result of improvements in
the techniques of production, especially the development of labour-saving
technology and the widespread use of water power and then steam power for
manufacturing. Many of the earlier inventions, especially those produced
before 1800, were mechanised alternatives to already existing manually operated machines. Later developments relied more on inventions by professional
engineers.

Between 1760 and 1800, there was a significant increase in the number of
patents that gave exclusive rights to their inventors. Between 1700 and 1760,
379 patents were awarded. In the 1760s, there were 205, in the 1770s, 294, in
the 1780s, 477 and in the 1790s, 647. These figures do not tell the full story,
however:

- Certain key technical developments pre-dated 1760. Coke smelting was
  developed by Abraham Darby in Shropshire in 1709, but it was not until the
  1750s that it was widely used. Thomas Newcomen's steam-atmospheric
  engine was invented between 1709 and 1712, but it too was not widely used
  until 1760. James Kay developed the flying shuttle in 1733. Its use increased
  the productivity of weavers, but it was 30 years before advances were made
  in spinning techniques.

- Registering patents was expensive and, as a result, some inventions were not
  patented. Samuel Crompton, for example, did not register his spinning
  mule until 1780. From the 1760s, there was a growing awareness of the
  importance of obtaining patents and the danger of failing to do so. This
  may account for some of the increase of patents registered from 1760.

- Many of the patents covered processes and products that were of little economic importance, such as medical and consumer goods. Some patents
  represented technological breakthroughs, while others improved existing
  technologies.

Despite these reservations, there were important groupings of technological advances after 1760. James Kay's flying shuttle speeded up the process
of weaving, but this produced a bottleneck caused by the shortage of
hand-spun thread. The mechanisation of spinning after 1764 reversed this
situation. Innovations in spinning thread included James Hargreaves' jenny
(1764), Richard Arkwright's water frame (1769) and Samuel Crompton's mule

In what respects did
trade play an
important role in the
development of the
British economy after
1780?

In what ways does the
information about
patents suggest that
historians have to be
careful about the
impact of inventions
on economic growth?

(1779). The new jennies allowed one worker to spin at least 8, and eventually 80, times the amount of thread previously produced by a single spinner. Productivity was further increased by Arkwright's and Crompton's inventions.

The problem was now weaving. Edward Cartwright's power loom, invented in 1785, did not initially resolve the problem as it was expensive and unreliable. Consequently the decades between 1780 and 1810 were ones of considerable prosperity for handloom weavers. The position of handloom weavers was only threatened after 1810 when the power loom was modified to make it more efficient.

In 1700 in the iron industry, charcoal was used to smelt iron. It had become increasingly expensive, causing Britain to rely on cheaper, better quality European imports. Although Abraham Darby perfected coke smelting in 1709, it was not until demand for iron rose rapidly after 1750 that coke became the popular fuel for smelting. The stimulus for expansion in the iron industry came from demands for weapons for the wars with France and the American colonies in the 1750s and 1770s, and especially between 1793 and 1815. This led to further technological change, especially the reverberatory furnace (1766), which used coal rather than the more expensive coke, and the puddling and rolling process (1782–84) that made **wrought iron** cheaper. The new technologies led to a four-fold growth in the production of **pig iron** between 1788 and 1806, a significant reduction in costs and thus virtually put an end to expensive foreign imports. The 'hot-blast' of 1828 further reduced costs.

Pig iron was the term that applied to iron taken from the furnace and cooled in moulds. It was then reheated and beaten by the blacksmith at the forge to remove impurities and turned into **wrought iron**.

Rising demand for iron stimulated developments in the coal industry. Here the major technological developments were led by the need to mine coal from deeper pits. Pumping engines, first Newcomen's and then Watt's, helped in this process. Sir Humphrey Davy's safety lamp helped to improve safety underground. Increases in productivity were, however, largely the consequence of employing more miners.

The development of steam power in the eighteenth century was gradual. Newcomen's engine was used for pumping water out of mines. Watt trebled the efficiency of Newcomen's engine by adding a separate condenser in the mid-1760s. Though older means of generating energy remained important, the application of steam power to mining, iron-making, the railways and especially the booming cotton industry meant that it was the dominant form of energy by 1850.

Historians have emphasised the importance of the steam engine to the Industrial Revolution, but this has been played down by recent writers. Wind and water remained important as sources of energy. Windmills were used for grinding corn, land-drainage and some industrial processes. Water power was very important and remained so until the mid nineteenth century. Before 1800, most textile mills were water powered, but by 1830, 2,230 mills used water power as against 3,000 using steam. The metalwork, mining, paper-making and pottery industries continued to use water power.

Geographical diversity

The pace and geographical distribution of economic change after 1780 was uneven. This was partly the result of differences in climate and ease of access to raw materials. Enclosure (see Chapter 1) was based on the better soils of central and eastern England, while Lancashire developed into the cotton-producing centre because of its coal resources, water and access to the sea so raw cotton could be easily and cheaply imported from the United States.

Dynamic growth took place in economic regions that specialised in par-ticular industries. Cotton was based in south Lancashire and parts of the joining counties of Derbyshire and Cheshire. Wool was dominant in the West Riding of Yorkshire. Iron dominated the economies of Shropshire and south Wales. Staffordshire was internationally renowned for its pottery. Birming-ham and Warwickshire specialised in metal-working. Tyneside was more diverse, with interests in coal, glass, iron and salt. With its huge population and sophisticated manufacturing and service sectors – docks, warehouses, engineering, shipbuilding, silk-weaving, luxury trades, the machinery of government and the law, publishing and printing, financial centre and enter-tainment – London was an economic region in its own right.

Deindustrialisation (the process by which some industries disappeared) was also regional in character. After 1780, the West Country and East Anglia textile industries declined. The iron industry disappeared from the Weald in Kent and the Cumberland coalfields. Industries in these areas were far less competitive because of their limited raw materials and poor communications. Their resultant lower profits meant they were less able to take advantage of newer, more productive technologies.

Regional growth or decline depended on a range of factors. Growth depended largely on access to water power as an energy source or as a means of processing, on easy access to coal and other raw materials, and on an ample labour force.

Investment

Britain was a relatively wealthy country in the mid eighteenth century with a well-established banking system. This enabled people to build up savings, thus providing them with capital to invest. Between 1750 and 1770, there was growing investment in roads, canals and buildings and in enclosing land. This process continued from 1780 through to the 1850s, with investment in trans-port, enclosure, expansion of the textile and iron industries and, after 1830, in the development of railways:

- The annual rate of domestic investment rose from about £13 million in the 1780s to over £40 million by the 1830s.
- The ratio of gross investment to the gross national product rose from 6 per cent in the 1770s to 12 per cent by the 1790s, where it remained until 1850.
- Widespread capital investment was largely confined to small, though important, parts of the economy. Capital investment increased in farming, communications and textiles, especially cotton, and in iron and steel. The rest of the economy was often undercapitalised relative to these industries.

Capital investment in farming was largely spent on enclosures, drainage and buildings. Landowners ploughed back about 6 per cent of their total income into the land. This figure rose to about 16 per cent during the French Wars when high wheat prices encouraged investment in enclosure. With the onset of depression, investment declined after 1815 and did not revive until the 1840s.

In the 1780s, a third of all investment was in farming; by 1850, this had fallen to an eighth. By contrast, there was a rapid growth of investment in industry and communications. Annual investment in industry and trade rose from £2 million in the 1780s to £17 million by 1850. Between 1780 and 1830, there was an annual investment of £1.5 million in canals and roads and for the improvement of docks and harbours. These figures were dwarfed by investment in railways, which peaked at £15 million per year in the 1840s, accounting for 28 per cent of all investment. The increase in the availability of capital to invest allowed economic growth to occur.

What were the main features of capital investment between 1780 and 1850?

Social factors

British society in the eighteenth and nineteenth centuries was profoundly conservative, with highly traditional structures. Yet it was able to generate changes in many areas of economic life. By 1780, British society was capitalist in character and organisation. Its aristocracy was remarkably open, allowing the newly rich and talented to move into its ranks. It was possible for the most successful merchants, professionals and businessmen in each generation to become part of landed society. In France, where social climbing was discouraged, there was political and social discontent and, ultimately, political revolution. In Britain, where social climbing was possible, there was an industrial revolution instead.

Until 1830, the key to economic growth was the growing domestic demand for consumer goods. Possessing and using domestic goods enhanced social status and displayed social rank. Growing consumption influenced trade and economic growth. Lower food prices after 1780 may well have stimulated a consumer boom as people had more disposable income. There was a dramatic increase in the number of permanent shops in major urban centres and many of the characteristics of modern advertising emerged in the form of circulars, showrooms and elaborate window displays. Changing patterns of consumption created an environment in which manufacturers could exploit known and growing demand.

Finally, entrepreneurial skill and enterprise played a major role in the development of the economy in the late eighteenth and early nineteenth centuries. Entrepreneurs did three things:

- They organised production.
- They brought together capital (their own or others') and labour.
- They found markets for their products.

They often combined the roles of financiers, capitalists, managers, merchants and salesmen. Three main explanations for the role entrepreneurs played in economic change have been identified by historians:

- There was a change in the ways people viewed social status from one where it was the result of birth to one where it related to what individuals achieved – status was based on what you did, not who you were. This was a reflection of the openness and mobility of British society.
- Many first-generation entrepreneurs seem to have had the crucial experience of Nonconformity in common. It encouraged a set of values favourable to economic enterprise.
- Entrepreneurs were able to effectively exploit advances in technology and industrial organisation. Most entrepreneurs were not pioneers of major innovations or inventions, but they realised how best to utilise them. This allowed them to manufacture and market goods within a highly competitive consumer society.

What was the role of the entrepreneur after 1780?

Conclusions

There was no blueprint for the Industrial Revolution. Population growth stimulated demand that entrepreneurs were able to satisfy. Investment in industry often brought good returns. The state made little attempt to control growth. Foreign trade provided the raw materials and profits that could be invested in enterprise. The social structure was adaptable and flexible. Each of these factors contributed to making Britain the first industrial nation.

What was the nature and extent of change?

The view that the Industrial Revolution represented a dramatic watershed between an old and a new world has recently been questioned by historians. It is now generally accepted that growth was considerably slower and took longer than was previously believed. Recent research suggests the following:

- Change in the economy was two-dimensional. There were dynamic industries, like cotton and iron, where change occurred relatively quickly and that can be called revolutionary. In other industries, change took place far more slowly.
- Between 1750 and 1850, the British economy experienced rapid and, by international standards, pronounced structural change. The proportion of the labour force employed in industry (mining, manufacturing and service) increased, while the proportion employed in farming fell.
- Much employment in industry continued to be in small-scale, handicraft activities producing for local markets. These trades were largely unaffected by mechanisation and experienced little or no increase in output per worker. Increased production was achieved by employing more workers.
- The cotton textiles industry, though dynamic and high profile, was not typical and there was no general ascendancy of steam power or the factory system in the early nineteenth century, nor was economic growth caused by a few ground-breaking inventions. The overall pace of economic growth was modest. There was no great leap forward for the economy as a whole, despite the experiences of specific industries.
- By 1850, Britain was the 'workshop of the world'. High productivity in a few industries enabled Britain to dominate world trade in manufacture. Half of all the goods sold in the global market came from Britain. This was achieved by more workers entering into the industrial and manufacturing sectors. The cotton and iron industries existed alongside other industries characterised by low productivity, low pay and low levels of exports.

Mechanisation

Although new machines for textile production, especially cotton, were introduced over a short time, their widespread use was delayed until the 1820s. There were three main reasons for this:

- First, the new technologies were costly and often unreliable. Modifications were necessary before their full economic benefits could be realised.
- Secondly, many workers resisted the introduction of the new technologies and some employers continued to use handworkers because they were cheaper than the new machines. This was particularly evident in the Yorkshire woollen industry that lagged behind cotton in applying new technology.
- Finally, the original spinning jennies were small enough to be used in the home, but Arkwright's water frame was too large for domestic use and needed purpose-built spinning mills that required a substantial amount of capital.

These early factories used water power, though the use of steam engines increased steadily. By 1800, a quarter of all cotton yarn was spun using steam power. It was not until after 1815 that factories combined powered spinning and weaving. By 1850, some factories were employing large numbers of workers, but many remained small. In Lancashire in the 1840s, the average firm employed 260 people but a quarter employed fewer than 100. The mechanisation of the textile industry did not happen overnight, but was a steady progression as technological innovation and modification took place.

By 1800, about a fifth of all mechanical energy in Britain was produced by steam engines. Steam power was a highly versatile form of energy and its impact on British industry was profound. It allowed industry to move into towns often on or near to coalfields where it could be supplied by canal, significantly reducing costs.

How important was technical advance to the Industrial Revolution? Adam Smith (see Chapter 1) in *The wealth of nations*, published in 1776, seemed unaware that he was living in a period of technical change and mechanisation. For him, economic growth was achieved through the organisational principle of division of labour rather than the use of new technology. Historians have assigned greater importance to technical change, but have emphasised that its effect was neither immediate nor widespread until after 1800.

Transport

By 1750, Britain was already a highly mobile society. Travel may have been slow and sometimes dangerous, but it was not uncommon. Within 100 years, the British landscape was scarred by canals and railways and crossed by improved roads, and the movement of goods and people speeded up dramatically.

Britain's road system in the mideighteenth century was extensive, but underfunded. The £1 million spent annually was insufficient to maintain the road system necessary to growing trade. **Turnpike roads**, the first of which was established in 1663, grew slowly in the first half of the eighteenth century, when an average of 8 were established each year. From the 1750s, this increased to about 40 a year and, from the 1790s, to nearly 60. By the mid-1830s, there were 1,116 turnpike trusts in England and Wales, managing about a sixth of all roads.

Parallel to this organisational development, there were improvements in the quality of road-building, associated particularly with **Thomas Telford** and **John Loudon Macadam**. Spending on parish roads did not increase markedly, though there was a significant growth in spending by turnpike trusts. This reached a peak of £1.5 million per year in the 1820s. The problem was that improvements made to the road system were patchy and dependent on private initiatives.

From the 1550s, the parish was responsible for maintaining roads. This may have been adequate for dealing with local roads, but the major or trunk roads were not maintained very well. Local people thought that the people who used these roads should pay for their upkeep. The result was the development of **turnpike roads**, financed by private turnpike trusts, that people were charged to use.

Thomas Telford (1757–1834) was a Scottish civil engineer who built 1,600 km of roads, 200 bridges as well as canals, harbours and churches throughout Scotland and England.

John Loudon Macadam (1756–1836) was a Scottish road engineer who developed the first road surface to be largely wear-resistant.

The Barton Aqueduct, near Manchester, carrying the Bridgewater Canal over the River Irwell.

Despite this, there were significant reductions in journey times between the main centres of population. In the 1780s, it took 10 days to travel from London to Edinburgh; by the 1830s, it took 45 hours. This led to a dramatic increase in the number of passengers carried by a rapidly expanding coaching industry. All kinds of industrial materials and manufactured goods were transported on the roads as well. There was a significant growth of carrier firms (they transported goods across the country) after 1780. In London, for example, there were 353 firms in 1790 and 735 by the mid-1820s; in Birmingham there was a five-fold increase in the number of carriers between 1790 and 1830. These firms were, however, unable to compete with the canals or the railways and concentrated on providing short-distance transport of goods from canals and railway stations to local communities.

The major problem facing early industrialists was the cost of carrying heavy, bulky goods like coal or iron ore. The solution was to use rivers, coastal transport and, from the 1760s, canals. The first phase of canal development took place in the 1760s and early 1770s. The second phase, in the 1790s, has rightly been called 'canal mania' with the completion of several important canals and the setting-up of 51 new schemes. By 1820, the canal network, linking all the major centres of industrial production and population, was largely completed. The consequences of this expansion of canals were twofold:

- Canals dramatically enhanced the efficiency of the whole economy by making a cheap system of transport available for goods and passengers. As a result, the price of raw materials like coal, timber, iron, wood and cotton tumbled. The needs of farming, whether for manure or for access to markets for grain, cheese and butter, were easily satisfied where farmers had access to canals.
- The building of canals created massive employment and spending power at a time when growing industries were looking for mass markets.

It is difficult to exaggerate the importance of canals to Britain's industrial development between 1780 and 1830.

From 1830, railways were the epoch-making transport innovation. Between 1830 and 1850, 7,000 miles of track were laid, peaking in the 1830s and again between 1844 and 1847 when investment was at its height. Their economic importance lay in their ability to handle both major types of traffic – people and goods – that no other single mode of transport had previously been able to do. They offered lower costs and greater speed, which attracted passengers, mail and high-value goods.

The railways increased demand for coal, iron and bricks. In the 1840s, 30 per cent of brick production went into railways and, between 1830 and 1845, about 740 million bricks were used in railway construction. Towns grew up around established railway engineering centres at Swindon, Crewe, Rugby and Doncaster. Food could be transported more cheaply and arrived fresher. In addition, there is no doubting the social and cultural impact of railways. This is clearly supported by the statistics: 64,000 passengers were transported in 1843; by 1848 this had increased to 174,000. In the same period, those travelling third class increased from 19,000 to 86,000 per year.

Between 1780 and 1850, great output was achieved by the transport industry, as was the case in the manufacturing industry, by applying a rapidly increasing labour force to existing modes of production as well as using new techniques and applying steam-driven machinery. Historians have emphasised the importance of canals and railways in the eighteenth and nineteenth centuries in reducing transport costs. However, coastal and river traffic and the carriage of goods and people by road remained important – the horse was still the main means of transport well beyond 1850.

Economic growth and rates of development

The main indicator of long-term economic growth is a country's **gross domestic product** (GDP). During the eighteenth century, annual GDP

How far did roads, canals and railways provide the central plank for economic development after 1780?

A country's **gross domestic product** is the income it receives from goods and services.

growth in Britain rose slightly from just under 1 per cent per year to just over it. Between 1800 and 1850, growth increased to over 2 per cent per year.

Growth in GDP depends on three things: an increase in the workforce, an increase in capital investment and an increase in productivity. Britain's growing population accounted for the increase in the workforce after 1780. Increased capital investment is also evident after 1780. Between 1780 and 1800, capital investment rose by 1.2 per cent per year. This rose slightly to 1.4 per cent between 1800 and 1830 and, largely because of investment in railways, rose to 2 per cent between 1830 and 1850. Increasing productivity is more difficult to estimate accurately, although it is clear that significant growth did occur in agriculture and the manufacturing industries that used the new technologies.

Historians have long been concerned with trying to identify the nature of growth in the British economy. Which industries did well and why? Why did some regions fare less well than others? The debate about overall growth in the economy and the rates at which particular industries developed is largely statistical. The major problem historians face in trying to work out the precise nature of economic developments in the late eighteenth and early nineteenth centuries is the unreliability of statistical data. The result is significant discrepancies in modern estimates. For example, the growth in the production of coal in the late eighteenth century has been variously estimated as between 0.64 per cent and 1.13 per cent per year. The lower figure suggests modest rates of growth, while the larger supports arguments for revolutionary growth. The inaccuracy and incomplete nature of contemporary statistics and information make it very difficult to draw conclusions about specific industries or about the economy as a whole. The problem is made worse by the contrasting experiences of different industries and regions between 1780 and 1850. For example, the south Wales iron industry grew rapidly after 1785 with the application of the puddling and rolling process to wrought-iron-making, but after 1830 its growth rates were less than those of Scotland, which had reduced fuel costs and had increased its competitiveness by using the 'hot blast' in the smelting process.

Urbanisation

In 1780, regions remained largely rural. However, industrial growth led to increasing urbanisation and the late eighteenth and early nineteenth centuries saw the rapid expansion of towns that specialised in various industries. The concentration of specialised commercial and manufacturing industries, especially skilled labour, in and around towns was a major advantage for entrepreneurs and businessmen. They were helped by the expanding communication network of roads and canals and, after 1830, railways that provided cheap supplies of raw materials and fuel as well as the means to distribute finished products.

Economic change and population growth led to the rapid expansion of urban centres. Towns attracted rural workers hoping for better wages; they saw them as places free from the paternalism of the rural environment and flocked there in their thousands. For some, migration brought wealth and security. For the majority, life in towns was little different from life in the countryside and, in environmental terms, it was probably worse. The workers had exchanged rural slums for urban ones and exploitation by the landowner for exploitation by the factory owner.

Between 1780 and 1811, the urban component of England's population rose from a quarter to a third. This process continued throughout the century and by 1850 the rural–urban split was about even. The number of towns in England and Wales with 2,500 inhabitants increased from 104 in 1750 to 188 by 1800 and to over 220 by 1851. By 1800 England was the most urbanised country in the world and the rate of urban growth had not peaked. London, with its one million inhabitants in 1801, was the largest city in Europe. The dramatic growth of the northern and Midland industrial towns after 1770 was caused largely by migration because of industry's demand for labour. Regions where population growth was not accompanied by industrialisation or where deindustrialisation took place found their local economies under considerable pressure – they were increasingly uncompetitive and had higher levels of unemployment. Surplus labour led to falling wages and growing problems of poverty.

What impact did industrialisation have on towns?

Summary questions

1 Identify and explain any *two* factors which were crucial for industrialisation in the period 1780–1846.

2 Compare the importance of at least *three* issues that changed the British economy and British society in this period.

10 Responding to economic change

Focus questions

◆ Why were there so many problems in the countryside?

◆ What was the popular response to economic change?

Significant dates

1760s	Upsurge in enclosure of arable land
1795	Speenhamland system introduced
1799–1800	Combination Acts introduced
1811–15	Luddites attack mills
1816	Widespread rioting takes place
1824	Combination Acts repealed
1830	Swing riots take place
1834	Grand National Consolidated Trades Union formed

Overview

Between 1780 and 1850, economic change had far-reaching effects on British society. From being an overwhelmingly rural and agricultural society, Britain was transformed into a manufacturing and urban society. This chapter examines how and why this process occurred, its effects on rural and urban society and the ways in which working people responded to these changes.

Why were there so many problems in the countryside?

Rural change

Change in farming took place far more slowly than in the dynamic manufacturing industries. Output increased by less than 50 per cent between 1700 and 1800 compared to nearly 200 per cent in industry and commerce. Increased productivity in farming was the result of a combination of improved techniques of farming, mechanisation and the enclosure of large areas of land.

Farming techniques

The most important changes in farming came about through improved techniques of farming: the introduction of new crops, greater attention to soil fertility and improved livestock breeding.

- Fodder crops, such as turnips and swedes, which were used to feed animals in the winter, had been introduced from the Low Countries in the mid seventeenth century and were widely used by the 1750s. They were of major importance as they allowed large waste areas to be brought into cultivation. New **rotations** of crops were introduced and their use spread throughout the eighteenth century. The most famous of these was the four courses of wheat, turnips, barley and clover introduced in Norfolk in the late seventeenth century. By providing winter feed, the new crops were responsible for the increase in livestock production in the eighteenth and early nineteenth centuries.

- The supply of manure remained of critical importance in maintaining the fertility of the soil. Until 1850, the main source of manure was animal dung and farmers within reach of towns relied heavily on **town muck**. They also made use of industrial waste materials such as coal ashes, soot, waste bark from tanneries, bones, pulverised slag from ironworks, and marl and lime. Guano, the dried droppings of seabirds, began to be imported in 1835, but until the 1840s quantities remained small. Artificial fertilisers were introduced on a commercial scale in the 1840s.

    The importance of effective **drainage** was not recognised until the mid eighteenth century. The invention of a **tile-making machine** by Thomas Scraggs and mole or drainage ploughs in the 1840s allowed clay lands to be brought into more productive use.

- Livestock breeding improved considerably during the eighteenth and early nineteenth centuries. By the 1770s Robert Bakewell, who extended the work of earlier breeders, had emerged as Britain's foremost livestock expert. Bakewell's pre-eminence rested with his improved longhorn cattle and the New Leicester sheep. Though his sheep and cattle had defects he did succeed in producing animals that were ready for market more quickly.

Mechanisation of agriculture

Farming remained a labour-intensive industry with no dramatic breakthrough in mechanisation until after 1850, but advances in stock, drainage, fertilisers and crops highlighted the need for improved farm tools and

Crop **rotation** is a farming system whereby different crops are grown in the same field in sequence. In the open-field system, wheat was followed by barley or oats and the field was left uncultivated (or fallow) for a year to recover. This meant that valuable land was not being used. New rotations meant that leaving the soil fallow for a year was no longer necessary. The four-course or Norfolk rotation, for example, worked on a four-year cycle of wheat, turnips, barley and clover. Turnips provided fodder for cattle and clover helped renew the fertility of the soil through its ability to transfer nitrogen from the air into the soil.

Town muck, the product of the swelling urban population, was either given to farmers willing to take it away or sold by people who collected urban sewage.

Drainage was a major problem in clay soils as plants with waterlogged roots cannot grow in clay soils properly. Once drained, clay soils become very fertile.

The **tile-making machine** made it possible to produce underground drainage tiles cheaply.

What were the major changes in techniques of farming between the 1780s and 1850 and what effects did they have?

machinery. Before 1800, improvements in implements, other than ploughs, proceeded slowly. Mass-produced tools originated in the 1780s; by the 1840s, Robert Ransome of Ipswich was producing as many as 86 different designs of ploughs to suit local needs. From 1786, Andrew Meikle's threshing machine began to be used and horse-drawn reapers appeared in the early decades of the nineteenth century.

Mechanisation in farming was primarily a mid-nineteenth-century development. The threshing machine was first adopted in Scotland and by 1815 it was commonly used there and in north-east England. However, it was not in general use in the south or in Wales until after 1850. Seed-drills were increasingly advertised in newspapers after 1820. Reapers and mowing machines appeared in the 1850s, but only became widely used after 1870. In 1850, most British corn was still cut and threshed by hand.

The unreliability of the early machines partly accounted for this. Far more important was the cost of labour. In the north, where labour costs were higher because of competition from non-agricultural employment, the early adoption of powered threshing made economic sense. Machines were used less in the south where cheap labour was plentiful. Some farmers kept the old methods to provide **winter employment** and thus prevent throwing their regular men on to the parish for support.

Enclosure

England contains land suitable for many different kinds of farming. In areas where animal farming dominated, land was divided into fields, often bounded by stone walls. Other parts of the country, especially central England, were dominated by large open fields divided into strips. Enclosing land into smaller fields farmed by one farmer began in the seventeenth century, especially in eastern England. **Enclosure** did more than any other development to alter the face of the countryside. By 1780, large areas of Britain had already been enclosed. Enclosure improved the efficiency of farming and made it easier, and it brought into fuller use **wasteland**, marshes, heaths and hill-grazing. Enclosure also gave villages the opportunity to improve their road system, dig drainage channels, rebuild farmhouses, barns and byres, and plant new hedgerows to provide windbreaks and shelter for stock.

Many contemporaries believed that enclosure resulted in increased productivity in terms of both improved output and rent. Increases in grain output of 10 per cent occurred in Oxfordshire, Warwickshire and Northamptonshire when enclosed fields were compared with open ones. For the landowner, enclosure was a good investment as it led to increased productivity and higher profits. Rents were increased by between 15 and 20 per cent, but this was both a cause and a consequence of enclosure. From the 1770s until

Winter employment was often provided by farmers for their regular workforce, especially in southern England. This helped keep the parish poor rate (a tax landowners paid to support the poor) at a lower level, but also reflected the widespread belief that farmers had a paternal responsibility for their workers.

Enclosure was achieved either by agreement between the local landowners or, increasingly, by getting parliament to pass an Enclosure Act. Historians disagree about the impact of enclosure on rural labour. Some argue that farmers who had enclosed their land needed fewer workers. Others suggest that during and immediately after enclosure more workers were needed. In the longer term, the combination of enclosure and mechanisation led to a reduction in the agricultural workforce.

How did enclosure change the rural landscape?

Large areas of England consisted of **wasteland** which had not been cultivated before because it would have been unprofitable to do so. The new crops ended this practice by increasing the fertility of the soil and making it profitable to farm.

the end of the French Wars, prices of wheat rose. This too helped landowners, who often relied on fixed rents for income, to enclose land and renegotiate leases with tenants who had benefited from rising wheat prices. Farmers could borrow money to enclose their land, knowing that high wheat prices would enable them to repay their loans and still make a good profit.

After 1780, population growth increased the demand for agricultural products and this explains why enclosure became increasingly important. Prices increased more rapidly than in industry. This encouraged farmers to invest in change. British farming was highly capitalised by 1800. High-intensity arable farming was situated near the main centres of population from Lancashire to London. Lower levels of investment occurred where stock-breeding dominated.

Population growth also increased the supply of labour. In 1801, 36 per cent of the population of England and Wales was involved in agriculture, forestry and fishing. This represented an increase of about 8 per cent since 1750, compared to a 70 per cent increase in the total population. Although only slightly more people were working in farming, they were feeding more people. One person employed in farming in 1750 fed 1.7 people; by 1800, this figure was 2.5. The percentage of the total population employed in farming fell relative to other industries after 1800, but the number of people employed continued to rise until 1850.

Why did farming remain important until 1850 and with what results for the rural workforce?

A chronology of change

Between 1750 and 1790, there was a gradual but consistent increase in all food prices paralleled by gradual but accelerating enclosure. Wheat became the staple grain food – 89 per cent of Londoners were on a wheat diet by 1764. Potatoes were important in the demographic growth in Ireland and parts of Scotland. Home-grown food supplies were sufficient to feed the population until the 1770s, but after that substantial imports were necessary. Corn prices began to rise faster than other food prices and faster than wages. This stimulated further change in farming.

Food shortages began to be experienced more frequently. Local shortages and food riots were often caused by the failure to distribute supplies effectively. Between 1793 and 1815, the major problem facing farmers was the cost of labour. Many farmers were forced to rely on casual workers. This did not lead to widespread mechanisation because the capital investment necessary to buy new machines was high. After **1815**, labour costs began to decrease.

Prices of wheat fell dramatically after 1814 because of good harvests and this coincided with the demobilisation of thousands of soldiers. The low wheat prices led to agricultural distress which was greatest on the clay-land arable farms and least in dairy and stock-rearing districts or in areas like Kent

The end of the French Wars in **1815** saw up to a quarter of a million men being demobilised. They had to be absorbed back into the labour force at a time when both farming and industry faced depression. This caused considerable distress in rural England where there was a surplus of workers. Farmers needed to reduce their costs (at a time of falling wheat prices) to repay loans they had taken out during the war when prices were higher. Rural wages fell.

The **Corn Laws** are examined in detail in Chapter 3 and their repeal in Chapter 6.

In what ways did farmers respond to changing conditions and why?

Mixed farming
combined arable and animal production. This allowed farmers to spread the risk of farming across two areas. When arable prices were low, animal prices could maintain profits and vice versa.

In what respects was farming more successful in 1850 than in 1780?

It had been customary for **farm workers** to be hired for a year and given food, clothes, board and a small annual wage in return for work, only living out when they wished to marry.

Rural protest against the **Poor Law Amendment Act of 1834** is examined in Chapter 12.

where hops and fruit were important crops. Farmers sought support from the government in the form of protection or reductions in taxes. The **Corn Law** of 1815 was the result.

By the 1830s many farmers had adjusted their costs to lower prices or had moved across to **mixed farming**. The social cost of depression was most severe in areas where agricultural wages had fallen. Tariffs did little to protect arable farmers because the price of corn rarely fell below 80 shillings in this period and provoked a violent reaction which the Anti-Corn Law League capitalised on in the 1830s and 1840s.

By the mid-1830s, British farming had got through its depression. The introduction of inexpensive drainage techniques freed farmers of clay lands from high production costs. Farming generally became more scientific, producing more at a lower cost. From the mid-1840s until the 1870s, agricultural production rose at 0.5 per cent per year. There was a more intensive application of the techniques of mixed farming on the light soils of southern and eastern England and on the Lothian area of south-east Scotland. There was some shift on the clay soils, especially those in the north and west of England, to beef and dairy production. This led to higher productivity at lower costs. Railways reduced transport costs. Cheap food had become both an economic and a political necessity with the result that British farming was more productive in 1850 than it had been in 1780.

Agricultural distress

After 1780 there was growing rural poverty in southern England. In 1851, James Caird, in his study of British farming, divided the country into high- and low-wage areas. In northern and parts of central England, where industrialisation was widespread, farm labourers' wages were high. In southern England, where there were few alternatives to farm labouring, supply exceeded demand and wages were significantly lower.

Two main issues affected agricultural labourers in the late eighteenth and first half of the nineteenth centuries:

- There was a gradual move from **farm work** as a relatively secure occupation to one characterised by underemployment and seasonal work at planting and harvesting times.
- Levels of rural poverty increased, especially in southern England. The labour surplus led to falling wages for agricultural workers and an increasing reliance on relief from the Poor Law in the form of doles (money to supplement wages) before 1834, and the threat of being sent to the workhouse after the introduction of the **Poor Law Amendment Act of 1834**.

Agricultural labourers were rarely at the centre of protest in the eighteenth century, but this changed after 1780. The agricultural revolution, especially enclosure, upset traditional rural society. Fewer farm servants were hired and living-in disappeared. Labourers were paid by the day or week and were employed for short periods for harvesting, hedging, ditching and threshing. Although farmers tried to keep their regular workers employed in winter, they did not feel the same responsibility towards casual workers. There was chronic underemployment in rural England, especially after 1815. As a result, the social and financial gulf between farmer and labourer widened.

What were the main causes of protest in rural England after 1780?

In 1795, Berkshire magistrates introduced a system of relief, known as the **Speenhamland** system, to supplement the wages of labourers. Similar schemes were introduced across southern England. The name gave the various schemes a sense of uniformity that they did not possess in practice. Its attempt to redress low wages became part of the framework of labourers' lives, instead of being a safety net in hard times. The system encouraged low pay and did not fully make up the difference between high prices and low wages. Wartime farming transformed much of southern and eastern England into a region dominated by wheat production. Boom conditions ended abruptly in 1815: grain prices slumped while rents, fixed during wartime inflation, did not. Farmers were faced with falling profits and sought to reduce costs by cutting wages, which was quite possible in a labour market saturated by the demobilisation of the armed forces, or by using more economical methods like the threshing machine.

The **Speenhamland** system was named after Speen, near Newbury, where the Berkshire magistrates met in May 1795. See Chapter 12 for more discussion of this system.

Why were underemployment and unemployment endemic in southern England after 1815?

What was the popular response to economic change?

Between 1780 and 1850, the way in which working people responded to economic change was transformed. In 1780, people dissatisfied with economic conditions rioted. These riots were spontaneous, largely unorganised and short-lived. During the eighteenth century, there were protests about prices, enclosure, turnpike roads, the militia and against new technology. They were reactions to specific situations and their aims were generally limited.

By 1850, working people had developed organisations like trade unions and radical movements like Chartism that allowed them to campaign for better standards of living and for a say in government. In addition, they established co-operative associations and friendly societies to provide mutual aid.

Machine-breaking was nothing new in the 1810s. What was new was the scale of the protests and their organisation. It was made a capital offence in 1813.

Protest against technological change: Luddism

In 1812, there was a series of disturbances in the Yorkshire woollen industry where skilled workers formed secret organisations dedicated to **machine-breaking**. **Croppers** too felt that they had to make a stand against industrial change. The value of woollen exports had dropped from £12 million to £1 million a year because of the French Wars. Poor harvests had pushed up the

Croppers were highly paid workers, the aristocrats of the labour market, whose skills lay in neatly cutting off the nap of the cloth, using giant iron shears that weighed up to 60 lb.

price of food. Distress was intense and the poor relief system was put under immense strain. When a crude machine was invented on which an unskilled man and a boy could do in a day what it took a skilled cropper a week to accomplish, they took direct action.

For several months in the early part of 1812, **Luddites** attacked mills. They smashed the new cropping frames, but usually left other machines and property untouched. When William Horsfall, a local mill owner, was murdered in April 1812 as he rode home from market, popular feeling turned against the Luddites – smashing machines was one thing, killing a defenceless man in cold blood was something else.

The authorities saw in these attacks the threat of potential revolution. The area was swamped with spies and informers and a reward of £2,000 was offered for information that would lead to convictions. Eventually, a magistrate extracted a confession from one of the Luddites. This led to the arrest of the Luddite leaders, who were brought before a special judicial commission at York Castle in January 1813. Twenty-four men were found guilty and 17 were executed, 14 at the same time. The others were transported for seven years. Luddism was broken. As new machines were introduced, the number of skilled croppers in the Leeds area dropped from over 1,700 to barely a handful in five years.

Luddism was not a uniform movement. In Nottinghamshire, for example, it was a non-political, but particularly violent, movement, whereas in the northern counties, it had a political dimension with revolutionary undertones. These Luddites had contacts on the continent during the disturbances of 1811–12, but the scope and importance of such seditious activity have been questioned. Luddism was a complex movement concerned with protecting people's livelihoods at a time of major technological change. It is not surprising that the way in which workers saw the problem differed and the methods they used to resolve the problem varied. For some, the solution lay in political change; for others, traditional forms of machine-breaking seemed to offer a better solution.

Spontaneous protests

There were four major outbreaks of food riots between 1790 and 1820, all relating to harvest failure and high food prices.

The harvest of 1794 was about 25 per cent below that of 1793 and led to food shortages in the spring and summer of 1795. At the same time, many industrial workers were laid off because of the trade depression caused by the French War, which also disrupted grain supplies. These circumstances combined to produce a major crisis. There were a few riots in 1794 and early 1795 and, by March, major protests began to take place. In all, there were 74

Luddites were called after their leader, real or imaginary, known as King Ludd, after a probably mythical Ned Ludd.

What were the main aims of the Luddites and what methods did they use to achieve their aims?

disturbances. The authorities took action to increase the supply of food and to regulate prices. These measures were sufficient to prevent major problems in 1796.

Good harvests between 1796 and 1798 were followed by poor yields in 1799, which pushed up grain prices sharply. This coincided with the beginnings of another trade depression. Major disturbances occurred in late 1799 and early 1800 in the industrial centres of Lancashire, Yorkshire and the Midlands. Good weather reduced tensions and prices fell in anticipation of a good harvest in 1800. The crisis was ended by the government actively encouraging imports. However, widespread rain in August caused prices to increase. This had a marked effect on consumers, who believed that the harvest had been good and that prices had increased because of speculation in the grain market by farmers, dealers, shopkeepers and merchants. Major incidents occurred in London, which was unusual as the government always tried to maintain the food supply of the capital, as well as in southern England, the Midlands, Nottinghamshire, Derbyshire, Yorkshire and Lancashire. High prices lasted through the winter of 1800–01 when industrial recession was at its height. The government instructed magistrates to deal quickly with any protests and this action led to fewer riots.

Food riots in 1810–13 and 1816–18 were again caused by food shortages and high prices. Transporting food to areas with shortages often caused problems. Urban growth made this worse by concentrating people in large cities and towns without ready access to food supplies. There were disturbances in the south-west, but the major problem was in the industrial centres of Lancashire, Cheshire and Yorkshire, which were suffering from acute commercial distress.

Food riots were replaced by other protests aimed at defending living standards in the industrial environment. Food prices stabilised from the 1820s and, combined with imports, helped reduce the potential problems caused by poor harvests. The government realised that ensuring that towns and cities had sufficient food was important to prevent public disorder.

> When and where did the major food riots occur between 1780 and 1850? What were their major causes?

The 1816 riots

Industrial workers, townsmen and agricultural labourers took action in 1816 in ways not repeated in 1822 or 1830. There were three main areas of protest:

- There were incidents in some market towns because of high food prices, a continuation of the tradition of food riots, and strike action by textile workers over falling wages.
- In Essex, Suffolk and Norfolk, there were protests by agricultural workers over the use of **mole ploughs** and threshing machines, combined with demands for a subsistence wage.

> The **mole plough** made draining the soil easier. Its use resulted in unemployment because there was less need to dig drainage ditches.

- There were also disturbances involving agricultural labourers in the Fens over low wages and high food prices.

The diversity of rioters – one in three arrested was not an agricultural labourer and one in seven had some land – reflected the impact of enclosure, drainage and depression. The local authorities had limited resources to prevent riots from spreading and, especially in the Fens, there were too few gentry to act collectively. Magistrates made concessions to stop the protest, but the dramatic breakdown of law and order could not be tolerated by central government: Lord Sidmouth, the home secretary, ordered the military to be sent to Norfolk, Suffolk and the Fens. Magistrates who had made concessions were overruled and rioters were arrested. Five rioters were executed and this, as much as anything, ensured that rioting spread no further.

Disturbances in 1822

How did local and central government deal with the 1816 and 1822 disturbances?

Falling rural wages led to protests against unemployment that occurred in three areas in Norfolk in late February and early March 1822. They all involved the destruction of threshing machines and, in contrast to 1816, these attacks were not intended to draw attention to the plight of the labourer, but were a campaign to sweep the machines away. Local magistrates acted quickly and the use of the military drove the rioters underground.

The Swing riots of 1830

In the 1820s, pauperism, desperation and discontent were almost universal in agricultural areas. The problem of pauperism was worst in the counties where extensive enclosure had taken place. High levels of relief led to increasing attempts to cut the level of local poor rates. Between 1815 and 1820, Poor Law spending was 12s 10d per head; by 1830, it was 9s 9d. Between 1824 and 1830, rural crime – mainly poaching and food theft – had increased by 30 per cent.

What caused the Swing riots in 1830?

Following poor harvests in 1829 and 1830, the Swing riots (named after the mythic leader of the movement, Captain Swing) broke out in August and lasted until well into December 1830. They took several forms: Poor Law officials and workhouses were attacked, but the destruction of threshing machines was most widespread.

The major difference between the protests in 1816 and 1822 and those in 1830 was their scale. The Swing riots were not confined to a single area, but spread across most of southern and eastern England. The aims of the rioters were remarkably similar throughout the Swing counties: men demanded a minimum wage, the end of rural unemployment and tithe and rent reductions.

The leaders of the riots were often craftsmen, but the majority who took part were labourers, often paupers on poor relief. Many of the rioters were young married men whose concern was for a living wage.

The riots began slowly and, initially at least, machine breakers were given lenient sentences. This was interpreted by many rioters as tacit approval of their actions and led to the protests gathering momentum. Revolution in France in July gave rural protest a more threatening dimension than in either 1816 or 1822.

When the Whigs achieved power in mid-November, their first priority was to suppress the disturbances. Concerted local action, especially by the gentry of Wiltshire and Hampshire, the use of troops and the unwillingness of Lord Melbourne, the home secretary, to tolerate weakness or compromise on the part of local magistrates gradually restored order.

Why did the government react harshly to the rioters?

After Swing

The crushing of the Swing movement did not destroy the willingness of agricultural labourers to protest. There was widespread action against the Poor Law Amendment Act in 1835, localised protests in the form of arson, and rural trade unions began forming in the south.

Labourers became expert at slacking in undetectable ways. More seriously, they were in a position to steal from their employers, despite severe sentences if they were caught: sheep- and horse-stealing were capital offences until 1831 and arson remained so until 1837. Poaching was widespread in rural areas. Other forms of protest included firing stacks, burning farm buildings, pulling down fences, maiming animals and breaching drainage channels.

How did rural protest continue in the 1830s and 1840s?

How did the working class develop between 1780 and 1846?

After 1780, social values that had existed largely unaltered for several hundred years began to be challenged. British society before the Industrial Revolution and, in some areas, after it was based on face-to-face, often daily, contact between individuals of different social status who recognised their 'place' in the social structure and the duties and responsibilities their rank gave them. Social control was based on acceptance of social status. Population growth, the expansion of towns and the change from a rural to an urban economy shattered this ordered structure:

- People moved to towns because they perceived them to be free from the constraints of rural society as well as providing economic opportunities. As towns and cities expanded after 1820, they became places where paternalist values had little place.
- There were important changes in religious observance. There was declining support for the Church of England in towns and cities. In the countryside, the challenge to the Church of England from Methodism broke the link between squire, parson and labourer.

- Working people, especially artisans, began to group together in trade unions to negotiate for better conditions with their employers.

These conditions led to many working people becoming increasingly conscious of their own interests. This, in turn, resulted in the development of economic and political demands for better wages and the right to vote.

How was the working class structured by the late 1840s?

Variations in standards of living, wages and working conditions were as great in towns as they were in the countryside. Average urban wages were higher, but so were rents and food prices. Women's wages were well below those of men, and families dependent on a sole female wage earner were among the poorest people. Jobs guaranteeing a regular weekly wage, with little cyclical unemployment, were rare and jealously guarded. Cyclical unemployment was the norm for most workers and was a major factor in the labour market.

Casual workers

What was the nature of casual employment in 1850?

The urban population was organised in hierarchical terms, largely in terms of levels of skill. At the lowest end of this hierarchy were the genuinely casual workers. Work like hawking and street-trading, scavenging, street entertainment, prostitution and some casual labouring and domestic work fell into this category. Casual trades were largely concentrated in large cities, especially London. Low and irregular incomes condemned casual workers to live in rooms in slums.

Unskilled workers

Above the casual workers were a whole range of unskilled occupations where workers could be hired for just a few hours and could be laid off for long periods without notice. These included labourers in the building trades and factories, carters, shipyard workers and especially dockers. All towns had such workers, but they were especially important in port cities such as London, Liverpool and Bristol, and in industries like coal-mining or clothing that had a partly seasonal market. In Liverpool over 22 per cent of the employed population in 1851 were general, dock or warehouse labourers. They needed to live close to their workplace since employment was often allocated on a first-come, first-served basis. When in work, dockers earned high wages, but few maintained these earnings for any length of time and in a bad week many earned only a few shillings. Conditions changed little between 1780 and 1850. Unskilled workers were frequently in debt and regularly pawned clothes.

What were the major differences between casual and unskilled workers?

Skilled workers and artisans

By the1820s there were two broad types of skilled workers: artisans, who provided skilled labour in traditional industries like furniture-making, and skilled factory workers, whose jobs were largely the result of changes in the manufacturing economy. After 1820, factories provided regular employment, as did public services such as railway companies and many commercial organisations. Skilled manual labour was relatively privileged: it was regular and well paid. Those living in textile towns like Manchester, Bradford and Leeds and in metal and engineering centres such as Sheffield suffered less from poverty than those living in cities like Liverpool or London. Skilled engineering trades were among the earliest to unionise, along with artisans and craftsmen. They commanded higher wages and regular employment. This gave them many advantages – they could afford to rent a decent terraced house, sometimes in the suburbs, thus avoiding the squalor of Victorian slums, but had a long way to walk to work.

Who were the skilled workers in the mid nineteenth century?

Women at work

Three major issues can be raised about working-class women's work in this period:

- First, there was a sexual division of labour. Work done by women required few skills and had low status.
- Secondly, women were a cheap source of labour.
- Finally, the Industrial Revolution brought about a decisive separation between home and work. Industrialisation shifted production into the factories or workshops. Many women were tied to the home by children, yet needed money to support themselves and their families. For them, outwork or homework, a particularly exploitative form of employment, was often their only option.

Single women often entered domestic service, but married women had severely limited choices. Away from the textile districts most found work as domestic cleaners, laundry workers, or in sewing, dressmaking, boot- and shoemaking and other trades carried on either in the home or in small workshops where wages were always low.

Women were excluded from many areas of the economy, but they dominated others. The 1851 census suggests that just over a quarter of the female population was at work and that women made up about 30 per cent of the country's labour force. Yet four activities accounted for almost 90 per cent of women's work: domestic service accounted for two out of every five working women and the textiles and clothing industries provided employment for a similar proportion. About one woman in 12 worked in agriculture. What women did depended largely on the particular economic structure of the communities in which they lived.

Did women's work change between 1780 and 1850?

Men and women brick-making by hand.

Conclusions

Class provided an identity for workers who were no longer bound by paternalist values. It evolved in response to the growing population, greater social mobility, urban growth and new patterns of work based in the factory or workshop. The popular radicalism and conservatism of the 1790s marked its beginnings. Radicalism between 1815 and 1821 gave the working class some substance. However, there were significant divisions within the working class between skilled and unskilled workers, working men and women, and rural and industrial workers.

Radicalism

Political radicalism among the working classes was one response to the changes in the economy. Working people believed that if they could get the vote they would have greater control over the changes that were taking place. For example, a parliament elected by working people could pass laws to improve working conditions in factories or make the operation of the Poor Laws fairer. During the 1790s the corresponding societies, influenced by events in France, sought change until they were made illegal by parliament. Between 1815 and 1821 Henry Hunt mobilised widespread support for extending the vote to the working classes. Between 1830 and 1832 some working-class radicals worked with middle-class reformers in support of the Whig Reform Acts. Finally, between 1838 and the early 1850s, the Chartists, the largest popular movement of this period, tried to persuade parliament to accept the six points of its charter. Each of these agitations was unsuccessful and working people were still denied the vote in 1850. They had to wait until the Reform Acts of 1867 and 1884 before some were given the vote and until 1918 for all men over 21 to be allowed to elect their MPs.

Seeking fair wages: trade unionism

The 1799 and 1800 Combination Acts made trade unions illegal. The campaign for their repeal, led by **Francis Place**, began in the improved economic conditions of the early 1820s. It was successful and in 1824 the Acts were repealed. When the economy slumped briefly in late 1824, there were union-led strikes for wage increases. Employers blamed repeal for the strikes and called for the return of the Combination Acts. Place needed all his skills to prevent this. Instead, the Trade Union Act of 1825 was introduced: it allowed workers to form trade unions, but they were not allowed to 'molest' or 'obstruct' either employers or fellow workers.

Early trade unions were small, local organisations composed largely of skilled artisans. Many workers were convinced that small unions could never succeed as they were easy targets for employers who could bring in non-unionised workers and lock workers out of their workplaces. What was needed, some argued, were national or general unions representing all the workers in a particular trade from every part of the country.

The movement towards general unionism proceeded in a piecemeal fashion:

- John Doherty, an Irishman and leader of the Lancashire cotton spinners, formed a Grand General Union of Spinners in 1829.
- To achieve greater negotiating power, Doherty's next step was to try to unite all unions in all trades into a single union. He formed the National Association for the Protection of Labour (NAPL), also in 1829. The National Association lasted two years and claimed over 100,000 members from textiles, mining and 20 other trades from as far afield as Wales and the Midlands. It had its own newspaper, *The Voice of the People*. The NAPL collapsed when attempts to back up striking spinners in Ashton-under-Lyne failed.
- Other workers formed the Operative Builders' Union, transformed by Robert Owen into a National Building Guild of Brothers in 1833. More national unions followed among potters, textile workers and others.
- In October 1833, 40 villagers formed a branch of the Friendly Society of Agricultural Labourers in the Dorset village of Tolpuddle. Six members of the branch were charged under the **Unlawful Oaths Act of 1797** for threatening not to work until their pay was guaranteed. In March 1834, they were

Francis Place
(1771–1854) was a radical activist who campaigned against the Combination Acts with the support of Joseph Hume in parliament. He also helped draft the People's Charter.

Francis Place

The **Unlawful Oaths Act of 1797** was an act passed to deal with naval mutinies.

sentenced to seven years transportation to Australia. They became known as the Tolpuddle Martyrs.

- The Grand National Consolidated Trades Union (GNCTU) was established in February 1834. The inspiration behind the GNCTU was Robert Owen, though he did not take an active role until April 1834.

Robert Owen was a successful mill owner who was one of the first theorists to write about the nature of capitalist society and suggest alternative ways of organising society. In his *A new view of society*, published in 1813, he argued that society should be based on co-operative ideas with workers living together in communities. He unsuccessfully attempted to found a co-operative community in the United States between 1825 and 1829. Owen's ideas had considerable influence on the union movement between 1833 and 1835, even though he was regarded by many working-class leaders with suspicion.

By 1833, however, his ideas had been accepted to the extent that the term 'Owenite' was used to describe trade union activity between 1832 and 1834. At first Owen took little notice of trade unions. He thought that they were selfish organisations fighting for small gains such as wage increases. When he met unionists like Doherty in 1833 he was surprised to find out how 'business-like and encouraging' they had become. For a time he saw unions as a possible way of changing society. His enthusiasm was short-lived: by mid-1834 he had come to believe that confrontation not co-operation lay behind much union activity. This judgement reflected the increasing union concern with short-term industrial gains rather than the longer-term creation of a new moral world.

Why did Robert Owen play a peripheral role in the trade union movement?

Strikes spread across the Midlands and the north in the spring and summer of 1834 as a result of attempts by employers to reduce wages. Employers reacted with considerable ferocity and in Derby they forced workers to sign **the Document**: 'We, the undersigned, do hereby declare that we are not members of a trade union; that we do not and will not pay towards the support of any such association.' About 1,500 Derby workers refused and were locked out.

The aim of **the Document** was to force striking workers back to work and to reduce the power of trade unions.

In early 1834, trade union delegates met in London to discuss the Derby strike. Two organisations emerged from this conference: the Grand National Consolidated Trades Union and the Derby Fighting Fund. Help poured in to the Derby fund, but it was not enough and the workers were slowly starved into submission.

Owen watched these events approvingly, seeing them as a prelude to the creation of a co-operative society. In the summer of 1834, he briefly became leader of the GNCTU during the protests against the transportation of the

Tolpuddle Martyrs. Owen hoped that the GNCTU's huge membership – by June 1834 it claimed to have 500,000 members (in fact, it had around 16,000) – would give workers greater control over the running of the country. This was not the view of trade union leaders like James Morrison and James Smith, who were extremely hostile to employers and sought better wages and conditions, not a co-operative society.

This division between Owen and trade union leaders did not bode well for the future. In May 1834, the London tailors went on strike. Employers presented them with the Document and demanded they leave the GNCTU. This firm action by the employers led to the end of the strike as the tailors left the GNCTU. The London cordwainers followed in late June. The loss of these two unions was a severe blow and the GNCTU collapsed in August.

The high hopes of 1830–34 had come to nothing. Trade unionists abandoned the idea of a national organisation. Some turned their energies to new causes, such as factory reform, the anti-Poor-Law agitation or Chartism. Others set out again to build strong local or single-craft unions. Mass national unions were not successfully revived until the 1880s.

How far was the failure of general unionism a result of opposition from employers and government?

Self-help

Some workers, especially artisans and skilled factory workers, sought to protect themselves by setting up working-class voluntary associations. Friendly societies and savings banks encouraged workers to save money in good times to offset the effects of unemployment, sickness and, to some extent, old age. Co-operative societies gave workers greater control over their wages by providing good-quality, cheap food, while the working-class associations gave workers greater control over their lives.

Friendly societies

By 1800, there were about 7,200 friendly societies with 648,000 members, rising to a million by 1820. Friendly societies largely developed in areas where there was some industry. In 1821, 17 per cent of Lancashire's population belonged to friendly societies, compared to 5 per cent in rural counties. This can be explained by higher industrial wages, which made saving possible, but also by the fact that industrial workers felt a greater need to make provision against sickness than those who worked on the land. The main financial benefits expected by a member of a local friendly society were a weekly allowance when he was sick and a funeral payment for his widow.

Savings banks

Savings banks appealed to artisans and the lower sections of the middle classes. The Poor Law Amendment Act of 1834 stimulated an expansion of savings bank activity in the late 1830s, because workers could save money to tide them over in times of unemployment rather than go to the workhouse.

Savings banks were more attractive in rural than industrial areas. This reflected the persistence of paternalist attitudes since many banks were established by landlords, squires, parsons or other notable figures. Many of the accounts were small, indicating that the depositors were probably workers. However, nationally the two largest identifiable groups of savers were domestic servants and children. Savings banks did not meet the needs of the poorer groups in society because they were more concerned to get the support of the better paid skilled workers. This led to the emergence in the late 1840s and particularly the 1850s of the penny bank movement, which encouraged less wellpaid workers to save a small amount each week. Some temperance societies established penny banks to help those who could not use savings banks, but who might otherwise have drunk their money away. Considerable numbers of penny banks established in the 1850s centred on a church or chapel, a club or a workplace.

In what ways could working people save in this period?

Co-operatives

There were isolated attempts to form co-operative societies before 1844. Some were the result of the influence of Robert Owen. The development of the Rochdale Equitable Pioneers Society and the opening of their store in 1844 marked the beginnings of the modern movement. What made the Rochdale society different was its decision to divide the profits from sales among all the members who made purchases from the society. If the society failed, members would lose nothing, but if it flourished they would obtain further shares of the profit. This kept members loyal to the store and gave them an immediate interest in its success. This idea was widely imitated and, by 1850, more than 200 societies had been established, largely in northern England. Co-operatives increasingly became a way of improving the economic position of working people, rather than a way of changing society.

Conclusion

The success of the friendly societies, savings banks and co-operative societies in improving the social conditions of the working population was limited. There is ample evidence of their appeal: friendly societies had more members than trade unions into the 1870s. However, their appeal was limited to those who could afford to save. For millions of people a lifetime of hard work petered out in the poverty of old age and the prospect of ending their days in the workhouse.

In what respects did working people helping themselves have only a limited impact?

1 Identify and explain any *two* factors that influenced working-class responses to industrialisation between 1780 and 1846.

2 Compare the importance of at least *three* issues which determined working-class attitudes to change in the economy in this period.

11

Children, work and education, 1833–53

Focus questions

◆ How effective was factory reform in improving children's working conditions?

◆ How were working-class children educated?

Significant dates

1830	Yorkshire slavery letters written by Richard Oastler
1833	Factory Act introduced; first state grants to elementary schools
1839	James Kay-Shuttleworth becomes secretary to the Committee of Privy Council for Education
1842	Mines Act introduced
1844	Factory Act introduced
1847	Ten Hours Act introduced

Overview

Work in the mid nineteenth century determined two things: the way in which working people spent most of their waking hours, and the amount of money they had to spend. Work also shaped most other aspects of workers' lives: their standard of living, how healthy they were, the type of housing they lived in, the nature of their family and community life, the ways in which they spent their leisure time, and the social, political and other values they held.

How effective was factory reform in improving children's working conditions?

Children, factories and reformers

Factories and mills in the textile industry developed from the 1780s. By the 1820s, cotton was almost entirely produced in mills, though the woollen trade in Yorkshire moved more slowly towards factory production. The development of factories was sufficiently advanced by the 1830s to justify a serious and sustained effort by the state to regulate them. Conditions in factories varied considerably. Some mill owners built houses for their workers and provided them with libraries and schools, but many took little care of their workers. Sarah Carpenter, interviewed for the *Ashton Chronicle* in 1849 said, 'The master carder's name was Thomas Birks; but he never went by any other name than Tom the Devil. He was a very bad man – he was encouraged by the master in ill-treating all the hands, but particularly the children. Everybody was frightened of him. He would not even let us speak.' Some mills were well organised, others were not. Mills, especially, the smaller ones, were frequently insanitary and ill ventilated. Hours of work were long for both adults and children. Women and especially children were paid much less than adult males. There is ample evidence of exploitation and cruelty towards children, especially by fellow workers and factory owners.

What were conditions like in factories in the 1820s?

Contemporaries did not agree on how widespread the ill-treatment of workers was or to what extent individual cases were used as propaganda for the **Ten-Hour Movement**. There was a wide range of experience within factories. Many late-eighteenth- and early-nineteenth-century textile mills were rural and recruited labour from the local domestic industries. Families often moved together to a new factory so that all members of a household could be employed. A weaver used to the workings of a small weaving shed would be familiar with many aspects of the work environment, if not the scale, of a factory. Boys would be apprenticed to weaving, power-spinning or be employed in the machine shop; girls would work in the carding room before moving to other low-technology jobs within the mill. Generally, as new technology was adopted, men took control of the new processes in spinning and weaving, while women were left with the older machines and more poorly paid jobs.

The **Ten-Hour Movement**, sometimes called the Short-Time Movement, was established in late 1830 to campaign for a reduction in the number of hours worked in factories to ten hours a day. Support for the movement was mobilised through local short-time committees.

Increasingly, as factories became steam powered, workers moved from rural mills to towns. The new, large urban mills offered greater opportunities, and the greater availability and wider range of employment in towns provided workers with some insurance against economic depression and unemployment.

Factory work altered labourers' lives in a variety of ways. Most obvious was the loss of freedom and independence they experienced, especially those men who had previously been their own masters. Factory workers could no longer combine industrial work with agricultural labour or other activities. Many factory masters introduced rigid and harsh regulations to keep the workforce at their machines for long hours and to break their irregular work patterns.

What opportunities did factories offer workers? What did the workers lose?

Pressures leading to change

The early industrial reformers had little or no organisation and consequently the campaign for factory reform in the early nineteenth century achieved little.

Michael Sadler
(1780–1835) was a banker and Tory MP who introduced a bill in parliament in 1831 to limit the working hours of children. He lost his seat in the 1832 general election.

John Fielden
(1784–1849) was a textile manufacturer from Todmorden. Fielden argued that, if workers were paid a decent wage, this would be good for the British economy, as it would increase spending on manufactured goods. He also believed that low wages and long hours had a disastrous effect on the health of the workers.

Richard Oastler
(1789–1861), unlike most people in the factory reform movement, was a supporter of the Tory party. He strongly opposed universal suffrage and trade unions and was an enthusiastic supporter of the rigid class structure of the early nineteenth century. However, he believed it was the responsibility of the ruling class to protect the weak and vulnerable.

Tory radicalism was something of a ragbag of attitudes that emerged in the 1820s and 1830s. Tory radicals like Oastler took a moral view on issues like child labour and the Poor Law, arguing that society had a moral responsibility to remove social evils. They believed that the state should intervene by passing laws to regulate these issues.

In 1828, John Doherty, leader of the Manchester Spinners' Union, formed the Society for the Protection of Children Employed in Cotton Factories. Doherty's organisation had two goals: to ensure that existing legislation would be enforced, and to agitate for the passage of new factory laws. The organisation continued until 1831 when it changed its name to the Manchester Short-Time Committee. At the same time, the Short-Time Movement began in Lancashire. These local organisations were central to the Ten-Hour Movement.

The movement was most active in the first half of the 1830s, between 1838 and 1841, and again from 1844 until the passage of the Ten Hours Act in 1847. Demands for reductions in the working day exposed the hardships faced by children and provided a way of attempting to limit the working day of adults. In the *laissez-faire* atmosphere of the period, any direct attempt to achieve state regulation of the working hours of adult males was doomed to failure. However, because children aged 10–13 were an essential part of the workforce, it was hoped that restricting their hours would affect the rest of the workforce's hours. The reformers did not oppose child labour, but they were opposed to unregulated labour. They judged the success of legislation not by its direct effect on child labour, but by its indirect effect on the position of adult workers.

Substantial sections of the propertied classes – merchants, gentry and professional men – recognised that their interests and values were similar to those held by artisans. Their views cut across the political spectrum, from traditional Tories to Whigs, but they were all committed to a paternalistic model of society that, if necessary, might be promoted through state intervention. After 1830, demands for reform were supported by wide range of people:

- Many of those who financed the movement, like **Michael Sadler** and **John Fielden**, were well-established factory owners and members of the Tory urban elite. They favoured a paternalist approach to children.
- Many Tory landowners wanted to extend protection to working people and children.
- Clergymen like the Tory parson George Bull of Bradford and the Nonconformist minister Joseph Rayner Stephens (who led the Lancashire Short-Time Movement from 1834 onwards) were also prominent in the movement.
- There were the mill operatives themselves and their supporters, of whom **Richard Oastler** was the most prominent. In late 1830, he sent his celebrated letter to the *Leeds Mercury* on 'Yorkshire slavery' and he later followed this up with letters to the *Leeds Intelligencer* and the radical *Leeds Patriot* in which he spoke of the 'monstrous' nature of the factory system and the 'terrors' of child labour. Oastler developed a kind of **Tory radicalism**.

- There were the Tory humanitarians, among whom **Lord Ashley** (later the earl of Shaftesbury) was most active. They were concerned about the moral and religious deprivation of young workers and the ineffectiveness of existing protective legislation.
- Romantics, like the poets William Wordsworth and Robert Southey, and the journalist William Cobbett looked back to a pre-industrial 'golden age' and blamed the Industrial Revolution for alienating workers from the land and forcing children to play a major role in the workforce.
- A final group of reformers came to the fore in the debates over amendments to the factory legislation of the 1840s. They included active supporters of *laissez-faire* principles, such as **Thomas Babington Macaulay**. They argued for regulation on economic and moral grounds. Macaulay suggested that child labour damaged the health of youngsters who would consequently be unable to achieve their potential productivity later in life. Restricting child labour was a rational means of promoting investment in the country's future workforce.

Agitation and parliament

By early 1831, short-time committees had been set up in the West Riding, Lancashire and Scotland. Thousands of pamphlets, petitions and tracts were issued, as 'missionaries' travelled throughout the textile areas of England and Scotland to highlight the horrors of child labour in the mills.

The extra-parliamentary activities of the Ten-Hour Movement strongly supported those who tried to get legislation through parliament. A petition signed by over 130,000 people was presented to parliament in early 1832. Michael Sadler then introduced a ten-hour bill; the government's response was to ask him to chair a select committee to collect evidence in connection with his bill. The committee's work was cut short by the 1832 general election.

In the election, Sadler failed to win his seat and he was replaced by Lord Ashley as parliamentary spokesman for the campaign. Factory masters organised a vigorous lobby to resist further factory legislation, arguing that shorter working hours would help foreign competitors and lead to lower wages and unemployment.

The select committee's report was published in January 1833. It highlighted the stark realities of conditions in factories and led Lord Ashley to introduce a factory bill. The report was criticised as being somewhat one-sided as it only reflected the workers' views. The government felt that the employers should be consulted and delayed the bill by setting up a Royal Commission to investigate the employment of children in factories. It was led by John Southwood Smith and Edwin Chadwick; their appointment represented an even-handed approach to the issue. In appointing them to the Royal Commission, the

Anthony Ashley Cooper, 7th earl of Shaftesbury (1801–85), was elected to parliament as a Tory in 1826 and remained in the House of Commons until he inherited his title in 1851. He championed the factory movement and was largely responsible for the Mines Act of 1842.

Thomas Babington Macaulay was a historian and MP.

Which sections of society supported factory reform and why?

government ensured that recommendations made would be more acceptable to manufacturers than the select committee's proposals.

The Commission's report, produced in 45 days, looked at factory conditions far less emotionally than the select committee had done. Its conclusions were not based on humanitarian grounds, but on the question of efficiency. Chadwick argued that human suffering and degradation led to ineffective production and that a good working environment would lead to the health, happiness and efficiency of the workforce. The report accepted the factory owners' opposition to state intervention, but argued that children were not free agents and therefore needed protection. It did not extend the same argument to adults. Within a month Lord Ashley's delayed bill was defeated; later in the year (in August) Althorp, the Whig chancellor, introduced his own factory bill that became law.

The Factory Act of 1833 applied to all textile mills, except for those manufacturing lace and silk. Its main provisions were:
- barring children under 9 from all work;
- restricting the working day of children aged 9–14 to 8 hours a day (with a maximum of 48 hours in a week) with 2 hours at school a day;
- restricting young persons under 18 to a 12-hour day and a maximum of 68 hours in a week.

Four factory inspectors were appointed to enforce the Act. They were aided by a group of resident superintendents who could start prosecutions.

The impact of the Act

There was widespread evasion of the terms of the Act. Employers wanted to employ cheaper child labour, and parents wanted their children to work and bring in much-needed income. The effectiveness of the Act rested on the factory inspectors being able to enforce the regulations. Deciding the age of children was difficult – it was not until the civil registration of births (and marriages and deaths) in 1836 that this proved possible. In addition, the inspectors and their assistants were largely ignorant of factories and their conditions. During their first four years of operation, the inspectors aimed to establish working relationships with employers.

However, the inspectors soon broadened their activities, became more critical of conditions and applied the law with greater rigour. Figures for Lancashire and the West Riding of Yorkshire suggest that about three-quarters of prosecutions were successful between 1833 and 1855. Nevertheless, fines remained low. Horner began to argue for further state intervention and was highly critical of the exclusion of silk mills from the 1833 Act. Overall, however, he believed that the Act was successful.

> What were the main differences between the select committee and Royal Commission reports on factory conditions?

> What were the main terms of the 1833 Factory Act?

> What problems did the early factory inspectors face in making the law work?

Women working in a Manchester cotton factory, 1835.

Oastler was disappointed. The Act still allowed young people to work long hours and it imposed inspection and centralisation. Factory masters were not much happier. They believed state regulation would restrict their ability to compete effectively.

Although there were several attempts in the 1830s to have the legislation changed, they were unsuccessful. The extra-parliamentary movement may have been frustrated by what had been achieved and the 1833 Act may not have been based on any real moral principles, but it did mark an important stage in the emergence of effective factory legislation and underpinned the developments of the 1840s.

Legislation in the 1840s

Factory Acts

The pace of the campaign of the 1840s varied considerably. Lord Ashley introduced bills in 1838, 1839 and 1841 to include a ten-hour amendment, but they were unsuccessful. By 1840, the factory inspectors were also in favour of further reform and hopes rose among working people that the return of the Conservatives under Sir Robert Peel in 1841 would lead to reform.

However, Peel opposed the Ten-Hour Movement right up until the passage of the Factory Act of 1847. He accepted the argument of political economists that wages would fall under a ten-hour day and the cost of production would increase, thus pushing up prices. His approach was based on a genuine concern for the welfare of workers as he believed reform would see their wages fall. In 1841, however, this concern was mistaken as acceptance of the ten-hour principle. This led to widespread and misleading publicity, which raised and then shattered workers' hopes, and intensified their hostility to the government during 1842.

Class antagonism intensified during the industrial distress and disturbances of 1841 and 1842. Strikes in mid-1842 speeded government action. In March 1843, Sir James Graham, the home secretary, introduced a factory bill that would restrict children aged 8–13 to six hours' work a day, with three hours' daily education in improved schools which would be largely controlled by the Anglican Church. Peel and Graham agreed on the importance of improving educational provision for working children and making the educational clauses of the 1833 Act effective.

Fear and prejudice came together in the massive campaign by Nonconformist groups. Graham's proposal for state assistance in the education of factory children was thought by Nonconformists and Roman Catholics to favour the Anglican Church unfairly. Parliamentary and extra-parliamentary opposition resulted in the whole bill being withdrawn.

Oastler mounted a major campaign in the spring of 1844, but he was unable to graft a ten-hour clause on to the revised factory bill. This bill, with its contentious educational clauses removed, was reintroduced in early 1844. Lord Ashley introduced a ten-hour amendment that was carried with 95 Conservatives supporting it. Peel refused to accept the ten-hour amendment or even to compromise with eleven hours, threatening to resign unless the vote went his way, and so the ten-hour amendment was thrown out.

Nevertheless, the Factory Act of 1844 made considerable improvements to the working lives of women and children:

- Children aged 8–13 became 'half-timers', working six and a half hours a day.
- Dangerous machinery was to be fenced in.
- Women shared the young persons' 12-hour restriction.
- Factories were allowed to operate for up to 15 hours a day, effectively establishing a maximum 15-hour day.

The Act caused considerable disappointment in the textile towns. A series of conferences tried to revive the ten-hour bill in parliament and, after a winter campaign, Lord Ashley tried to introduce it in January 1846. However, the debate over industrial conditions was overshadowed by the controversy over the Corn Laws (see page 68) and Lord Ashley felt morally obliged to resign his seat because he did not approve of repeal. Fielden took his place as parliamentary leader of the campaign. Fielden pushed ahead with the ten-hour bill, but he was defeated in May. A further campaign was mounted in the autumn, but gathering industrial recession weakened the case for opposition because workers were needed for fewer hours. Whig attempts to compromise on 11 hours were defeated. Eventually Fielden triumphed in May 1847, with the Ten Hours Act receiving the royal assent in June. The 1847 Act restricted working hours for women and children in textile factories to 11 hours for the first year of its operation and then to 10 hours a day. It was hoped that the result of the Act would be the introduction of the ten-hour day for adult men. This was not the case and it was not until 1874 that the ten-hour day for adult men was eventually achieved.

From 1848, there were reports of evasions in Lancashire and of masters' campaigns to repeal the Act. Several employers resorted to the **relay system**, which meant that hours of work could not be effectively enforced. Gradually, a new campaign emerged to protect the Act, but it was increasingly obvious that it was divided. Lord Ashley and a 'liberal' group were prepared to accept compromise; Oastler was not. A test case on the illegality of the relay system was heard in early 1850 and failed.

The **relay system** involved children working, resting and then working again.

How was the Factory Act of 1847 evaded?

In 1850 another Factory Act was passed, which undermined the ten-hour principle:
- Weekly hours were increased from 58 to 60 hours.
- A working day of 12 hours, between 6 a.m. and 6 p.m., was established in return for banning relays.

Children only received their fixed day of ten hours in the Factory Act of 1853.

Mines Act of 1842

Peel opposed Lord Ashley over ten-hour legislation because he believed that the moral case for reducing the working day was weaker than the economic one for not doing so. However, he accepted the moral arguments of those who sought to introduce the Mines Act of 1842. Working conditions in collieries were dangerous, and children and women played an important part in mining coal. In 1840 a Royal Commission was established to investigate the working conditions of children in coal mines and factories. Its findings were horrific: children as young as five or six worked as 'trappers' (operating doors to ventilate the tunnels). The report also commented on the poor health of the mining community. Artists, employed to go underground, made sketches of workers and these appeared when the commissioners' report was published in 1842. Their sketches were graphic and had immense propaganda value – the public was shocked. Lord Ashley drafted a bill which became law at the end of 1842:

Under what circumstances was Peel in favour of changes in the law?

A picture, from the Royal Commission report, 1842, that shocked Victorian Britain: a girl with a belt and chain dragging coal tubs underground.

- The employment of women and girls underground was made illegal.
- Boys under 10 could no longer work underground.
- **Parish apprentices** aged 10–18 could continue to work in mines.

Parish apprentices were children, often orphans, from the workhouse.

There were no clauses on hours of work and inspection could only take place to check on the 'condition of the workers'. Many women were annoyed that they could no longer earn much-needed money. In 1850, a further Act widened the authority of colliery inspectors to enable them to check the condition of machines.

How were working-class children educated?

Before 1830 the state was not involved in funding education for children but, by then, few people believed that the working classes should not be educated at all. For those who believed in social control as a means of moulding public morals and social attitudes, education was a major concern in the 1830s and 1840s:

- First, education was seen as a means of reducing crime and the rising cost of punishment.
- Secondly, it was seen as a way of keeping the child, or the child when adult, out of the workhouse.

The employment of children in factories meant many were unable to attend school. New types of schools – factory schools, Sunday schools, evening schools and infant schools – were established to compensate for these factory-related developments. These new schools sought not only to teach morals, but also to mould their pupils to fit in with the needs of an industrial society. Schools placed great emphasis on continuous and regular attendance, with teachers making sure that children were kept busy by their allotted tasks. It was assumed that such regimentation of children would make them more willing to accept the discipline of factory work.

What were the main motives behind education for children in this period?

Types of school

Different types of schooling were available for children in the early and mid nineteenth century. Day schools operated much as schools do today, from Mondays to Fridays. Sunday schools were only open on Sundays. Many children did not attend school regularly. Even if children attended a day school, their parents frequently kept them away if they were needed for working on the land during harvests or to look after younger children so the parents could work, or if the parents could not afford to pay the fees. This influenced the amount of schooling children received. Where children lived also played an important part in the amount of education they had as some areas had more schools, of whatever type, than others.

Sunday schools

From the 1780s, working-class enthusiasts and middle-class reformers were concerned with extending the amount of time working-class children spent at school. Among the most successful enterprises were Sunday schools, which originated in the 1780s. In 1801 there were 2,290 Sunday schools, increasing to 23,135 in 1851, with over 2 million enrolled children. This meant that three-quarters of working-class children aged 5–15 attended school. Sunday schools fitted into working-class life for two main reasons:

- Sunday was the one day when schooling did not compete with work.
- Chapels or churches could be used as schoolrooms and teachers gave their services free, so that if fees were charged at all, they were very low.

This did not mean that working-class children always attended Sunday schools. Parents sometimes objected to the religious aspects of their teaching or could not or would not pay fees.

Voluntary day schools

The promotion of day schools led to the formation of two religious, voluntary societies. The **National Society** for Promoting the Education of the Poor in the Principles of the Established Church in England and Wales was formed in 1811 and, three years later, the British and Foreign School Society replaced the **Lancastrian Society**, which had been formed in 1808. The schools were run

The **National Society** was an Anglican body established in 1811 in opposition to the work of the Lancastrian Society. Its origins lay in the work of Reverend Andrew Bell (1753–1832) in Madras, India, in developing the monitorial (or Madras) system.

The **Lancastrian Society** was founded by supporters of the educational ideas of Joseph Lancaster (1778–1838) in 1808. Lancaster had developed the monitorial system independently of Bell, around the same time. In 1814, it became the British and Foreign School Society, a change that offended Lancaster. In 1818, he emigrated to North America, where he opened a number of schools.

Lancaster's monitorial school in Borough Road, London, 1805.

along religious lines: the National Society schools by the Anglicans and the British and Foreign School Society's schools by the Nonconformists. The effectiveness of these schools was not helped by their teaching methods:

- Both favoured the monitorial or mutual system of teaching, by which a teacher taught the older children (or monitors) who then passed on what they had learnt to groups of younger children. This system was designed to enable a single teacher to cope with very large groups of children.
- Teaching was mechanical in its approach, relying on rote learning and memorisation, but it was economical and this appealed to many contemporary adult observers. The reaction of the children who were taught this way was far less positive.

Private schools

Historians have identified a large sector of cheap, private day-school education run by private individuals outside the voluntary and Sunday school system. One in four working-class children was educated in this way. The reasons why many working-class parents rejected the new National and British schools and chose slightly more expensive private day schools were threefold:

- They had no taint of charity or of social control.

- They were not regarded as part of the authority system and parents could regard the teachers as their employees.
- They also fitted in with working-class lifestyles. Children were allowed to come and go to fit in with existing work patterns.

Conclusion

The expansion of these types of education resulted in the creation of a more literate working class. In 1833, Lord Kerry's Returns on Elementary Education showed that 1.2 million (about a third of all children in England and Wales aged 4–12) attended private and voluntary day schools. He also found that 1.6 million attended Sunday schools (0.5 million of these also attended day schools). Yet, it was not enough – by 1855, 39 per cent of children between 4 and 12 (1.5 million) were still not at school.

What types of schools were available for working-class children in the 1830s and 1840s?

The state and working-class education, 1833–50

Everyone agreed that education should have a religious core. Anglicans, as members of the established church, argued that any school supported by government funds should be controlled by the Anglican Church. Nonconformists and Roman Catholics hotly disputed this. It was for this reason that the two voluntary day school societies were joined by a third, the Catholic Poor School Committee, in 1849.

Public support for the voluntary societies' schools began with a grant of £20,000 in 1833 for school buildings. This was inevitably channelled through the two religious societies. The Factory Act of 1833, the Mines Act of 1842 and the Factory Act of 1844 limited the number of hours children could work. The idea behind this legislation was that if there was no work for children to do lawfully, they would go to school instead. The growth of education grants increased dramatically from the original £20,000 in 1833 to £370,000 by 1850. The continuation of central grants ensured the expansion of **Her Majesty's Inspectorate**.

Her Majesty's Inspectorate was responsible for inspecting schools to ensure the grant was properly spent.

Grants were the first form of state involvement in education, but during the 1840s other forms of central control over education were introduced, largely through the work of James Kay-Shuttleworth, secretary of the Committee of Privy Council for Education (the body set up to make sure that grants were used properly) between 1839 and 1849:

- He believed that better standards would only be attained through properly trained teachers. He set out to attract teachers of the right class and calibre by raising salaries. In 1846 teacher apprenticeships were introduced. From the age of 13, teacher trainees would receive a grant of £10, which increased to £20 when they were 18. They had to pass the Inspectorate's annual examination. Their role was to assist the master in teaching; he, in turn, would train them in class management and routine duties. Kay-Shuttleworth intended trainees to come from the upper working and lower middle classes and to form a social link between the children of labourers and the school managers, who were clergy or gentry.

- Kay-Shuttleworth believed that better paid and trained teachers were the key to better standards. Teacher training colleges formed the top rung of this ladder of recruitment. In 1839 there were 4 training colleges in the United Kingdom with courses lasting between six weeks and three or four months. By 1850 there were 29 colleges, partly financed through queen's scholarships (grants to help student teachers).

By 1850, attitudes were changing. Many people accepted that elementary education should be under state control. Some Nonconformists, especially the Congregationalists and Unitarians, continued to oppose state-funded education, but they were increasingly in a minority. By 1850, more than £370,000 was allocated by the state for education. Under Kay-Shuttleworth's successor, Ralph Lingen (1849–70), the work of the Education Department, as it became in 1856, steadily expanded.

In what ways did the state intervene in education in the 1830s and 1840s?

Summary questions

1 Identify and explain any *two* factors that determined the development of factory reform in the 1830s and 1840s.

2 Compare the importance of at least *three* issues that improved the lives of working-class children in this period.

From Speenhamland to the new Poor Law, 1830–47

Significant dates

1795 The Speenhamland system is introduced

1815 The French Wars end

1830 Swing riots take place

1832 Royal Commission set up to investigate the workings of the Poor Law

1834 Poor Law Amendment Act abolishes the old Poor Law system and replaces it with a new system based on the workhouse, Poor Law unions and central control through the Poor Law Commission

1834–38 Anti-Poor-Law agitation takes place

1845–46 Andover scandal occurs

1847 Poor Law Amendment Act reorganises the running of the Poor Law system by abolishing the Poor Law Commission and creating the Poor Law Board

Overview

Many people in the 1830s and 1840s saw poverty as part of the natural order of things. They made a distinction between the 'deserving poor', those for whom poverty was the result of circumstances often out of their control, and the 'undeserving poor', whose poverty was largely their own fault. After 1830, however, this gradually changed as society began to regard poverty as a state caused by the moral weakness of the individual. The poor, massed together in large towns, were regarded as a social menace. This attitude gave impetus to

A **pauper** was an individual who received benefits from the state through the Poor Law system. A labourer who was out of work and in receipt of benefits was termed an able-bodied pauper, and the sick and elderly in receipt of benefits were called impotent paupers. In times of economic distress, many poor people were likely to become paupers.

Sometimes called justices of the peace, **magistrates** were judges in the local courts, but also had important administrative functions. They tended to be leading property owners.

The **poor rate** was paid by all rate payers (inhabitants and landowners). The amount collected varied in each parish.

overseer of the poor At least two people were appointed by the vestry each year to collect the poor rate and supervise its distribution.

After 1662 **legal settlement** was granted after 40 days' residence and the parish was then responsible for poor relief if needed. Itinerant workers had to carry a certificate from their own parish stating that they would be taken back.

What was the old Poor Law and how did it operate?

Poor Law reform in 1834. Relief continued to be offered, but only in the workhouse, where the **paupers** would be made less comfortable than those who chose to stay outside and fend for themselves. The thinking behind reform was that those who were genuinely in need would enter the workhouse, rather than starve.

Why was there increasing opposition to the old Poor Law?

The Speenhamland system and the old Poor Law

The old Poor Law was introduced in 1598 and 1601. Until 1834, it remained a varied system that catered for the material needs of paupers. It had been designed when England was a rural society in which work and employment were seasonal. Industrialisation and growing urbanisation from the mid eighteenth century, combined with the economic and social impact of the French Wars after 1793, resulted in changing attitudes. Many believed that the Poor Law was in need of reform.

The parish, supervised by the local **magistrates**, was responsible for collecting the **poor rate** and the income was distributed to needy parishioners by the **overseer** or was used to pay for paupers' medical treatment.

In the seventeenth and eighteenth centuries, poor relief was usually given in the form of outdoor relief: money, food, clothing or other goods were given to paupers who continued to live in their own homes. The able-bodied paupers were sometimes given work. Parishes developed different ways of paying relief such as pensions, dole, bread allowances or payments in kind.

A system of indoor relief, given in workhouses, originated in the 1720s. Early workhouses were largely intended for the sick, the elderly and orphans. The Workhouse Act of 1723 allowed parishes to join together to establish workhouses to share costs. By 1815, there were 2,000 workhouses with between 20 and 50 inmates each. The workhouses cost around a quarter of all Poor Law expenditure, but helped only 1 pauper in 12. Gilbert's Act of 1782 allowed parishes to join voluntary unions that administered the Poor Law and employed paid officials. By 1834, there were about 70 voluntary Gilbert Unions, involving over 900 parishes.

The Poor Law Act of 1601 stated that paupers could only obtain relief in their parish of **legal settlement**. However, this allowed migrant workers and vagrants to move to a new parish and quickly obtain the right to receive relief, which placed a considerable financial burden on parishes. The Settlement Act of 1662 (known as the settlement laws) tightened these rules, allowing paupers to be removed from one parish to the parish in which they were born. It has been estimated that around 15,000 people were still being removed each year by the 1850s.

In the 1790s, economic distress led to the introduction of 'allowances in aid of wages'. This was generally known as the Speenhamland system. Berkshire magistrates met in the Pelican Inn at Speen in May 1795 and devised a system that supplemented wages. The allowance was paid from the poor rates and was based on the current price of bread, the amount of the applicants' wages and the size of their families. The same idea was used across southern and eastern England, but it operated only occasionally in a few parishes and was often abandoned. Nevertheless, the Speenhamland system was significant because it symbolised (to those opposed to the old Poor Law) the inefficiency and increasing cost of the existing system. In particular, there was a widespread belief that the system encouraged larger families than people could afford.

Pressures leading to change

The old Poor Law provided no clear answers to certain critical questions:
- Should unemployment be regarded as an offence or as a misfortune?
- Should relief be administered as a deterrent, as a dole or as a livelihood?

To those who believed in free-market principles, the settlement laws and outdoor relief limited the ability of people to move around in search of work. The Poor Law also came under attack from other quarters:
- The Reverend **T. R. Malthus** demanded its abolition. He argued for the need to delay marriage (reducing the number of children in families) and for an end to both the settlement laws, which distorted the free market, and to the Speenhamland system, which, he believed, encouraged the married poor to have children they could not afford.
- The economist David Ricardo maintained that the more relief was given to the poor, the less money would be available for wages.
- The growing cost of relief was also a cause for concern: Poor Law spending trebled during the French Wars and had reached £8 million by 1817. The cost of relief fell in the early 1820s, but rose again, reaching over £7 million in 1831 and £8.3 million in 1832 and 1833.

Landowners and tenant farmers bore the brunt of these higher rates. The Swing riots of 1830 (see page 138) were the final blow to the old system: many believed that if the existing, expensive system could not deliver social stability, then it should be reformed

By the early 1830s, opinion on the Poor Laws was broadly divided into three groups:
- Humanitarians, radicals and paternalistic Tories were among those who wished to retain the Poor Laws. They believed that there was a strong argument, based on humane social responsibility, for providing a measure of social security for the labouring poor.

What was the Speenhamland system and why did contemporaries criticise it?

T. R. Malthus (1766–1834) was a clergyman who published his *Essay on the principles of population* in 1798, with a second edition in 1803. Those who supported his ideas were known as Malthusians. Malthus argued that population rose faster than the resources necessary to sustain it. Unless population growth was limited, he suggested that there would be a subsistence crisis with widespread famine and disease. This would then cut population back to its natural level. The Great Famine in Ireland in the 1840s is often cited as the classic case of a Malthusian crisis.

Thomas Malthus (1766–1834).

Edwin Chadwick
(1800–90) was the
leading social reformer of
the 1830s and 1840s. An
inspired administrator, he
laid the foundations of
reform of the Poor Law,
factories, the police and
public health. This did not
make him popular, a
problem made worse by
his inability to manage
people.

What different
attitudes were there to
Poor Law reform?

Edwin Chadwick
(1800–90).

The **workhouse test**
meant that all relief had to
be given in the workhouse,
ending the practice of
outdoor relief.

- The second group, which was similar in composition to the first, wished to modify the existing system. Although they were motivated to some degree by the same sentiments as the first group, they wished to reduce the cost of the Poor Law.
- The third 'progressive' group, consisting of individuals like **Edwin Chadwick**, political economists and supporters of Malthus, was the most influential. Its supporters believed that labourers should operate within a free-market economy and that the Poor Law should be a deterrent to those who were able to work, but who were unwilling to under the existing system of relief.

The third group had the better of the argument. By the early 1830s, it was widely believed that the Poor Laws encouraged laziness and vice. The Whigs decided that it was necessary to look at the existing system and set up a Royal Commission in 1832.

What was the thinking behind the Poor Law Royal Commission and the Poor Law Amendment Act of 1834?

The 1832 Royal Commission

A Royal Commission was set up in 1832 to investigate the workings of the Poor Law. Twenty-six assistant commissioners were appointed. They toured the country, submitting reports on the provinces and gathering replies to the Town Queries and Rural Queries surveys that had been sent out in August 1832. Just how selective they were in their collection of evidence is a matter of considerable debate. However, the conclusions they reached did reflect the preconceived views of the leading commissioners, especially Edwin Chadwick and the economist Nassau Senior.

The Commission's report, published in 1834, reflected contemporary opinion that the Poor Law *was* the cause of poverty. Chadwick argued that the Speenhamland system was demoralising and that it pauperised rural labourers because it removed the fear of hunger and led to idleness. He believed that, if the system was scrapped, the idle pauper would be forced to seek work.

The motives of those who framed the Poor Law Amendment Act were clear. Chadwick argued that the old Poor Law hindered productivity. He wanted to drive the able-bodied poor into the open labour market. This would reduce levels of poor relief and, as a result, provide capital for economic development and increase productivity.

The Commission's report established the three main principles of the new system:

- the **workhouse test**;

- 'less eligibility', which meant that those who were unable or unwilling to make provision for themselves would only be able to obtain poor relief on terms less favourable than those obtained by the lowest paid worker in employment;
- administrative centralisation with uniformity of provision.

What do you understand by less eligibility and the workhouse test? How were they linked?

The workhouse test was used to put less eligibility into practice. If an individual wanted relief, it would only be available in the workhouse and it would be less than the wages paid to an independent worker. It was believed that this would remove the attraction of the Poor Law for the able-bodied pauper. Chadwick believed that the able-bodied poor did not need looking after and that this was not the intention of the old Poor Law. For this reason, the report recommended that outdoor relief would not be offered. Chadwick accepted that the old, ill and orphaned needed support and planned for them to be housed separately in the new workhouses, which would operate under strict rules. The report was not concerned with reducing poverty, but with deterring pauperism.

What conclusions did the Royal Commission come to?

The new Poor Law, 1834–47

The Poor Law Amendment Act closely followed the recommendations of the Royal Commission's report. It was introduced in April 1834, becoming law in August:
- Parishes were to be grouped together to form Poor Law unions, which would be administered by professionals and salaried officials. They would be responsible to an elected boards of guardians. Parishes continued to pay for the relief of their own poor, but this money was to be paid into a common fund, administered by the unions.
- The Act dealt with paupers, rather than the poor, through the medium of the workhouse test. Paupers were those who were in receipt of relief from the Poor Law system.
- Unions were also subject to the central control of the Poor Law Commission, a three-man body of which Chadwick was secretary. The Commission was responsible for ensuring that the new system was operated in the same way throughout the country.

What were the main elements of the Poor Law Amendment Act of 1834?

Although the Poor Law Amendment Act legislated for all relief to take the form of indoor relief, it was not practical to abolish outdoor relief completely. However, relief for those unwilling to fend for themselves was to be based on the belief that pauperism resulted from defects of character and that there was always work available if it was sought strenuously enough. These values were adopted for the rest of the century. The sense of shame at the acceptance of relief, the stigma of the workhouse and the dread of the pauper's funeral

What change in attitudes to poverty was reflected in the 1834 Act?

Political economists were those economists who argued for an economy operated on the principles of the free market.

Patronage was a system of appointing people to government positions that was based on social position rather than merit or ability.

were central features of the lives of the working population. The 1834 Act embodied the ideas of the **political economists**, but its opponents saw it as an abuse of the poor.

Introducing the new system

Patronage was at the heart of government in the 1830s and, as a result, Chadwick was not appointed one of the three central commissioners of the Poor Law Commission, largely because of his middle-class origins. However, he did persuade the government to accept him as permanent secretary to the Commission. This proved an unworkable solution because only one of the three commissioners sympathised with Chadwick's views. This meant that from 1837 the Commission paid little attention to Chadwick's advice and that as a result he had little influence over the policies and direction of the Commission.

Consequently, the Poor Law administration was divided into two camps. Most of the assistant commissioners supported Chadwick. However, they were under the direction and in the power of the anti-Chadwickian Commission. This had a damaging effect on the administration of the system. Chadwick suffered most: public opinion held him responsible for the Commission's policy, over which he had no influence.

It was not possible to implement the Act as Chadwick had intended. The Act was based on Chadwick's report, yet his investigation into the problem of the rural poor was seriously flawed. On critical matters like rural wage rates, actual numbers of unemployed and regional variations, very little reliable data was collected. In addition, Chadwick had little understanding of the nature of urban poverty or how the old Poor Laws operated in towns and cities where relief was seen as a temporary measure to help workers who were unemployed because of a slump in trade until the economy revived and they were back in full-time work.

The administrative aspect of the Act also suffered from critical weaknesses:

- The first was the independent status of the Commission. The new Poor Law was criticised in parliament, where the commissioners had few supporters. This total separation from parliament made the Commission weak, confused and subject to political pressures.
- The second weakness was the power still left to local authorities. Chadwick did not fully implement centralisation for two reasons: first, he believed that a national (as opposed to a local) poor rate would be too expensive; secondly, he expected that local guardians who wanted to reduce the cost of the poor rates would accept and act on the instructions issued by the central Commission. In fact, this was a recipe for conflict between central and local government.

What were the major administrative weaknesses of the new system?

The weaknesses of the Act were not wholly Chadwick's responsibility. The recommendations of the Royal Commission were modified as the Poor Law Amendment legislation went through parliament, something over which Chadwick had little control. Central government had removed coercive powers over the local unions from the hands of the commissioners. This meant that the Act gave far more freedom to local unions than had been intended. The 1834 Act did not define the political status of the Poor Law Commission or its relationship to local institutions. Its independence from central political control meant that it lacked the necessary authority to impose its will on the Poor Law unions which also left it vulnerable to attacks in parliament. The Poor Law Amendment Act of 1847 (see below) largely remedied these deficiencies.

Despite the important deviations from Chadwick's original proposals, much of his work survived and, in a few instances, his most serious errors were corrected; for example, the local **dietaries** were allowed instead of those produced by the commissioners.

One of the most important achievements of the 1834 Act was that it laid the foundations of modern central government: the basis of centralisation had been established.

Dietaries were the lists of prescribed meals.

In what respects did the 1834 Act mark the foundations of the modern state?

How did the new Poor Law work in practice?

Administration

The Poor Law Amendment Act was implemented with speed and determination. Nine assistant commissioners were appointed; by 1836, this figure had risen to 16. By the end of 1835, 2,066 parishes had combined to form 112 unions and, by December 1839, 13,691 parishes out of approximately 15,000 had been incorporated into 583 unions.

The reduction in costs was considerable. By 1838, the commissioners reported that the country had been saved about £2,300,000 'direct annual taxation'. Although costs began to rise after 1837, they did not reach the levels of 1834. This was a success for those who wanted to reduce costs. For those who saw the 1834 Act as a means of social control, there were also claims of success. By 1835, the commissioners said they were providing better relief for the aged, infirm and sick, and had improved the education of pauper children as well as the industry and moral habits of the able-bodied paupers.

The southern counties felt the impact of the new Poor Law even before the new unions were created. Some places took the opportunity to reduce poor relief radically. The Uckfield Union in Sussex reduced its costs in one year from £16,643 to £8,733, of which only £5,675 was spent on the poor, the remainder being used to build a workhouse. Immediate reductions occurred in other areas, if not on the Uckfield scale. In east Yorkshire, expenditure fell by 13 per cent in 1835 and by 27 per cent between 1834 and 1837. Parishes were still responsible for collecting the poor rate to cover the cost of their own paupers. This made it difficult for unions to develop effective financial strategies and it was a problem not solved until the 1860s when they became responsible for collecting the poor rate.

The commissioners wanted the unions to consist of a circle of parishes situated around a market town and some unions did conform to this pattern. Many did not. In some rural areas, assistant commissioners were often only given the support of the landed aristocracy and gentry as long as the assistant commissioners made the estate the area of the union. Where this occurred (as, for example, in Woburn, Bedfordshire, where the dukes of Bedford owned land), landowners were able to control migration of labourers into parishes and so limit the poor relief that was paid out. There were, therefore, considerable differences in the size, shape, population and wealth of the unions. Instead of introducing administrative uniformity, the 1834 Act introduced a period of considerable diversity and experiment in local administrative areas.

The workhouses

The well-regulated workhouse was the centrepiece of the new system. Creating the Poor Law unions was straightforward, but the building of workhouses was far more contentious. The Poor Law Commission could order the extension of existing workhouses, but it could not insist on the building of new ones. In the 1830s, 350 workhouses were built, largely in southern England. There was far more resistance in the industrial north and in parts of Wales. The Leeds guardians, for example, refused to build a new workhouse until 1859, while the building of workhouses in north Wales was delayed by the determined opposition of the Caernarfon guardians.

Chadwick had never intended that the deterrent workhouse test should apply to all. The new workhouses were intended for orphans, the old and the infirm; existing parish workhouses were to be used for the separate treatment of the young and the able-bodied. He hoped to house lunatics, the blind and other special categories separately. This proved impractical as a single large workhouse was more efficient. The result was that the 'deserving poor' were treated little differently from the 'undeserving' able-bodied.

Who was the workhouse intended for? How did this work out in practice?

The commissioners never intended the workhouses to be places of repression for the able-bodied. Nevertheless, the inmates were put to heavy work, subjected to discipline (including the banning of tobacco and alcohol), and men and women were separated. The workhouses were seen by the working class and critics of the new system as 'prisons without crime'. Dietaries published by the commissioners were sufficient, but food was stodgy and

The women's yard of a workhouse. A typical drawing of the late 1830s.

monotonous. Although inmates had to wear workhouse uniforms, the commissioners resisted the attempts of some guardians to clothe unmarried mothers in yellow as a badge of shame.

Indoor relief in the workhouse was the feature of the 1834 legislation that caught the attention of contemporary opinion. It was seen by working people as humiliating and the stigma of going to the workhouse remained throughout the century. However, over 80 per cent of paupers remained on outdoor relief after 1834. In 1837, 11 per cent of all paupers had been workhouse inmates; by 1844, the figure was no more than 15 per cent. Despite Chadwick's and the Act's intention, it proved impossible to outlaw outdoor relief and it remained central to the new system.

The Victorian workhouse was faced with the impossible task of providing a refuge for the weak, while deterring the scrounger. This was the dismal view of contemporary critics in the 1830s and 1840s, such as *The Times* and the novelist Charles Dickens. The picture of the workhouse presented by its early opponents suggested a life of horror: for even the mildly awkward, there were savage beatings and solitary confinement in the most unsuitable of cells. For the majority, existence was endured on a starvation diet, families were ruthlessly separated, accommodation was overcrowded and unhealthy and daily life was a monotonous routine supervised by unsympathetic officials. Finally, for those who died in the workhouse, the end was a pauper's burial without dignity or respect.

For the modern historian the picture is not so entirely bleak. Most historians accept the conclusions of David Roberts that the sensational stories of cruelties were largely false. In a number of cases, such as the flogging of young girls at the Hoo workhouse or the **Andover scandal**, the local authority could be shown to have ignored the directives of the central authority. However, this did not entirely excuse the inadequacy of the supervision that allowed such incidents to take place.

Just how cruel workhouses were is a question obscured by propaganda and myth. They were often overcrowded, but their nature varied. The characters of the master and matron, the union boards and the regional Poor Law assistant commissioner were crucial. The new workhouses were often less crowded and insanitary than those built before 1834. The most resented deterrent of the new Poor Law, and the most obvious contrast with the old system, was the strict monotonous workhouse routine and the growing stigma attached to being a pauper.

As a result of the Andover scandal, the government decided that the Poor Law Commission must go, partly to placate public opinion, but also because it had done its work. The poor rates had been cut, outdoor relief for the able-bodied had been reduced, and almost the whole country had been unionised. The time had come when the Poor Law commissioners could be replaced by a body with fewer powers and one that was directly responsible to parliament. When the Act that had extended the life of the Poor Law Commission ran out in 1847, it was not renewed. The Poor Law Amendment Act of 1847 set up a new body, the Poor Law Board.

Why was there widespread opposition to the introduction of the new Poor Law?

The old Poor Law provided some flexibility in dealing with poverty. It was regarded by many labourers as their right in times of hardship. It was not

The **Andover scandal** was highly publicised. At Andover, work was hard, discipline strict and the diet scanty. The work the paupers did was to crush bones and, eventually, hunger led to them to eat the marrow from decomposing bones. In March 1846, a select committee of the House of Commons was established to investigate the scandal and the conduct of the Poor Law commissioners.

How were workhouses organised?

surprising that the introduction of the 1834 Act and especially the workhouse test provoked widespread hostility and opposition.

Rural opposition

Although the 1834 Act had a relatively easy passage through parliament, it came up against some opposition. In his pamphlet *The legacy to labourers*, William Cobbett described the Act as an attack on the right to relief and an assault on the traditional arrangements between the propertied and the poor. Others saw it as an attack on the independence of local government. Working-class radicals saw it as part of an assault on the livelihood of the poor by a penny-pinching government.

Why was there general opposition to the 1834 Act from radicals like William Cobbett?

The first reaction to the implementation of the Act came in agricultural areas where it was greeted with hostility. There were numerous disturbances in East Anglia and the southern counties. This situation was aggravated by a hard winter that forced many unemployed labourers to apply for relief. Attempts to separate male and female paupers under the new regulations were seen as part of a Malthusian plot to stop the poor from having children. There were also rumours that workhouse food was laced with an anti-fertility sub-stance and even that it was poisoned. The most serious disturbances took place in Suffolk, where strong local feeling was more evident than in many other parts of the country. Anglican clergymen also openly opposed the new law. The landed gentry were in a difficult position. There was often consider-able local sympathy for the rioters, and many gentry and parsons petitioned against the Act. However, they would not condone the use of violence or threats against the new system.

Historian Anthony Brundage suggested in the 1970s that there was consid-erable continuity between the old and new systems: the new guardians and Poor Law officials were often the same men who had operated the old system. He also argued that the 1834 Act strengthened the authority of the landed classes by increasing their control over how the system operated in practice. Poor Law unions were created quickly, despite opposition, and were used to maintain a largely deferential society. However, the historian Peter Mandler argues that continuity in practice and personnel did not necessarily mean continuity of principles for the landed classes. Some farmers accepted the principles of *laissez-faire*, while other retained their deferential attitudes and both played a role in the acceptance of the new arrangements in rural England.

Reactions varied from locality to locality, but there was little serious vio-lence. The disturbances did little to change the implementation of the Act; by mid-1836 the new system was operating across the agricultural south. The rural movement never gained the support or the success it achieved in the north.

What form did opposition take in rural England and why was it unsuccessful?

Urban opposition: the north

Initially the Act was received favourably by the powerful provincial northern press because they felt it was irrelevant to the industrial areas, where poor rates were much lower than in the southern agricultural areas. However, implementation of the Act in the north from the end of 1836 aroused serious and sometimes violent opposition, largely because of the first signs of depression there. Much of the opposition was organised by Tory radicals such as Michael Sadler and Richard Oastler (see p.150) who attacked the Poor Law as the 'catechism of Hell' and the workhouses as '**bastilles**'. These middle-class Tory reformers, already prominent in campaigning for factory reform, provided an organisation against the new Act that the resistance in the south lacked. The campaign stressed the Christian duty of the rich to assist the poor.

The sensitivity of the assistant commissioner to local circumstances was central to the degree of opposition that occurred. In the north-east, Sir John Walsham was able to get the new system accepted. By contrast, in Lancashire and the West Riding, Charles Mott was more confrontational and this led to widespread opposition. The *Halifax Guardian* opposed the Poor Law as 'unEnglish, pernicious and wicked' and published accounts of the ill-treatment of the poor. Riots by local ratepayers at Todmorden led to the military intervention to keep order. In Stockport, the workhouse was attacked. All this delayed the introduction of the new system: it was not introduced into Leeds until 1844 and Liverpool was given permission to return to the former system of administering relief under its own local Act.

By 1838, the violent phase of resistance had died down. In 1839, the campaign began to disintegrate as working-class resentment was appeased by the continuation of outdoor relief. Chartism began to attract the more radical agitators. The anti-Poor-Law movement in the north was a temporary alliance between the working and middle classes against what was seen as an unjust law.

Opposition to the 1834 Act did little to delay its implementation in southern England, but in the north it delayed effective implementation until 1838 and, even then, local concessions meant that outdoor relief remained important. The intentions of the 1834 Act were significantly diluted in practice. The northern campaign demonstrated that exerting pressure through the press, pamphlets and meetings did make a difference. This stands in contrast to the more traditional, less organised and less effective reactions in the agricultural areas.

Further reform

Between 1837 and 1842, Britain lay in the grip of hunger and industrial depression. It was consequently impossible to operate the new Poor Law as

The Bastille was the French castle in the centre of Paris that was attacked by the Parisian mob on 14 July 1789, an attack which signalled the beginnings of the French Revolution. It was seen as a symbol of royal oppression. The workhouses, often surrounded by high walls, looked like prisons and so acquired the name of **bastilles**.

What form did opposition take in northern England and why was it more successful than the south?

Chadwick had intended. Opposition to the Poor Law became a central theme of Chartism (see Chapter 14) and the Chartists undertook a ceaseless campaign against the Commission. It was soon clear that outdoor relief could not be abolished.

This was recognised in 1842 when the Commission devised the Labour Test Order that allowed outdoor relief as long as the paupers did some work. Increasingly the unions moved away from abandoning outdoor relief. It is clear that the principles underlying the 1834 Act were not widely applied. The workhouse test was generally ignored, with even the rural unions moving against it from the 1840s because administering indoor relief was so much more expensive than outdoor relief.

Why did attitudes to outdoor relief change in the early 1840s?

The life of the Commission was extended for five years in 1842, but its days were numbered. Critics gained strength from a series of mistakes, epidemics and scandals, provoking public demands for reform of the worst abuses. The Andover scandal of 1845–46 was the last straw. When the Commission came up for renewal once more in 1847, it was replaced by a Poor Law Board consisting of a president, accountable to parliament, and two secretaries, one of whom might be an MP, as set out in the Poor Law Amendment Act of 1847.

The 1847 Act had two great merits. First, it remedied the weakness caused by the old Commission's independent status. The government was now genuinely responsible for the implementation of the Poor Law and there was a proper channel between the Board and parliament. Secondly, it silenced the long agitation against the new Poor Law and meant that the new Board could undertake a common-sense policy of gradual improvement. It was aided in this by the improved economic situation and by the fact that the settlement laws were also removed in 1847.

How was the central administration of the Poor Law changed in 1847?

Summary questions

1 Identify and explain any *two* factors that helped strengthen the case for the reform of the Poor Laws in 1834.

2 Compare the importance of at least *three* issues that determined the problems facing the new Poor Law between 1834 and 1847.

Chadwick and public health, 1830–54

Significant dates

1831–32	First outbreak of cholera
1842	Chadwick's Sanitary Report appears
1848	Public Health Act passed
1848–49	Second outbreak of cholera
1853–54	Third outbreak of cholera
1854	Chadwick dismissed from General Board of Health

Overview

William Sproat, a keelsman from Sunderland, was not well known. Yet his death on 26 October 1831 had a dramatic effect on the attitudes of contemporary society to public health. On the previous Saturday, believing he was recovering from an attack of diarrhoea and against his doctor's advice, he ate a mutton chop for dinner. He then walked to his boat, but had to return home as he was suffering violent stomach cramps. When Mr Holmes, his doctor, visited him on Sunday morning he was clearly very ill. Later that day Holmes consulted two other doctors and they agreed that Sproat had Asiatic cholera. Others may already have died from cholera that summer in Sunderland, but local doctors either had not recognised the disease or were reluctant to admit that cholera had finally arrived.

The numbers who died of cholera during the four epidemics of 1831–32, 1848–49, 1853–54 and 1866 were small compared to the numbers of those killed by many other contemporary diseases. However, cholera was the shock disease of the century. The *Quarterly Review* saw it as 'one of the most terrible pestilences which have ever desolated the earth'.

Why was the urban population vulnerable to epidemic diseases in the first half of the nineteenth century?

In 1800, there was little understanding of what caused disease, and death from diseases that are preventable today was common. Children were especially vulnerable and levels of infant mortality were high: one in seven children died before the age of one. The importance of personal hygiene was not understood and lice and fleas were an accepted part of people's lives. Those in authority, especially in towns, recognised that disease was a problem and took rudimentary steps towards public health by cleaning the streets, providing communal water pumps and sewers to remove human waste. However, there was little grasp of what caused disease and little attempt was made to combat it. The problem of public health was made worse by the rapid industrialisation and urbanisation of the late eighteenth and early nineteenth centuries. In 1801 only 14 towns had more than 25,000 people, but by 1841 this had risen to 41. Towns and cities concentrated large numbers of people in a small space, making the spread of disease easier and putting considerable strain on already existing public health provision.

How unhealthy was it to live in cities and why?

It was unhealthy to live in Victorian cities. The chances of illness and premature death varied considerably, however. Who you were – which social class you came from, where you lived, how much you earned and how well you were fed – mattered. Contemporary opinion was most concerned about infectious diseases. Diseases like **typhus** and influenza killed large numbers of people in both rural and urban areas, but particularly affected the malnourished of the urban slums. Smallpox became less of a threat, partly because of a vaccination developed by Edward Jenner in the 1790s. Typhus and typhoid fever were common in London and epidemics occurred in all major towns in 1817–19, 1826–27, 1831–32, 1837 and 1846–47, coinciding with periods of economic slump and high unemployment.

As towns grew, polluted water became a general problem and was the cause of many diseases such as infantile diarrhoea, dysentery, typhoid fever and especially cholera. Contaminated food also spread cholera. Infectious diseases like **tuberculosis**, typhus and cholera were concentrated mainly in inner-city slum districts. Cholera was more deeply feared than any of the other diseases because it sometimes spread to the middle- and upper-class areas.

Typhus, spread by body lice, affected mainly adults. Common in the nineteenth century, it became epidemic during economic depressions and poverty crises and was strongly associated with poor living conditions.

Spread by a bacillus through droplet infection from coughs or saliva, **tuberculosis** is not highly contagious. Its spread is encouraged by a combination of poverty, malnutrition and overcrowded living conditions. Though not immune, the middle class were better able to withstand tuberculosis than the poor, malnourished working class.

In what ways was the health of the working population affected by poor living conditions?

Victorian slum housing in London.

What was the impact of such high rates of infectious disease?

Children were particularly vulnerable to disease, especially to the effects of diarrhoea, dysentery, diphtheria, whooping cough, scarlet fever and measles. By the end of the nineteenth century, infant mortality still accounted for a quarter of all deaths.

Death rates, already high in most towns, went up in the 1830s and 1840s: from about 19 per 1,000 in 1831 to 22.4 per 1,000 by 1838 and to over 25 per 1,000 in 1849, a cholera year. The figures for individual towns were starker. In 1831 the death rate for Bristol was 16.9 per 1,000, rising to 31 per 1,000 by 1841.

There were also marked differences in the average age of death between professional, trade and labouring populations. In 1842, in Liverpool, these figures were 35, 22 and 15 years respectively, compared to rural Rutland's 52, 41 and 38 years respectively.

Death was only one of the effects of disease. For a poor family struggling to pay rent and buy food, illness (whether fatal or not) imposed additional strains. There were medical bills to pay, medicines to buy, extra heating costs and, if the mother was taken ill, the problem of childcare. There is little doubt that the high level and concentration of infectious disease were a significant extra burden for working-class families in the Victorian city.

In what ways was illness a problem for working-class families?

Why did housing and clean water pose problems?

The influx of working people into towns created a housing crisis. Back-to-back houses, cellar dwellings and cheap, poorly built housing of various kinds were constructed to house the new arrivals. Even so, supply could not keep up with demand. An affluent skilled worker might have lived in a two- or three-storey house with two rooms on each floor and an associated yard and workshop. However, few workers could afford to live in such houses and, by 1830, many houses were multi-occupied. Working-class families frequently lived in a single room or cellar without proper sanitation or water supply. In London, lodging houses were common and in the poorest districts as many as 15 people would sleep in one room.

Contemporaries tended to focus on the horrors of urban living, but the situation was little different for the rural poor. There were rural as well as urban slums. The main difference was the density of urban living. Living literally on top of or beneath neighbours in a multi-occupied house or tenement was a new experience for many, requiring adjustments in lifestyles and daily routines.

The major problem was that most new houses did not have adequate drainage, nor did they have sewerage or a water supply. The water companies were unwilling to spend their profits cleaning polluted rivers and springs and central and local government had yet to see the provision of clean water as one of their responsibilities. By the late 1820s, for example, the Thames had become highly polluted. Despite this, the water companies continued to praise the state of the river, a case of profit outweighing the needs of public health.

The problem of London's water culminated in the 'great stink' of 1858. The duke of Newcastle had sounded the alarm in July 1857, warning that 'the river was like a vast sewer, and unless something was done before long to purify it, it would engender some frightful plague among the two and a half million who inhabited the metropolis'. A year later there were suddenly 'strange stories flying of men struck down with the stench and of all kinds of fatal diseases, upspringing on the river's banks'. Parliament took action to bring London's water under central control. The London experience was paralleled in many industrial towns where rivers were invariably open sewers. Unpolluted water was in short supply.

In what respects was there a 'housing crisis' by the 1830s? Why did it occur?

What were the major constraints on effective public health reform?

Governing towns

Before 1835 many of the growing industrial towns did not have a town council. Where councils existed, they were often inefficient and unaccountable for the ways in which they used the local rates. In towns without town councils, power was in the hands of the parish vestry which was elected by property owners. Local communities in the 1830s and 1840s had little effective control over building, sewers and the piping of water. The 'improvement commissioners', appointed under a Local Improvement Act, undertook reform of the cleaning and lighting of streets. By 1830 there were about 350 of these acts in around 200 boroughs or municipal corporations. The problem was that each commission dealt with a specific area of health, not the whole package. Each borough remained separate and did not share joint responsibilities. This led to confusion and a lack of co-ordination.

The rapid growth of the urban population outstretched the abilities of this unreformed system. Urban reform (see Chapter 4) began with the Municipal Corporations Act of 1835. It provided for elections of town councils every three years by ratepayers, but contained no specific proposals regarding public health. It did, however, allow rates to be levied for street lighting, fresh water supply and sewage disposal, but implementing this required a **Local Act of parliament**. The chaotic nature of local government made effective reform difficult. Added to this was self-interest: water companies and builders were in search of profit. Builders exploited demands for cheap housing and paid little attention to drainage, ventilation or water supply. Private landlords were reluctant either to pay for sanitary improvements, largely because of the cost, or to accept responsibility for the health of the working classes.

Much as they might have wished to, neither local nor national politicians could ignore urban living conditions. The debate centred around who was responsible for public health. At the local level, there were groups whose concern was to improve their own conditions – the outbreak of cholera was a

Local Acts of parliament, like the Liverpool Municipal Act of 1846, were passed by parliament to deal with problems in a particular place. They were private pieces of legislation and were often introduced on behalf of the local urban council by a local MP.

significant spur for them to act. The central state was, however, reluctant to become involved in public health reform: the *laissez-faire* attitudes of the period meant that central government did little except when it was forced to. The outbreak of epidemics eventually forced the government into action. The outbreak of cholera in 1831 led to the creation of the Central Board of Health and 1,200 local boards. The Cholera Act of 1832 allowed local boards to finance anti-cholera measures from the poor rates. Finally, the Public Health Act of 1848 (see below) occurred partly as a result of the return of cholera.

There was an increasing amount of statistical and other information on the nature of urban conditions, linking poor living conditions with disease. Such evidence on its own, however, did little to persuade local ratepayers to spend money on improving housing and sanitation for the working class. The impact of cholera in 1832 and 1848 brought home, especially to the middle classes, the fact that disease could affect all classes. The poor were blamed for the disease, but it was in the interests of the middle classes to improve conditions and prevent it from recurring. Intervention was also justified through economic self-interest: reducing levels of disease would bring about a more efficient workforce and thereby benefit industrialists and entrepreneurs.

What were the major public health problems in the 1830s and 1840s?

Why reform took so long

Public health reform was slow in coming for a variety of reasons:

- First, there were major technical problems associated with a lack of medical understanding of disease and with the civil engineering solutions required for larger sewers and treatment plants. The knowledge that germs caused disease did not become widespread until the 1870s and 1880s. Nevertheless, people did not have to know *why* the cesspool and the soil-heap caused disease; they only had to establish that there was a connection between the two. More difficult were the civil engineering problems related to the building of water and sewerage systems that could provide a pure water supply and remove liquid sewage. There was a tension between the politicians who were responsible for finding local solutions to problems but who lacked the necessary technical expertise, and between the public health experts themselves who disagreed over the nature of public health problems. This led to disagreement over how reform should best be accomplished; for example, there was considerable disagreement over whether local or national solutions were needed.
- The second reason why reform was delayed was the problem of cost. Sewerage was not a popular subject and resources for it were scarce. Controlling spending was important for local government. This cut across party lines and could limit local action. Concern about the high cost of public health was linked to the question of who should pay for improvements.

The issue of cost raised important ideological questions. If social amenities were paid for from the rates, then wealth was being redistributed via local taxation – the few funding reform for the benefit of all. Property owners, in particular, objected to paying twice: they spent money on their own sanitary needs and were then asked to pay taxes to provide for the needs of the less well off.

The debate was decided on largely political grounds. At local level there were four broad groupings: the council itself, property owners, ratepayers and vested interests like water companies. Councils were often concerned to bring public health under one administrative body. This brought them into conflict with existing municipal organisations like water commissioners, commissioners for sewers and improvement commissioners. Ratepayers often objected to the rising cost of local taxation and commercial organisations were resistant to any change that affected their profitability.

Local disagreements about who should wield power with regard to public health were dominated by the wider debate about the proper role of the central state. Local councils were concerned that they would lose control over their own affairs if central government took a more active role. As far as they were concerned, central control meant that their local democratic rights to run their communities would be eroded. The different local bodies may have been unable to reach agreement on the issue of public health, but they were united against the threat of central government intervention.

What were the issues that dominated the public health debate?

The constraints affecting public health were not fully resolved until the 1860s and 1870s. By then, many of the civil engineering problems had been resolved. There was a growing recognition, locally and nationally, that public health could only be established if a national approach to the problem was undertaken.

How was public health reformed?

From the late eighteenth century local authorities had started becoming aware of the threats posed to public health by poor sanitation and housing. By the 1830s a significant number of local surveys had been undertaken that identified the urban environment as a threat to health, including James Kay's famous survey of Manchester, *The moral and physical conditions of the working classes*, published in 1832.

A city or town wishing to introduce public health measures needed to persuade parliament to pass a Local Act authorising it to raise local taxes to pay for the improvements. It was not until the 1840s that the largest cities obtained Local Acts to deal with their public health problems. These Acts represented attempts by local communities to respond to the need for better sanitary conditions. The alternative was central government legislation for what town councils saw as local issues. The Leeds Improvement Act of 1842 arose, in part, from an attempt to avoid the provisions of national legislation. Manchester and all the other major cities followed suit. The Manchester Police Regulation Act of 1844 strengthened the powers of the city's corporation over public health. Leeds needed a further Act in 1848 to build a system of sewers, and Manchester obtained a further 10 Acts before 1858 to deal with other public health issues. The most important advances, however, were made by the Liverpool Sanitary Act of 1846. This effectively made the corporation a health authority and allowed it to appoint an engineer, an Inspector of Nuisances and, in W. H. Duncan, the country's first medical officer of health. These three cities also addressed the problem of water supplies. By 1852 Leeds had brought the town's water supply under public control. In 1847 Liverpool purchased the town's private water companies and Manchester began work on its Longdendale reservoir scheme. In 1848, the City of London did likewise and appointed Sir John Simon as its medical officer of health. Control over public health was, in these cities, kept firmly in local hands.

Local authorities were unwilling to accept centrally imposed legislation like the Public Health Act of 1848. As a result, they tried to find solutions to public health problems, though these were often an uneasy combination of appeasing vested interests, keeping down costs and maintaining council control. There is little evidence of long-term planning by local councils.

> Why was intervention in public health issues more acceptable after 1840?

Intervention at national level

During the 1840s there were two contradictory trends in public health policy. Some people wanted to extend central control. Others wished to call a halt to central intervention. The public health movement had to operate against the pressures produced by these opposing forces. However, the development of long-term strategies for improving the public's health demanded national policies. The campaign for improving urban conditions was dominated by Edwin Chadwick.

Chadwick's sanitary policies tried to tackle all aspects of the problem. He thought out an administrative structure at both central and local level that was related to basic environmental and geographical factors. This comprehensive planning won him a number of enemies – any such plan was bound to antagonise powerful vested interests, especially local government, landlords and the water companies. Chadwick's plans suffered from his dogmatic style and showed his usual inability to compromise or to modify his ideas.

Awakening political interest

The creation of the Poor Law Commission in 1834 and the office of **Registrar-General**, responsible for the civil registration of births, marriages and deaths,

> The Registration of Births, Marriages and Deaths Act 1836 resulted in the introduction of civil registration for England and Wales. From 1 July 1837 copies of entries for births, marriages and deaths have been placed in the General Register Office run by the **Registrar-General**. Civil registration was not introduced in Scotland until 1855.

in 1837–38 resulted in national statistical evidence on the issue of public health, especially causes of death. Chadwick's Poor Law Report of 1834 had assumed that by imposing the workhouse test the cost of poor relief would fall. In his first few years as secretary to the Poor Law Commission, however, Chadwick found that a significant proportion of relief was given to widows and children of male breadwinners who had died, often from disease. Chadwick concluded that unnecessary ill health and death had the effect of increasing the cost of relief. This led directly to his 1842 Sanitary Report (see below).

The first step towards public health reform was to produce evidence of the effects of insanitary conditions that could not be challenged. Lord John Russell, the home secretary, asked the Poor Law Commission for its comments on the links between disease and environment in the worst areas of London. Following reports produced for the Poor Law Commission, the House of Lords established an inquiry into sanitary conditions under Chadwick's chairmanship in 1839.

How did Chadwick seek to raise the profile of public health in the late 1830s?

Chadwick attempted to obtain as much information as possible. Questionnaires were sent to Poor Law assistant commissioners all over the country. About 1,000 Poor Law boards of guardians gave evidence on sanitary conditions. Prison officers, employers, rural and urban doctors also contributed. Chadwick himself visited the main urban centres. This was the most comprehensive survey of public health undertaken to date and resulted in the *Report on the sanitary conditions of the labouring population of Great Britain*, produced in July 1842.

The 1842 Sanitary Report

The 1842 Sanitary Report made a deep impression on public opinion – about 100,000 copies were sold within a year. It was a damning indictment of the sanitary condition of Britain. Several points stand out:

- The statistical evidence collected showed a clear link between poor environmental conditions and disease.
- It established a close correlation between poor housing, poor sewerage and polluted water supplies, and high levels of disease, high death rates and low life expectancy.
- It demonstrated that social evils were the result of insanitary living conditions and maintained that low moral standards (such as prostitution, crime and drunkenness) were the *result* of the physical environment, not the other way round.

As part of the research for the 1842 Sanitary Report, Chadwick also investigated the problem of burying people in towns. Many existing town cemeteries were overcrowded and decaying corpses contributed to urban sanitation problems. In 1843 Chadwick published a report on **interments**, in which he argued for the separation of burial grounds from urban areas.

Chadwick believed that disease was carried by impurities in the atmosphere (the **miasmic theory**) and that the great challenge was to get rid of impurities before they could decompose. He put it briefly: 'All smell is, if it be intense, immediate acute disease.' For Chadwick, the key to solving the whole problem of public health was the provision of a sufficient supply of pure water driven through pipes at high pressure. This would provide drinking water and also make it easier to clean houses and streets. He suggested that sewage could be collected in towns and used as fertiliser in the surrounding fields. It was the very completeness of his solution that presented problems.

Many water companies provided water only on certain days of the week and at certain times. They did not provide it either in the quantities or at the pressure that Chadwick desired. Many houses in poorer districts had no water supply at all, nor did they have proper means of sewage disposal. Where sewers did exist, they were often very badly designed. Chadwick wished to replace existing constructions with a smaller type, developed by **John Roe,** that could be flushed more effectively.

In addition to his first two basic ideas (the supply of clean water and the collection of sewage), Chadwick maintained that nationwide policies for public health should be provided by central government and put into practice by local authorities.

The contrast between the government's reaction to the Poor Law Report in 1834 and its reaction to the Sanitary Report of 1842 was unmistakable. In 1834 legislation had rapidly followed the report because it reflected the widely held views of an important cross-section of society. In 1842, by contrast, Chadwick's views were ahead of political opinion: it was four years before the first national public health laws were passed and six before the comprehensive legislation envisaged by Chadwick was passed.

Towards comprehensive legislation

The report may have outraged public opinion, but this was not translated into political action by parliament. There was widespread concern at the cost of public health reform and the impact it would have on the relationship between central and local government. Local authorities did not want to relinquish their power to make decisions for their communities. In addition, central government did not see sanitary reform as a major priority in the early and mid-1840s. Dealing with the threat from Chartism, problems in Ireland and the Corn Law controversy were regarded as more important.

Government action was limited to introducing two minor and largely ineffective pieces of legislation in 1846. The Nuisances Removal Act and the

Interments are burials in graveyards.

The Royal College of Physicians did not support the **miasmic theory**. Though germs had not yet been isolated, many doctors in the 1850s believed they existed. They believed in the theory of contagion and concluded that dirt and smells were harmless. They regarded the views of sanitary reformers as unscientific. We now know that germs do exist and that they breed faster in dirty conditions. In the early 1850s neither theory could be proved and each appeared to exclude the other.

John Roe was engineer to the Holborn and Finsbury Commission of Sewers. His advice was that drains should be closed pipes not open and that sewers should be capable of being flushed with water to prevent them silting up.

What were the main features of the 1842 Sanitary Report?

Nuisances were public health hazards like insanitary drains.

Joshua Toulmin Smith (1816–69) was a constitutional lawyer who published *Local self-government and centralisation* in 1851 in which he argued strongly in favour of democratic local government untramelled by central control.

What circumstances led to the delay between the publication of the Sanitary Report in 1842 and national legislation in 1848?

Diseases Prevention Act allowed local magistrates to prosecute those responsible for **nuisances**. Both were permissive Acts, allowing but not forcing local authorities to act, and many simply ignored them. The following year, the Town Improvement Clauses Act and the Town Police Clauses Act defined the obligations of towns to lay water supplies and drainage schemes and to control nuisances.

Despite political reluctance to introduce legislation, Chadwick had established the case for public health reform. His vision of a more hygienic Britain had impressed the House of Lords and he played an important, if unofficial, role in the Royal Commission on the Sanitary State of Large Towns and Populous Districts (1844–45).

Other developments helped Chadwick to spread his public health message. Southwood Smith, a doctor involved in the 1839 inquiry into sanitary conditions, founded a pressure group known as the Health of Towns Association in December 1844. By now the public health controversy had polarised into two groups, what contemporaries called the 'Clean Party' who favoured reform and those against it, the 'Dirty Party' or 'Muckabites'.

Reform was proving slow, but increasingly Chadwick's vision began to gain support from those in authority concerned about the nation's health. In 1847 Lord Morpeth attempted to introduce a comprehensive public health bill, but it aroused so much opposition that it failed. The following year he re-introduced the bill, this time successfully. In the interim a second epidemic of cholera had begun and people were therefore more prepared to accept central direction. The Act was again attacked by vested interests and those opposed to centralisation and loss of local democracy, led by **Joshua Toulmin Smith**. The debate was not whether action was necessary, but whether central or local government should take action. As a result the scope of the 1848 legislation was reduced.

The Public Health Act of 1848

The Public Health Act of 1848 had three main provisions:
- It established a General Board of Health with a lifespan of five years and with three commissioners (Lord Morpeth, Lord Shaftesbury and Chadwick, with Southwood Smith as medical officer).
- It allowed for local Boards of Health to be established if 10 per cent of ratepayers petitioned the General Board. A town council would have to set up a local board if the death rate in the town was higher than 23 per 1,000.
- It made provision for the local Boards of Health to take over the powers of water companies and drainage commissioners. They were given wide powers to deal with sewage and drainage, to ensure that streets were swept,

watered and repaired, to erect public conveniences and to clean and purify 'unwholesome houses'. They could levy a rate and had the power to appoint a salaried medical officer. They also had the power to pave streets, but this was not compulsory.

What were the main features of the Public Health Act of 1848?

The implementation of the Act appeared to be fairly straightforward. It was clear and unambiguous and initially had widespread public support. However, the Act had several important weaknesses:

- The General Board was essentially an advisory and co-ordinating body, rather than an initiator of reform. It could force local authorities to establish a local board of health, but only if there was a public petition or high mortality rate. The cholera epidemic of 1848–49 reinforced the argument for central action, but it caught the Board unprepared for the demands of the task and the Board did not deal with the cholera outbreak very effectively. The Interment Act of 1850, which gave the General Board of Health power to construct and manage public cemeteries, illustrates its problems. There was furious opposition to the legislation and, as a result, it was forced into constant battles with the Treasury over even minor items of spending. The General Board lacked sufficient political authority, had no independent financial powers to raise taxes and was losing public support. This increased its ineffectiveness.

Why was the General Board of Health unsuccessful in introducing effective public health measures?

- The Act was permissive in character and most towns by-passed the legislation by obtaining Local Acts of parliament to avoid central interference.

London was not affected by the legislation; by 1850 it was clear that the government was not prepared to extend the powers of the General Board to cover the capital city. This proved a major weakness of political will and represented a major setback for Chadwick's case for comprehensive reform. If public health reform was impossible in London, it is not surprising that other major cities and towns resisted central direction.

The scale of the General Board's operations was modest. Only 182 local boards were established by 1854 and only 13 had begun work on waterworks and sewerage schemes. By 1858 only 400,000 of the county's 2.5 million people came under Boards of Health.

There was growing opposition to the General Board in the whole country as a result of its inability to cope with the cholera epidemic and the threat it posed to local democracy. Opposition to the Board was mounting. Lord Seymour, who was hostile to Chadwick, replaced Lord Morpeth on the General Board in March 1850. In addition, neither Chadwick nor the Board had many supporters in the House of Commons and they had a growing number of opponents, especially Sir Benjamin Hall, champion of local democracy, and Thomas Wakley, the editor of *The Lancet*. *The Times* orchestrated feelings against the Board and Chadwick. The Board should have ended in 1853, but it was given a year's extension because of the return of cholera.

Chadwick produced a report on what had been achieved, but he was critical of the various vested interests. Chadwick knew that the 'Dirty Party' was bent on his destruction. Hostility from town councils, private cemeteries and water companies, landlords, ratepayers, parliament and from *The Times* and *Punch* focused on Chadwick, who was seen to be bullying the nation into cleanliness.

Chadwick was dismissed on 12 August 1854 and never held public office again. The General Board continued, but whatever limited influence it had once had, ceased after Chadwick's dismissal. In 1858 it was abolished and replaced by a Medical Department of the Privy Council. This body continued the statistical work begun by the General Board of Health, but never attempted the centralised direction that had led to the Board's destruction.

Conclusions

Public health was far more complex than the pioneers of the 1840s had envisaged. For Chadwick, public health was simply a matter of better sanitation and water supply. In reality, the problem had far wider environmental causes – pressure of population, bad housing and poor nutrition – and Chadwick consistently underestimated the importance of medical questions, especially what could be achieved by preventive medicine. The Sanitary Act of 1866 placed all the responsibilities of the 1848 Act squarely on local authorities. It was mandatory, but there was no central control and no inspectorate. It faced little opposition as there was a greater public awareness of public health hazards and the need to do something about them than there had been in the early 1850s. Local control achieved what centralisation had failed to do.

Summary questions

1. Identify and explain any *two* factors that determined developments in public health between 1830 and 1854.

2. Compare the importance of at least *three* issues that held back the development of effective public health reform between 1840 and 1854.

14 Chartism

Focus questions

- Why did Chartism develop in the late 1830s?
- How far can Chartism be seen as a 'class' movement?
- Why did Chartism fail to achieve any of its objectives by 1850?

Significant dates

1815   Corn Law introduced

1832   Reform Acts introduced

1834   Poor Law Amendment Act introduced

1837   Beginnings of Chartism

1838   Formation of the Anti-Corn Law League

1839   Newport rising

1841   Conservatives win general election

1842   'Plug Plot' occurs

1846   Corn Laws repealed

1848   Kennington Common meeting takes place

Overview

Parliamentary reform triumphed in 1832. The 'floodgates of democracy' that Peel said would accompany parliamentary reform were opened. The Reform Acts of 1832 gave the vote to the middle classes, but gave nothing to the working population. This 'betrayal' was felt deeply. It was made worse by factory and Poor Law reform. Increasingly, many working-class radicals felt that, until they were given the vote, no aspect of their lives could be improved. The result was the emergence of Chartism in the late 1830s.

Why did Chartism develop in the late 1830s?

The **unstamped press** published illegal newspapers. This was an attempt by radicals to provide cheap newspapers to working people.

Stamp duty was paid on newspapers and journals. It was seen as a 'tax on knowledge' and led to illegal unstamped newspapers being printed.

The **GNCTU** or Grand National Consolidated Trades Union was a short-lived national union formed in 1834.

In what ways did Whig policies contribute to the development of Chartism?

What were the aims of the Chartists?

Feargus O'Connor (1796–1855) was Chartism's most influential and, arguably, destructive leader. He led the movement between 1838 and 1848. He owned and edited the Chartist newspaper *Northern Star* and dominated the militant northern section of the movement.

Chartism emerged as a political movement because of the policies of the Whig government. Between 1830 and 1836, the Whigs attacked the **unstamped press**: over 700 sellers of radical journals were prosecuted. This resulted in widespread opposition to the government, even after **stamp duties** were reduced in 1836. The Whigs also took a firm stand against trade unionism, especially the **GNCTU** and the Tolpuddle Martyrs in 1834. The workhouse became the symbol of Whig cruelty. In Scotland, the alliance between middle-class radicals and trade unionists broke down when the members of the Glasgow cotton spinners' union were arrested in July 1837, on suspicion of arson and murder, as the middle class was not prepared to support law-breakers. This led to a working-class campaign in their support throughout Scotland and northern England.

Another reason for discontent was that parliament made no real improvements in working conditions. The Factory Act of 1833, though it regulated the working day of children in the textile industry, left adult hours unaltered. Many of the northern delegates to the Chartist convention in 1839 (see p.191) entered politics through the Ten-Hour Movement and the campaign against the new Poor Law. By 1838, this campaign was beginning to decline and gradually activists in the north turned to a wider-based radicalism. The frustrations of factory reformers swelled the rising Chartist tide. In the spring of 1838, the People's Charter was published. Its 'six points' – annual parliaments, equal electoral districts, payment of MPs, universal manhood suffrage, vote by ballot and the abolition of property qualifications – were demanded to secure political equality.

The key figure in channelling separate grievances into a general demand for further parliamentary reform was **Feargus O'Connor**. He was able to win support from the middle-class Birmingham Political Union and the artisan London Working Men's Association. The unity of Chartism should not be exaggerated: Chartism was fuelled by a widespread sense of resentment, but all levels of the movement had different emphases, tactics and organisations.

How far can Chartism be seen as a 'class' movement?

Support for Chartism came from across the country and from people who had a wide range of jobs. Its power base lay in the textiles districts of the east Midlands, the West Riding of Yorkshire and in southern Lancashire. Chartism was stronger in industrial villages and medium-sized towns like Stockport and Bradford than in the major provincial centres of Manchester and Leeds, where the effects of depression were less marked. However, Chartism was also a force in other areas, like south Wales, the Black Country and parts of the West Country, where there had been little organised radicalism before. In the first national petition, which called on parliament to grant the Charter, 19,000 signatures came from London, compared to 100,000 from the West Riding. Mass metropolitan support for Chartism came only in the 1840s. In other areas, support was limited. In Ireland, cities like Belfast, Cork and Dublin had Chartist organisations, but the Catholic Church's suspicion that Chartism would undermine society meant its impact was limited. Chartism was weak in rural areas where deference remained strong. Despite this regional and local diversity, there was a real sense of national unity in the movement, especially between 1839 and 1842, and in 1848.

A wide range of urban and industrial workers was involved in the movement. Economic conditions, especially the widespread depression of 1837–38, were only partly responsible for this, though they were of major importance. Of the 23 local associations who responded to a questionnaire distributed by the 1839 convention, only two stressed the vote as a general grievance. The majority complained of low wages, expensive food, scarcity of work and economic hardship. Although contemporaries saw Chartism as a 'knife and fork' question of fair wages and prices, it was more than this. The economic slump of the late 1830s only added to the workers' general sense of political frustration and despair.

Considerable support came from domestic **outworkers**. Economic conditions for textile handloom weavers, linen-spinners and wool-combers in Yorkshire were chronically depressed. In Scotland, handloom weavers were the major force behind Chartism. The move to demands for political answers to their economic grievances was motivated by the belief that, without the vote, there would be no improvement in their situation.

Outworkers worked largely in their own homes.

Factory workers played a more active role in Chartism than in previous radical movements. Here, too, their initial motivation was economic, springing from the widespread unemployment of the late 1830s.

Factory workers and miners occupied an intermediate position between the rank-and-file outworkers and the artisans and small shopkeepers who formed most of the leadership. In Suffolk and Essex, for example, tailors, shoemakers and building artisans looked to agricultural labourers for mass support. In Bath, artisans provided the leadership, and the declining cloth trade the rank and file. In Aberdeen, there was a similar balance between handloom weavers and a small articulate artisan leadership. Craftsmen were prominent in the movement, partly because of their long tradition of political radicalism. Economic considerations increased levels of artisan involvment. In the clothing, furniture and building trades, the artisans' economic position was deteriorating or at least vulnerable. The growing market for low-quality goods and falling prices compelled employers to cut their costs. Only a few skilled trades, like bookbinding and watchmaking, were able to maintain their prosperity and remained aloof from Chartism.

Women were involved in Chartism to an unprecedented extent. This strong female involvement (up to a third of those who signed the first petition in 1839 were women, and the petition on behalf of the transported **John Frost** in 1841 was organised by women) was not motivated primarily by the question of women's suffrage. Women acted in support of men and of their communities. In the early years of the movement, there were over 100 female radical associations, and a general commitment to women's suffrage and the improvement of women's education were accepted by many radicals. By the mid-1840s, the growing respectability of parts of the movement meant that radical papers mentioned women less.

The Chartist movement aimed to make the Charter the basis of the British political system by giving the working class the vote. Radicals maintained that the conditions of working-class life would never improve until the six parts of the Charter had been granted. Although there were different radical groups, what held them together was their acceptance of the Charter as the basis for change.

Chartism: a chronology

The Chartist movement did not rise to a peak and then decline; rather it peaked on three occasions: between 1838 and 1840, in 1842 and in 1848. There were, however, important differences over how the Charter should be put into effect which created local, as well as national, divisions.

Phase 1: 1838–41

In June 1836, the London Working Men's Association (LWMA) was formed, with **William Lovett** as secretary. The Charter emerged out of a tradition of London artisan radicalism that went back to the corresponding societies in the 1790s (see Chapter 2), with the assistance of a small group of middle-class radicals. Thomas Attwood revived the Birmingham Political Union (BPU) in 1837, which initially called for household suffrage, but soon supported universal suffrage. The LWMA and BPU drummed up support for the Charter in Scotland and northern England.

Feargus O'Connor realised that success would prove difficult for a movement based exclusively in London. During the winter of 1836–37, he broadened the base of his support from London, Lancashire and Yorkshire to Nottingham, Newcastle and Scotland. By mid-1838, he exercised considerable

John Frost (d. 1877) was an ex-mayor of Newport and leader of the Newport rising in 1839.

What different types of people supported Chartism? Why did they do this?

William Lovett (1800–77) was born in Cornwall and moved to London in 1821. He soon immersed himself in various radical activities. In 1836 he founded the London Working Men's Association from which emerged the Chartist movement. He helped draft the Charter and from 1838 he was a leading Chartist, though he soon quarrelled with O'Connor. From 1842 he was increasingly marginalised in the movement and in later life turned to teaching, writing and supporting liberal causes, especially the importance of working-class education.

dominance over northern popular radicalism through his newspaper, the *Northern Star*, and founded the Leeds-based Great Northern Union in April 1838. O'Connor recognised that his union alone could not win reform and that he would have to work with the LWMA and BPU.

What was the role of Feargus O'Connor in the early development of Chartism?

The Convention, 1839

From September 1838, a series of regional meetings elected delegates to a national convention. The convention finally met in London in February 1839. About half its 54 delegates were working men, the remainder were radical gentry or small employers. Divisions emerged almost immediately: should the convention regard itself simply as a means of managing the first petition or should it set itself up as 'the people's parliament'? As the language of militants became more extreme, many of the moderate delegates, principally those from Scotland and Birmingham, returned home. It was the issue of violence and the closely connected issue of co-operation with the middle classes (who generally opposed violent protest) that did most to divide the convention delegates. When Melbourne's government resigned in May 1839, the **national petition** could not be presented to parliament and the remaining 35 delegates to the convention moved to Birmingham. They discussed various strategies for what would happen if the Charter was rejected, but no agreement was reached. Decisions were left to local associations.

The **national petition** would have been presented or delivered to parliament by a sympathetic MP, debated in the House of Commons and then a vote taken on whether to accept it or not.

This was, in part, a response to the hardening of government policy. Initially Lord John Russell, the home secretary, resisted those demanding repression of the Chartists. By mid-1839 this had changed and drilling was banned, lord-lieutenants were given powers to raise and arm special constables, and 6,000 troops were stationed in the **northern district** in response to the threat of an armed rising. The Metropolitan Police was deployed to rural Wales and put down rioting Chartists at Llanidloes in mid Wales in May. On 12 July, the House of Commons rejected the Charter by 235 votes to 46. Leading figures in the London and Lancashire movements were arrested and the tempo of arrests increased after a riot in Birmingham in July over the failure of the government to grant the Charter.

England was divided into military districts. The **northern district** broadly covered the area north of the River Trent.

The convention, reduced in size by resignation, differences of opinion and now arrests, moved back to London. After the government's failure to grant the Charter, the convention finally had to face up to the issue of violence and resistance. On 17 July it voted to hold a general strike, despite letters from local associations questioning the wisdom of taking this step during a severe trade depression. On 24 July, following consultations with 63 Welsh, Scottish and English associations which showed support from only 9, the decision was reversed. The convention was dissolved in September and the initiative for the continuity of the movement passed to the local associations.

How far can Chartism be called a united movement?

The Newport rising, 1839

Henry Vincent
(1813–78) was the leading Chartist in the West Country and south Wales. He took up the cause of temperance in 1841.

Agents provocateurs were spies who tried to prompt radical groups, in this case the Chartists, into taking direct action.

In what ways were economic rather than political considerations central to Chartist concerns in 1838–39?

Meetings were held in the early autumn of 1839 to co-ordinate a national rising, but in the event, the only one occurred in south Wales. On the night of 3–4 November 7,000 miners and ironworkers marched in three columns to Newport to release **Henry Vincent** from prison. There is also evidence that they were intending to launch a massive uprising to create a people's republic in the Welsh valleys that they hoped might spread to other parts of Britain. Troops opened fire, killing at least 22 and wounding about 50. The rest fled in confusion and many were arrested in the next few days. Over 250 people were tried in the last mass treason trial in British history. Death sentences were handed down to the three leaders, though these were later commuted to transportation for life to Australia.

The Newport rising was not a small-scale affair or the work of Whig *agents provocateurs* or simply a 'monster demonstration', as earlier historians have concluded, but was the product of a radical political culture in an area where class divisions were clear. Further risings were planned after Newport, but came to nothing.

Declining fortunes, 1840–41

After the Newport rising, the Chartists assumed that the government would adopt repressive policies against them and that this would result in violent protest. However, the government did not act as expected. Initially, Russell adopted a conciliatory stance, giving the Chartists time to alienate moderate supporters by their militant language. Consequently, the initiative quickly moved to the government and the Chartists found themselves on the defensive, caught between defeat or revolution. By late 1839, it was clear they could not defeat the state by force. At the local level, sympathetic handling defused potentially explosive situations. **General Napier,** for example, met Lancashire Chartist leaders and promised to keep troops and police away from a major rally as long as it was peaceful.

By the summer of 1840, Chartism was in disarray. Divisions began to emerge. The Chartist church movement, an attempt to combine Christianity and radicalism that began in Scotland, spread southwards, flourishing in the Birmingham area and in the West Country. Lovett launched the National Association for Promoting the Improvement of the People, stressing education and self-help. Henry Vincent toured the country after his release from prison in early 1841 on behalf of **teetotal Chartism**. In Leeds and other provincial cities, Chartists became involved in local government. In Nottingham, Chartists took up the Poor Law issue again. A degree of unity and national organisation was provided by the National Charter Association (NCA) formed in July 1840, largely at O'Connor's instigation.

Sir Charles Napier
(1782–1853) commanded the northern district between 1839 and 1841 and was not unsympathetic to the Chartists.

Teetotal Chartism was a working-class movement linking Chartism and the temperance movement.

The NCA remained the major national organisation for the next decade. It was very much O'Connor's organisation and this led to significant personal opposition. Consequently, many Chartists, including Lovett, refused to join. By the end of 1840, fewer than 70 local associations were affiliated to the NCA. These were concentrated in Lancashire and Yorkshire, the Nottinghamshire–Derby area and in London. Nevertheless, during 1841, O'Connor claimed 50,000 members from 401 localities. He feared Chartism would fragment, with some reason: Lovett's Association had considerable middle-class backing, while Chartists in Leeds had become local councillors.

Phase 2: 1842–47

Some Chartists turned to the Complete Suffrage Union (CSU), launched by Joseph Sturge in Birmingham in April 1842. Sturge wanted to reconcile the middle classes and working classes through the repeal of class-based laws. He believed that denying the vote to most people was unconstitutional and unchristian. This stance attracted the middle classes and those Chartists, like Lovett, who had been alienated by the violence of 1839–40. At its first meeting, the moderate nature of the CSU was emphasised when O'Connor's supporters were excluded. By late April 1842, there were 50 local associations of the CSU and it presented a rival parliamentary petition to that of the NCA.

O'Connor initially attacked the CSU, but as he began to recognise the tactical advantage of a brief alliance with middle-class radicals, he came out in favour of class collaboration in July 1842. By the autumn, under pressure from Chartist hardliners, he had reversed his position. At a CSU conference in December, packed with Chartist delegates who supported O'Connor, the middle-class radicals insisted on introducing a new bill of rights for universal suffrage, instead of the Charter. Lovett was not prepared to accept this and temporarily joined with O'Connor in opposing the CSU. Neither Lovett nor O'Connor could envisage Chartism without its Charter, but it was an alliance that would last only until the CSU was defeated. This led to the immediate withdrawal of the majority of the middle-class delegates. Class collaboration ended and O'Connor's grip of the Chartist movement tightened.

The Plug Plot, 1842

The second convention met in Birmingham in April 1842 to launch the second national petition. The number of delegates was limited to 24 from English constituencies and 25 from Welsh and Scottish ones. The petition was better organised and contained 3 million signatures. However, the result was the same as it had been for the first petition: rejection by the House of Commons by 287 to 46 votes on 1 May. This created much bitterness, a situation aggravated by the worst economic recession of the century.

In July and August 1842 up to half a million workers were involved in the series of strikes that swept across many of the industrial districts of the north and the Midlands. Miners on the north Staffordshire coalfields struck in July, followed by a rash of strikes in the Lancashire textile industry in response to wage cuts. Strikers travelled through the county drawing out the plugs of factory boilers so that they literally ran out of steam and would not function, hence the name the 'Plug Plot'. Within days, the strikes had spread across the Pennines into Yorkshire and north into Scotland. By September, 15 English and Welsh and 8 Scottish counties were affected.

The degree of Chartist involvement in the strikes varied. Although many of those who spoke at strike meetings were Chartists who had few connections with the textile trades, Chartist leaders were caught unawares. They soon exploited the strikes for their own ends, however. A series of regional trade conferences held in August provided the Chartists with an opportunity to take over the strike movement. Consequently, there was a widespread adoption of the Charter as one of the strike's main aims. The extent to which Chartists were involved varied regionally. In Manchester, Glasgow and London there was some convergence of Chartist and trade union activity. In Yorkshire, where trade unions were weaker and less widespread, local Chartists exercised strong influence over tactics. Generally, however, Chartist leaders were too divided to take full advantage of the situation.

The unions had problems co-ordinating the strikes and the different attitudes of Chartists prevented the NCA from taking on this role. Tension eased in September because of improving economic conditions. The 1842 harvest was good, trade revived and employers agreed to cancel wage reductions.

The strike movement had two adverse effects on the Chartists. First, Peel and his home secretary, Sir James Graham, blamed the Chartists for the strikes. A wave of arrests followed in September and harsh sentences were handed out. In Staffordshire, for example, of 274 cases tried, 154 men were imprisoned and 5 men transported for life. By early 1843, there was less need for harsh treatment. Peel and Graham recognised, as Russell had done in 1839–40, that pushing repression too far would alienate public opinion and create public sympathy for the Chartists. In addition, trade union disappointment with Chartism increased. To unionists, the issue was economic rather than political and, for them, the strikes were partially successful. Wage levels were restored and, in some places, increased to the 1840 levels, while in the cotton districts, trade unionism emerged on a more organised and confident basis.

Confrontational tactics had failed in 1839–40 and again in 1842. Mass arrests and imprisonment sapped the strength of the Chartist movement and the relative economic prosperity of the years between 1842 and 1848 helped to dampen the enthusiasm of the rank and file. The agreement between Lovett and O'Connor in late 1842 over the CSU proposals was short-lived. Lovett had no intention of working with O'Connor and gradually he and others withdrew to pursue their objectives by peaceful means. O'Connor emerged firmly in control of the formal Chartist movement, which he promptly led off in entirely new directions.

What different tactics were used by the Chartists in an attempt to achieve their aims?

Different directions, 1842–47

Lovett placed increasing emphasis on educating the working population. Henry Vincent and others continued their work on temperance. Other diversions took the form of increased trade union activity, support for the Anti-Corn Law League and for European republicanism. These represented attempts by radicals to find alternatives to Chartism, though they generally failed to gain mass support. In Leeds, Chartists were elected to the Board of Surveyors for Highways and as Poor Law guardians. In Sheffield, there were 22 Chartists on the council. In Rochdale, Chartists took control of the Board of Guardians from 1844, ensuring that the new Poor Law was not fully applied before the 1870s. Skilled and prosperous workers, organised in strong trade societies, distanced themselves from Chartism as improved trade after 1842 saw a temporary revival of national unions among workers in cotton and mining.

The Land Plan

Increasingly O'Connor turned his attention to the land question. The Land Plan provided a major outlet for frustrated Chartists. It was a highly attractive proposition as it offered a means of restoring the independence and self-reliance of artisans. The idea was to raise capital for a land company from the purchase of shares at 3d or more a week. With the cash, land would be purchased, made into smallholdings complete with the necessary buildings and rented to shareholders chosen by ballot. Much of the initial support came from the industrial north and Midlands, but enthusiasm for the Plan soon spread south. Momentum gathered once O'Connor purchased his first site near Watford. On May Day 1847, the first tenants moved into O'Connorville. Subscriptions soared and the National Co-operative Land Company bought further estates. Over £100,000 was collected from about 70,000 subscribers, though only 250 ever settled on the two-acre allotments.

The company and its associated Land Bank were plagued by legal difficulties. In May 1848, parliament appointed a select committee to investigate the Land Company. Although there was no evidence of fraud, the accounts were confused and inaccurate and this further weakened the scheme. O'Connor found that the flow of share capital was drying up and, after exploring alternative means of saving the scheme, he finally wound the company up in 1851.

Phase 3: 1848

For both contemporaries and historians, 1848 was a watershed in the history of the Chartist movement. It is certainly true that after 1848 Chartism lost whatever unity it had had, with even O'Connor willing to accept limited household suffrage and leaders such as **Ernest Jones** and Harney moving towards socialism.

The winter of 1847–48 was a severe one. Commercial crisis and growing economic distress led to increasing Chartist activity. The authorities were uneasy at Chartist plans to present a third petition. There were fears that the revolutions sweeping across Europe would infect Britain, especially since some Chartists had been in contact with European radicals.

In March 1848, Chartists highjacked a middle-class radical meeting in London that had been called to demand the abolition of income tax. Attempts by police to break up the demonstration led to three days of rioting. Similar disturbances took place in Glasgow and Manchester. Although there was a Chartist presence in each case, disorder and crimes were largely committed by non-Chartists, but the Chartists were guilty by association in the eyes of property owners.

Forty-nine delegates were elected to the third convention that first met in London on 4 April. The convention planned a peaceful demonstration on Kennington Common on 10 April, to be followed by a procession to present the petition supporting the Charter to parliament. O'Connor's personal position had been strengthened by being elected MP for Nottingham in 1847 and he hoped that the petition would contain five million signatures.

There were fears that the demonstration proposed by the convention would tie down the army at a time when Irish radicals threatened rebellion. Strong precautionary measures were thus taken by the authorities. Eight thousand troops were drafted into the capital to support thousands of special constables. The procession was banned, but the meeting went ahead. The government's firmness frightened O'Connor into asking his supporters to disperse peacefully after the meeting. The meeting was ridiculed by many as a 'fiasco' and two days later, O'Connor faced further disapproval when his petition was found to contain less than two million genuine signatures.

The convention continued to sit, initially undaunted by the rejection of the petition. Soon, internal disagreement, mutual suspicion and recriminations increasingly paralysed the convention and its dissolution quickly followed.

On 2 June, *The Times* concluded, 'Chartism is neither dead nor sleeping. The snake was scotched not killed on the 10th of April. The advancing spring

Ernest Jones (1819–69) was the son of a wealthy cavalry officer. He joined O'Connor in 1846 and stood as a Chartist candidate for parliament. He was imprisoned in 1848 for advocating 'physical force' and in the 1850s became one of the leaders of Chartism.

The earliest photograph of a mass demonstration, taken by William Kilburn at the great Chartist meeting, Kennington Common, April 1848.

has brought with it warmth, vigour and renovation.' It was right: the summer of 1848 saw further Chartist activity, arrests, trials and several riots, against the background of events in Ireland. The focal points of government concern were Bradford in May and London between June and August. Police broke up meetings in the East End on 4 June and the Chartists called for a day of protest on 12 June. The government responded with a heavy display of force at the mass meeting held on Bishop Bonner's Field in London.

The authorities certainly believed that the Chartists posed a real threat in 1848. They saw the daily meetings and riots, and received reports of drilling and military-style marches from the rural areas. Prompt action by the government put O'Connor in the position of having to back down. His hold over the movement was broken and other leaders simply did not have his authority. Just as in 1838 and 1842, Chartism was contained from without and was critically weakened from within. Chartism's failure in 1848 was not one of ideas, but of will. The united 'mass platform', already weakened, disintegrated.

Chartism lingered on for a further decade, displaying vigour in some areas of the country, but it had ceased to be a mass movement. Nevertheless, its journals still flourished and Ernest Jones achieved a following among craftsmen, especially in London, resentful at the growing influence of trade unionism. Chartists continued to be active in local politics, but by 1860 organised

What policies did successive governments adopt towards Chartism?

Chartism was dead. The last convention gathered in 1858. Two years later, the NCA was formally wound up.

Why did Chartism fail to achieve any of its objectives by 1850?

Repeated failure sapped the momentum of the Chartist movement. To sustain its support, the movement needed to maintain a widespread belief that success was possible. The events of 1839 seriously damaged its capacity to do this. The defeat of the strike in 1842 and the crushing failure of 1848 completed the process. The authorities had inflicted the most damaging psychological defeat on any popular reform movement of the century.

In part, this was a result of the organisational weakness of the movement. Its lack of administrative experience was clearly exposed by the ways in which the conventions were organised and financed. Rejection of the three petitions shows how little parliamentary support the Chartists had. The reforming movement of 1830–32 and the activities of the Anti-Corn Law League, both of which used similar tactics to Chartism to gain support, were successful because these movements had parliamentary allies. With little parliamentary backing or solid middle-class support, the Chartist movement found itself with three choices: giving up, raising and maintaining public support or opting for less peaceful methods. This divided leadership and rank and file, creating bitterness and a lack of tactical direction. Chartists could agree on the Charter, but on little else. To Lancashire cotton workers, Chartism held out the prospect of economic improvement and factory reform. To the London artisan, it pointed the way to political equality.

The Chartist leaders also had different objectives. For Lovett, the vote was part of a general programme of social improvement; for Ernest Jones, Chartism was equated with socialism; and for O'Connor, the franchise was the political counterpart to his schemes for land reform. Loss of momentum within the movement meant that Chartism could not maintain any unity of purpose.

Economic conditions played an important role in the Chartists' failure to maintain unity. The difficulty of staying unified, except during economic slumps, was universally recognised by contemporaries. The changes that occurred in the policies and attitudes of government, in part the result of Chartism, can be seen as evidence of its partial success. The movement drew attention to social problems and the need to tackle them and there was some resultant liberalisation of state policies in the 1840s. This simply weakened the Chartist case that only a reformed parliament would improve the conditions of the working population.

A final explanation for the demise of Chartism lies in the consolidation of industrial capitalism that had occurred by 1850. In the previous 50 years, industrial change had created militancy among the working population, who believed that political reform alone could arrest or reverse this process. By 1850, this battle had more or less been lost and Chartism remained relevant only in places like Halifax and Bradford where the woollen and worsted trades still fought rearguard actions against mechanisation. Militancy was associated with the early stages of industrialisation. Chartism was crucial in the shift from older forms of popular protest to the development of new ones, like the general strike and pressure-group activity, that were more effective in a mature industrial urban society.

What explanations have been given for the end of Chartism?

Chartism was the first organised, mass movement of the working population in British history in terms of its geographical and occupational breadth and the unprecedented involvement of women. But it did not draw on trade unionism in any formal way or bridge the gulf between rural and urban workers. It did not mark a vital stage in the inevitable progress of organised labour. Chartism was motivated by 'knife and fork' issues, but it was also concerned with the dignity of the individual and the 'rights of man'. It looked back to the campaigns of the 1790s and forward to the emergence of socialism as a political force from the 1880s.

Summary questions

1 Identify and explain any *two* factors that determined the beginnings of Chartism in 1838.

2 Compare the importance of at least *three* issues that explain why the Chartists had not achieved their aims by 1848.

The condition of England, 1832–53

◆ What problems were raised by children in this period and how effectively were they tackled?

◆ Why was poverty such an issue?

◆ What were the pressures leading to changes in the public health system?

◆ How radical were labouring adults and to what extent and why did they fail to achieve change?

Overview

In 1839 Thomas Carlyle published an essay on Chartism in which he posed the question: 'Is the condition of the English working people wrong, so wrong that rational working men cannot, will not, and even should not rest quiet under it?'

This question encapsulated a debate which had been taking place for some time throughout British society. Economists, politicians, popular theorists and workers' leaders were all concerned with the nature of the new industrial economy and its effects on workers and on society as a whole. While industrialisation had brought wealth to the nation, this wealth had not been distributed evenly. The effects of urbanisation, industrial growth and agricultural revolution upon children, the family and the poor were widely acknowledged to be negative.

Economic arguments about the correct path for the future in Britain formed around two different schools of thought. The supporters of one set of ideas argued that the creation of a free market was central to the country's continued prosperity. Following the ideas of Adam Smith, Malthus and Ricardo, they argued that living standards for all would improve if market forces were freed to allow increased competition. The other set of ideas centred around a philosophy of government associated with Jeremy Bentham. He accepted that the free-market economy could have positive effects, but argued that state intervention was necessary to ensure that the interests of different communities were catered for. Bentham called for all institutions to be judged on whether they were economic, efficient and, most importantly, brought 'the greatest happiness of the greatest number'. His followers, known as Utilitarians, recognised the need for state intervention as long as it was geared to the needs of individuals.

Contributing to the debate were the anti-capitalist theories that were popular at the time. Writers such as Thomas Paine, Thomas Spence, Charles Hall, Robert Owen and Thomas Hodgskin all challenged Smith's ideal of equal individuals pursuing their own interests. They based their arguments on a co-operative rather than a competitive view of society. These theories were very popular with the Chartist movement.

While all these ideas were very different, their aims were the same: to improve conditions for children, families, workers and the poor in the new industrial economy. The document sections that follow reflect the ways in which these opposing theories affected the direction of political thought, social activism and economic policy for more than 20 years.

Document study: What problems were raised by children in this period and how effectively were they tackled?

1 Attitudes to factory reform

1.1 Joseph Birley's defence of the existing factory system

Every station in life has, more or less, its abuses – and workers in the Cotton Factories are not exempt. Isolated cases, some true, some coloured, some entirely false, some out of date, are no proof of general suffering. It neither is the practice nor can be the interest of the owners of Factories to enervate or otherwise injure the persons they employ . . . on the contrary, it is necessary that they be alert and attentive; for attention, and not hard labour, is their constant duty . . . Tales of sorrow, got up for a Parliamentary Committee, cannot establish the justness of a sweeping accusation . . . If [manufacturers] be vilified and fettered as ignorant, meddling enthusiasts and philanthropists are now attempting, but not at their own expense, establishments for spinning and weaving will still flourish – but not in Great Britain.

Source: Joseph Birley, *Sadler's Bill. Cotton Branch*, 6, 7, Manchester, 1832

1.2 A manufacturer's protest against reform

The first and immediate consequence of limiting the ages of children employed to 'under 9 years' will be to throw out of employment all that class of hands. This is perhaps the most cruel stroke to the poor man which could have been inflicted . . . this threatened invasion of the rights of the parent over the child is an infringement of the liberty of the subject and a direct violation of the home of Englishmen . . . the quantum of good produced in mills and factories will be diminished in direct proportion to the curtailment of the hours of labour.

Source: A letter to Sir John Cam Hobhouse, Bart., MP, on 'The Factories Bill', 1832

1.3 A defence of the Ten-Hours bill

[The government] could not refuse to protect children. But they are 'political economists' and though, as men, they could not longer screw up their minds and hearts as far as to sacrifice any more limbs and lives of infants, the science would not suffer them to invade the 'freedom of industry' by involving the adult in that protection which they were obliged to give to the child . . . We have nothing to fear from foreign competition. It is the greatest humbug that Englishmen were ever made to believe in; but from competition amongst ourselves we have everything to fear; and if we do not restrain ourselves in time, or the legislature do not restrain us, we shall very soon destroy ourselves . . .

Source: John Fielden, *The curse of the factory system*, London, 1836

1.4 An extract from one of Richard Oastler's 'Yorkshire slavery' letters

Thousands of little children, both male and female, *but principally female*, from seven to fourteen years, are daily compelled to labour from six o' clock in the morning to seven in the evening with only – Britons, blush while you read it! – *with only thirty minutes allowed for eating and recreation*. Poor infants! Ye are indeed sacrificed at the shrine of avarice, *without even the solace of the negro slave*; ye are no more than he is, *free agents*; ye are compelled to work as long as the *necessity* of your needy parents may require, or the cold-blooded avarice of your worse than barbarian masters *may demand*! Ye live in the boasted land of freedom, and *feel* and mourn that *ye are slaves*, and slaves without the only comfort which the negro has. He knows it is his sordid, mercenary master's interest that he should *live*, be *strong* and *healthy*.

Source: Richard Oastler, *Leeds Mercury*, 16 October 1830

Document-study questions

1 From 1.4 and your own knowledge, what can you learn about the problems faced by working children in 1830?
2 How useful is 1.1 as evidence of the arguments against factory reforms?
3 Compare and explain the objections made in 1.2 and 1.3 to reform of factory conditions in the 1830s.
4 Using all the sources and your own knowledge, explain how far you would agree with the view that, during the 1830s, the debate on factory conditions was between those who took a moral stance and those who placed their faith in economic arguments.

2 The Mines Act of 1842

2.1 An extract from Lord Ashley's address to parliament in support of the Act

Lord *Ashley* . . . Sir, it is not possible for any man, whatever be his station, if he have but a heart within his bosom, to read the details of this awful document without a combined feeling of shame, terror and indignation. But I will endeavour to dwell upon the evil itself, rather than on the parties that might be accused as, in great measure, the authors of it. An enormous mischief is discovered, and an immediate remedy is proposed . . . Much, no doubt, may be left for future legislation, but there are some of the evils of so hideous a nature, that they will not admit of delay . . . evils that are both disgusting and intolerable, disgusting they would be in a heathen country and perfectly intolerable they are in one that professes to call itself Christian. The first provision then, which I shall propose, will be the total exclusion of all females from mines and collieries . . . I think that every principle of religion – I think that every law of nature calls for such a step; and I know no argument that can be raised against it, unless one of the most unworthy and of a completely selfish character.

Source: *Parliamentary debates*, third series, volume lxiii, columns 1321, 1336–37, 7 June 1842, House of Commons

2.2 An extract from Joseph Hume's address to parliament in support of reform

Mr *Hume* was sure that the noble Lord the Member for Dorsetshire would experience the most hearty co-operation from those who sat near him, in carrying out the measure which he had just introduced to their notice. The tale he had unfolded could not but give rise to the most painful reflections . . . He believed that none of the enactments proposed by the noble Lord would be objected to. The question as to age would be, perhaps, a solitary exception but on every other point they were free from those objections which on other and similar occasions had seemed to him to exist to interfere between the master and the workman.

Source: *Parliamentary debates*, third series, volume lxiii, column 1356, 7 June 1842, House of Commons

2.3 An extract from Lord Londonderry's address to parliament opposing reform

Lord *Londonderry* denied that such inhuman practices as had been stated prevailed, at least, in the collieries of Durham and Northumberland . . . Now, who were the commissioners, and what were the feelings with which they entered on the enquiry? . . . It appeared . . . that these gentlemen came to this inquiry fresh from the factory commission, with all the prejudices which that commission was likely to excite . . . Their instructions were to examine the children themselves, and the mode in which they collected their evidence – communication with artful boys and ignorant young girls and putting questions in a manner which in many cases seemed to suggest the answer, was anything but a fair and impartial mode . . . Again, he thought the manner in which the report had been accompanied by pictures of an extravagant and disgusting, and in some cases of a scandalous and obscene character, was not as should have been adopted in a grave publication, and was more calculated to excite the feelings than to enlighten the judgement . . .

Source: *Parliamentary debates*, third series, volume lxiv, column 539, 24 June 1842, House of Lords

2.4 An extract from the earl of Radnor's address to parliament opposing reform

The earl of *Radnor* . . . Women and children might be employed in collieries and might be improperly or indecorously employed, but the condemnation of the system . . . was not altogether a sufficient ground for passing an Act of Parliament to carry out such a desire . . . It seemed to him, that the chief argument in favour of this bill was, not the hardship of the system, but its indecency. Now if we began to legislate for the purpose of checking what was indecent or indecorous, they might cut out for themselves more work than they would be able to perform . . .

Source: *Parliamentary debates*, third series, volume lxv, column 584–85, 25 June 1842, House of Lords

Document-study questions

1 From 2.1 and your own knowledge, what can you learn about the problems faced by working children in mines in 1842?

2 How useful is 2.3 as evidence of the arguments against reforming conditions in mines?

3 Compare and explain the objections made in 2.2 and 2.4 to reform of mining conditions in the 1840s.

4 Using all the sources and your own knowledge, explain how far you would agree with the view that the debate on mining conditions was between those who took a Christian stance and those who recognised the economic realities of mining.

5 From the illustration on page 156 and your own knowledge, explain what effect this picture was intended to have and why it and similar illustrations were included in the 1842 report on child labour in mines.

3 Why educate the working classes?

3.1 An extract from a speech given to the governors and directors of the public charity schools

If a good direction be not given to the knowledge afforded by the few to the many . . . then our Altars, our Throne and the just property of individuals will be soon trampled on. If one part of the instruction given, be not to learn truly to labour, to get their own living and to do their duty . . . I very much fear that the results of the Education given, will be discontent, idleness and vice . . . It is not, however, proposed . . . that the children of the poor should be educated in a manner to elevate their minds above the rank they are destined to fill in society . . .

Source: Montague Burgoyne, *Address to the governors and directors of the public charity schools*, 1830

3.2 An extract from a letter from Reverend Gilderdale to Lord Brougham

Are then the advocates of a Christian Education enemies to the diffusion of knowledge? We answer emphatically, no. We know that ignorance is unfavourable to morality; we therefore rejoice in the spread of useful information, and in the expansion of the public mind. But we would not teach science to the exclusion of religion: – we would make that *primary* and *fundamental* which is first in importance: – we would not occupy the scanty opportunities of the poor with *human* learning and leave them destitute of that which is *divine*: – we would not educate man for *time* only, but for *eternity* also.

Source: Reverend J. Gilderdale, *Letter to Lord Brougham*, 10 March 1838

3.3 An extract from a book written by leading Chartists

Convinced of the *importance* of an improved system of education, we think there needs little to convince any one of the necessity of its being made as *general* as possible; for, if the effects of ignorance are so generally detrimental to happiness, the remedy must be sought for in the general dissemination of knowledge . . . What, but the superior cunning and ingenuity of the few, and the ignorance of the many, have led to the establishment of our landed monopoly in its present state . . . Public education ought to be a *right* – a right derivable from society itself, as society implies a *union for mutual benefit*, and, consequently, *to provide publicly security and proper training of all its members*.

Source: William Lovett and John Collins, *Chartism: A new organisation of the people*, London, 1840

Document-study questions

1 From 3.1 and your own knowledge, what can you learn about the main reasons for educating the poor in 1830?
2 How useful is 3.2 as evidence of educational thinking at this time?
3 Compare and explain the objections made in 3.2 and 3.3 in favour of educating the poor.
4 Using all the sources and your own knowledge, explain how far you would agree with the view that the debate on how far the poor should be educated was determined by the notion of education as social control.

1 The implementation of the reformed Poor Law

1.1 Workhouse dietaries (Men)

1. Breakfasts – 6 ozs. Bread and 1 1/2 ozs. cheese. Dinners – Sundays 5 ozs. meat and 1/2 lb. Potatoes. Tuesdays and Thursdays, ditto. Other days 1 1/2 pints soup. Supper – days on which there was meat for dinner, 6 ozs. bread and 1 1/2 pints broth; other days, 6 ozs. Bread and 2 ozs. Cheese.
2. Breakfasts – 6 ozs. Bread and 1 oz. cheese. Dinners – Sundays 16 ozs. Meat pudding plus vegetables; Mondays, 7 ozs. Bread and 1 oz. Cheese; Tuesdays and Fridays, 16 ozs. suet Pudding plus vegetables; other days bread and cheese as Mondays. Supper – 6 ozs. Bread and 1 oz. Cheese.

Source: Poor Law Commission, *Second annual report*, 1836

1.2 Workhouse rules of conduct

Any pauper who shall neglect to observe such of the regulations herein contained as are applicable to and binding on him;
Or who shall make any noise when silence is ordered to be kept;
Or shall use obscene or profane language;
Or shall threaten to strike or to assault any person;
Or shall refuse or neglect to work, after having been required to do so;
Or shall play at cards or other games of chance . . .
Shall be deemed DISORDERLY.

Source: Poor Law Commission, *Seventh annual report*, 1841

1.3 Dickens on the Poor Law

The members of the Board are very sage, deep philosophical men; and when they came to turn their attention to the workhouse, they found out at once what ordinary folks would never have discovered . . . the poor people liked it! It was a regular place of public entertainment for the poorer classes; a tavern where there was nothing to pay; a public breakfast, dinner, tea and supper all the year round . . . 'Oho!' said the Board, looking very knowing, 'we are the fellows to set this to rights; we'll stop it in no time.' So they established the rule . . . of being starved by a gradual process in the House or by a quick one out of it. With this view they contracted with the water works to lay on an unlimited supply of water; and with the corn-factor to supply periodically small quantities of oatmeal; and issued three meals of thin gruel a day, with an onion twice a week and half a roll on Sundays. They . . . kindly undertook to divorce poor married people . . . and instead of compelling a man to support his family, took his family away from him and made him a bachelor. There is no saying how many applicants for relief . . . might have started up in all classes of society, if it had not been coupled with the workhouse; but the Board were long-headed men and provided for this difficulty. The relief was inseparable from the workhouse and the gruel, and that frightened people.

Source: Charles Dickens, *Oliver Twist*, London, 1838, pp. 16–17

Document-study questions

1   From 1.1 and your own knowledge, what can you learn about the operation of the new Poor Law in 1836?
2   How useful is 1.3 as evidence of the operation of the new Poor Law in the 1830s?
3   Compare and explain the impressions given in 1.2 and 1.3 of what conditions in workhouses were like in the 1830s.
4   Using all the sources and your own knowledge, explain how far you would agree with the view that the ways in which workhouses operated in practice and the ways in which some people believed they operated were substantially different.

2 Anti-Poor Law agitation

2.1 William Cobbett speaks out against the new Poor Law

This bill will totally abrogate all the local government of the kingdom: the gentlemen and the magistrates will be totally divested of all power, tending to uphold their character, and to secure their property, and their personal safety in the country. I have talked to twenty gentlemen, farmers and attorneys; every man of them has said: If this bill be attempted to be put into execution, there will be a revolution in England; and I am so firmly persuaded of the soundness of their opinion, that I should look upon such result as something inevitable.

Source: *Weekly political register*, 3 May 1834

2.2 Account from W. J. Gilbert of Devon

The leaders of the opposition are to be found amongst the constant overseers (gentlemen accustomed to accept the office for £5 a year, and quit it with a well-furnished purse); the little shopkeeper, at whose house the poor were paid, and who received the amount for old debts and encouraged new, from which the pauper never got free; the beer-shop keeper, at whose house great part of the relief was expended; and the little farmer or the lime-kiln owner, whose influence at the vestry enabled him to pay one half his labour from the parish funds, under the name of relief in aid of wages, or to speak correctly, relief in aid of vestrymen. Wherever disturbances have taken place, they have been traced to the instigation of some or one of these parties. In the north of the county, where there were some disturbances, we found that the poor people were acting under the grossest deception . . .

Source: Poor Law Commission, Second annual report, Appendix B, No. 9, 1836

2.3 An extract from a speech given by Reverend J. R. Stephens against the new Poor Law

The people were not going to stand this, and he would say, that sooner than wife and husband, and father and son, should be sundered and dungeoned, and fed on 'skillee' – sooner than wife or daughter should wear the prison dress – sooner than that – Newcastle ought to be, and should be – one blaze of fire, with only one way to put it out, and that with the blood of all who supported this abominable measure . . .

Source: From R. C. Gammage, *History of the Chartist movement*, 2nd edn, London, 1894, p. 64

2.4 An extract from Richard Oastler's book in which he condemns the new Poor Law

Christian Reader.

Be not alarmed at the sound of the Title. I can not bless that, which GOD and NATURE CURSE. The Bible being true, the Poor Law Amendment Act is false! The Bible containing the will of God, – this accursed Act of Parliament embodies the will of Lucifer. It is the Sceptre of Belial, establishing its sway in the Land of Bibles!! DAMNATION, ETERNAL DAMNATION to the accursed Fiend!!

Source: Richard Oastler, *Damnation, eternal damnation*, London, 1837, frontispiece

Document-study questions

1   From 2.1 and your own knowledge, what can you learn about opposition to the new Poor Law in 1834?
2   How useful is 2.2 as evidence of opposition to the new Poor Law in the 1830s?
3   Compare and explain the reasons given in 2.1 and 2.2 for opposition to the new Poor Law.
4   Using all the sources and your own knowledge, explain how far you would agree with the view that the agitation against the new Poor Law was fought largely on the question of the rights of the poor.

1 Urban conditions

1.1 Manchester in the 1790s

In some parts of the town, cellars are so damp as to be unfit for habitation . . . The poor often suffer from the broken state of cellar windows. This may be a trifling thing but the results to the inhabitants are of the most serious kind. Fevers are among the most usual effects, and I have known consumption [tuberculosis] which could be traced to this cause . . . rheumatic complaints which prevent people from every kind of employment, are often produced in the same manner . . . I have often seen that fevers prevail most in houses exposed to the effluvia [smell] of dung hills in such situations. In a house in Bootle Street, most of the inhabitants and people are very ill, in consequence of their situation in a blind alley, which excludes them from light and air. Consumption, distortions and idiocy are common in such recesses.

Source: John Aitkin MD, *A description of the country from thirty to forty miles around Manchester*, Manchester, 1795

1.2 Manchester in the 1830s

The greatest portion of those districts inhabited by the labouring population, especially those situated beyond Great Ancoat Street, are of very recent origin and suffer from a lack of proper municipal regulations and do not have common sewers. The houses are ill drained and often ill ventilated, unprovided with privies [toilets] and in consequence the streets which are narrow, unpaved, and worn in deep ruts become the common receptacle of mud, refuse and disgusting odours . . . The houses in such areas are often ill provided with furniture and an air of discomfort pervades them . . . they are often dilapidated, badly drained, damp, and the habits of their tenants are gross . . . they are ill-fed, ill-clothed and uneconomical . . . There is no common slaughterhouse in Manchester and those that exist are in the narrowest streets. The drainage of these slaughterhouses, deeply tinged with blood and other animal matter, frequently flows down in the common surface drains of the street and stagnates in ruts and pool.

Source: J. P. Kay, *The moral and physical conditions of the working classes in Manchester in 1832*, Manchester, 1832

1.3 Greenock in 1842

In one part of Market Street is a dunghill – yet it is too large to be called a dunghill. I do not misstate its size when I say it contains a hundred cubic yards of impure filth, collected from all parts of the town by a person who deals in dung. It is never removed . . . The proprietor has an extensive privy attached to his concern . . . which is just off the public street. It is enclosed in front by a wall, the height of the wall is over twelve feet and the dung over-tops it. Its malarious moisture comes through the wall and runs on to the pavement. The smell all round the place in summer is horrible. There is a block of houses next to it which is four storeys high. Every article of food and drink must be covered, otherwise if left out for a minute the flies attack it and render it unfit for use, from the strong taste of the dung hill left by them.

Source: Dr Laurie, 'Description of Greenock', Parliamentary papers: House of Lords, vol xxvi, 1842, pp. 46–47

1.4 The River Aire* in 1840

The river . . . is charged with the contents of about 200 water closets and similar places, a great deal of common drains, the drainings from dung hills, the Infirmary (dead leeches, dressings from patients etc.), slaughter houses, chemical soap, gas, dung, old urine, wash with all sorts of decomposed animal and vegetable substances from an area of drainage . . . amounting to about 30,000,000 gallons per year of the mass of filth with which the river is loaded.

Source: Quoted in Derek Fraser, *The development of the British welfare state*, 2nd edn, London, 1986, p. 91

* The River Aire provided up to 70 per cent of the drinking water for Leeds.

Document-study questions

1 From 1.2 and your own knowledge, what can you learn about urban conditions in the 1830s?
2 How useful is 1.3 as evidence of the need for public health reform in the 1840s?
3 How far do 1.1 and 1.2 explain the impact of urban conditions on working people?
4 Using all the sources and your own knowledge, explain how far you would agree with the view that the nature of urban problems was well known by the early 1840s and that public health reform was limited mainly by the reluctance of government to legislate.

2 Support and opposition for reform

2.1 Disease and health

In general, all epidemics and all infectious diseases are attended with charges, immediate and ultimate, on the poor rates. Labourers are suddenly thrown, by infectious disease, into a state of destitution, for which immediate relief must be given. In the case of death, the widow and children are thrown as paupers on the parish . . . There is no disease which brings so much affliction into a poor man's family as fever . . . It most commonly attacks the heads of the family, those upon whose daily labour the subsistence of the family depends . . . Out of the total number of persons in London who received parochial relief during the last year, more than one-fifth were the subjects of fever . . . It is plain that this disease is one of the main causes of pressure on the poor rates . . .

Source: Reports of the Poor Law commissioners, 1838–39

2.2 Local government and sanitation

The utter failure of the system of local self-government for sanitary purposes is notorious to all who have taken any pains to inquire into the subject . . . Drainage, especially, which is of vast importance to health, cannot be carried out by parishes. It presupposes an extensive area selected for that special object, surveyed and laid out with a scientific skill and judgement which few parishes have at their command, and which popular election is unlikely to ensure . . . We look upon local self-government . . . at least for sanitary purposes . . . as a popular delusion, condemned by common sense and every day experience . . . We would rather trust to the central government than to local authorities.

Source: *Fraser's Magazine*, 1847

2.3 Property owners give evidence to the General Board of Health inquiry

Good sewerage may increase our personal comforts and conveniences but if it tends to deprive us still more of our now scanty living, we fear the introduction of it . . . The principal cause of nuisances in the township is the dereliction of duty on the part of the owners of property, in not constructing proper conveniences for the occupiers of their dwelling houses. And is the public at large to be taxed because these individuals fail to perform their duty?

Source: Chartist evidence to the General Board of Health inquiry into the North Staffordshire Potteries District, 1851

2.4 Support for reform in parliament

Mr Urquhart said he had an objection to the bill, not to its intent and object, but to the establishment, for the purposes of promoting the public health, of an organisation which he thought tended to increase the mode of foreign government which was known by the name of 'centralisation'. Mr Mackinnon . . . denied that this was a centralising bill. The Government merely reserved a superintending influence, but the operating parts of the bill would be in the hands of local authorities.

Source: Report on the Commons debate on the second reading of the Public Health bill, *The Times*, 22 February 1848

Document-study questions

1 From 2.4 and your own knowledge, what can you learn about opposition to public health reform in the late 1840s?

2 How useful is 2.2 as evidence of the failure of public health reform in the 1840s?

3 Compare and explain the attitudes towards public health reform contained in 2.3 and 2.4.

4 Using all the sources and your own knowledge, explain how far you would agree with the view that the unwillingness of many to legislate for public health reform was due to self-interest.

Document study: How radical were labouring adults and to what extent and why did they fail to achieve change?

1 Criticism of Feargus O'Connor

1.1 Lovett on O'Connor

I regard Fergus O'Connor as the chief marplot of our movement . . . a man, who, by his personal conduct joined to his malignant influence in the *Northern Star*, has been the blight of democracy from the first moment he opened his mouth as its *professed advocate* . . . Not possessing a nature to appreciate intellectual exertions, he began his career by ridiculing our *'moral force humbuggery'* . . . by his constant appeals to the selfishness, vanity, and mere animal propensities of man, he succeeded in calling up a spirit of hate, intolerance and brute feeling, previously unknown among Reformers . . .

Source: William Lovett, *The life and struggles of William Lovett*, London, 1876, pp. 294–97; R. H. Tawney edn, London, 1967, p. 245

1.2 Gammage on O'Connor

His broad massive forehead . . . bore evidence . . . of great intellectual force. To assert that he possessed a mind solid and steady was to say too much, no man with an equal amount of intellect was ever more erratic. Had the solidarity of his judgement been equal to his quickness of perception he would intellectually have been a great man, but this essential quality of greatness was lacked, hence his life presents a series of mistakes and contradictions . . . No man in the movement was so certain of popularity as O'Connor. No man was so certain to lose it after its attainment. It was not until he proceeded to speak that the full extent of his influence was felt . . .

Source: R. C. Gammage, *History of the Chartist movement 1837–54*, 2nd edn, London, 1894, p. 45

1.3 Adams on O'Connor

Next to this fault was the disposition [among the leaders] to quarrel. But quarrelling was almost inevitable when not one man but many men, desire to become dictators. It was almost equally inevitable when such a man as Feargus O'Connor, who had few of the qualities of a powerful leader save extraordinary force of character, had acquired absolute dominion over the cause . . . The common notion of O'Connor outside the ranks of his personal followers was that he was a charlatan and a humbug – an adventurer who traded on the passions of the people for his own profit and advantage. A correcter notion would have been that he was a victim of his own delusions . . .

Source: W. E. Adams, *Memoirs of a social atom*, London, 1903, pp. 203, 208–09

1.4 Epstein on O'Connor

O'Connor has often been severely criticised for having exerted an undemocratic, 'dictatorial' control over the Chartist movement. However, as David Jones has suggested, 'the problems which he faced deserve greater attention'. The central problem of national Chartist leadership was the maintenance of radical working-class unity. The magnitude of this task should not be forgotten. With remarkable forbearance, energy and enthusiasm O'Connor battled to overcome the divisions and sources of fragmentation within the working-class movement . . . In the early 1840s, the vulnerability of Chartism's national unity was tested. Both from outside and within the Chartist ranks the movement was faced with a series of 'rival' or alternative agitations . . . Several weeks before the publication of his attack [early spring 1841] on the quadruple alliance of church, teetotal, knowledge and household-suffrage Chartism, O'Connor explained his position: 'I do not object to Chartists being religious – to Chartists being teetotal – to Chartists thirsting after knowledge, or to Chartists voting out of, and living in, their own houses'. His opposition was based rather upon his fears that these various tendencies might become splinter groups, dissipating the movement's strength . . .

Source: James Epstein, *The lion of freedom: Feargus O'Connor and the Chartist movement 1832–42*, London, 1982, pp. 236, 240

Document-study questions

1 From 1.1 and your own knowledge, what can you learn about contemporary attitudes to Feargus O'Connor?
2 How useful is 1.3 as evidence of Feargus O'Connor as a self-seeking politician?
3 Compare and explain the attitudes towards Feargus O'Connor contained in 1.2 and 1.4.
4 Using all the sources and your own knowledge, explain how far you would agree with the view that Feargus O'Connor's involvement in Chartism was negative rather than positive.

Further reading

General texts

E. J. Evans, *The forging of the modern state: early industrial Britain 1783–1870*, London, 2nd edn 1996, N. McCord, *British history 1815–1906*, Oxford, 2nd edn 1998, and Michael Turner, *British politics in an age of reform*, Manchester, 1999, are good introductions. R. Pope (ed.), *Atlas of British social and economic history since c.1700*, London, 1989, provides a valuable visual dimension.

Chapter 2: William Pitt, 1783–1801

J. W. Derry, *Politics in the age of Fox, Pitt and Liverpool: continuity and transformation*, London, 1990, covers the period from the 1780s through to the late 1820s. Eric J. Evans, *William Pitt the Younger*, London, 1999, is brief and L. G. Mitchell, *Charles James Fox*, Oxford, 1992, examines his major protagonist. H. T. Dickinson (ed.), *Britain and the French Revolution 1793–1815*, London, 1989, provides all students will need.

Chapter 3: Tory dominance and decline, 1812–30

E. J. Evans, *Britain before the Reform Act 1815–1832*, London, 1989, contains text and documents. John Plowright, *Regency England: the age of Lord Liverpool*, London, 1996, is eminently accessible. Norman Gash, *Lord Liverpool*, London, 1984, and P. J. V. Rolo, *George Canning*, London, 1965, are the only modern biographies.

Chapter 4: The Whig reforms, 1830–41

E. J. Evans, *The Great Reform Act of 1832*, London, 2nd edn 1995, is an accessible starting-point. R. Stewart, *Party and politics 1830–1852*, London, 1989, covers Whigs and Tories. There are valuable biographies of the key Whig politicians: E. A. Smith, *Lord Grey 1764–1845*, Oxford, 1990, L. G. Mitchell, *Lord Melbourne 1779–1848*, Oxford, 1996, and John Prest, *Lord John Russell*, London, 1972.

Chapter 5: Redefining Toryism

Paul Adelman, *Peel and the Conservative party 1830–1850*, London, 1989, contains text and documents. Eric J. Evans, *Sir Robert Peel: statesmanship, power and party*, London, 1991, and T. A. Jenkins, *Sir Robert Peel*, London, 1998, are good short reassessments.

Chapter 6: Peel and Ireland

Roy Foster, *Modern Ireland 1600–1922*, London, 1987, and K. T. Hoppen, *Ireland since 1800: conflict and conformity*, London, 2nd edn 1999, are good studies. Paul Adelman, *Great Britain and the Irish question 1800–1922*, London, 1996, is designed with the beginner in mind. On the famine, see Christine Kinealy, *The great calamity: the Irish famine 1845–52*, Dublin, 1994, and *A death-dealing famine: the great hunger in Ireland*, London, 1997.

Chapter 7: Britain at war, 1793–1815

Three chapters in H. T. Dickinson (ed.), *Britain and the French Revolution 1789–1815*, London, 1989, consider diplomacy, strategy and public finance.

Chapter 8: Foreign policy, 1814–41

C. J. Bartlett, *Defence and diplomacy: Britain and the great powers 1815–1914*, Manchester, 1993, and John Lowe, *Britain and foreign affairs 1815–1885: Europe and overseas*, London, 1998, provide an overview. C. J. Bartlett, *Castlereagh*, London, 1966, and Muriel Chamberlain, *Lord Aberdeen*, London, 1983, are valuable on the 1810s and 1820s. Muriel Chamberlain, *Lord Palmerston*, Cardiff, 1987, is readable and short.

Chapter 9: The first industrial nation

Phil Chapple, *The industrialisation of Britain 1780–1914*, London, 1999, and Kenneth Morgan, *The birth of industrial Britain 1750–1850*, London, 1999, are good places to begin. Pat Hudson, *The Industrial Revolution*, London, 1992, is of major importance as a summary of recent research on both economic and social history.

Chapter 10: Responding to economic change

John Stevenson, *Popular disturbances in England 1700–1832*, London, 1991, is the best introduction. P. Adelman, *Victorian radicalism: the middle-class experience 1830–1914*, London, 1984, and D. G. Wright, *Popular radicalism: the working class experience 1780–1880*, London, 1988, look at different responses to change. E. P. Thompson, *The making of the English working class*, London, 1968, is a controversial classic.

Chapter 11: Children, work and education, 1833–53

J. T. Ward, *The factory movement 1830–1850*, London, 1962, is the most detailed study but must now be supplemented by Robert Gray, *The factory question and industrial England 1830–1860*, Cambridge, 1996. Eric Hopkins, *Childhood transformed: working class children in nineteenth-century England*, London, 1994, and Pamela Horn, *Children's work and welfare 1780–1880*, London, 1994, provide valuable insights into children's work and how and why it changed. W. B. Stephens, *Education in England 1760–1914*, London, 1998, is the best introduction to the subject. M. Sanderson, *Education, economic change and society in England 1780–1870*, London, 2nd edn 1991, is a briefer bibliographical study.

Chapter 12: From Speenhamland to the new Poor Law, 1830–47

David Englander, *Poverty and Poor Law reform in 19th century Britain 1834–1914: from Chadwick to Booth*, London, 1998, and Peter Murray, *Poverty and welfare 1830–1914*, London, 1999, are the most accessible books on the subject. Alan Kidd, *State, society and the poor in nineteenth-century England*, London, 1999, is broader. Derek Fraser (ed.), *The new Poor Law in the nineteenth century*, London, 1976, and M. E. Rose, *The relief of poverty 1834–1914*, London, 2nd edn 1985, are useful on the introduction and operation of the 'new' Poor Law. The workhouse is discussed in N. Longmate, *The workhouse*, London, 1974, and M. Crowther, *The workhouse system 1834–1929: the history of an English social institution*, London, 1984. Michael Rose (ed.), *The English poor laws 1780–1930*, Newton Abbot, 1971, contains useful source materials.

Chapter 13: Chadwick and public health, 1830–54

The development of town and city can be approached through A. Briggs, *Victorian cities*, London, 1968. R. Rodger (ed.), *The Victorian city: a reader in British urban history 1820–1914*, London, 1994, collects together important papers and has an excellent introduction that puts urban growth in its context.

On urban conditions and the problems of public health, see A. S. Wohl, *Endangered lives: public health in Victorian Britain*, London, 1985. R. A. Lewis, *Edwin Chadwick and the public health movement 1832–1854*, London, 1952, is an essential work on Chadwick and should be read in conjunction with S. E. Finer, *The life and times of Sir Edwin Chadwick*, London, 1952, and A. Brundage, *England's 'Prussian Minister': Edwin Chadwick and the politics of government growth 1832–1854*, Pennsylvania, 1988.

Chapter 14: Chartism

E. Royle, *Chartism*, London, 3rd edn 1996, R. Brown, *Chartism*, Cambridge, 1998, Harry Browne, *Chartism*, London, 1999, and John Walton, *Chartism*, 1999, are good places to begin. Dorothy Thompson, *The Chartists: popular politics in the Industrial Revolution*, Aldershot, 1984, is more detailed. Norman McCord, *The Anti-Corn Law League*, London, 1968, is the standard study of Chartism's opponents.

Document study: The condition of England, 1832–53

General studies of social reform include U. Henriques, *Before the welfare state*, London, 1979, D. Fraser, *The evolution of the British welfare state*, London, 2nd edn 1985, Keith Laybourn, *The evolution of British social policy and the welfare state*, Keele, 1995, and Michael Willis, *Democracy and the state 1830–1945*, Cambridge, 1999. E. Evans, *Social reform 1830–1914*, London, 1978, is a useful collection of documents.

Index